A heritage of light

A heritage of light

Lamps and lighting in the early Canadian home

LORIS S. RUSSELL

University of Toronto Press

Published on the occasion of the Centennial of Canadian
Confederation and subsidized by the Centennial Commission.

Ouvrage publié à l'occasion du Centenaire de la Confédération
Canadienne, grâce à une subvention de la Commission du Centenaire.

SBN 8020 1530 1

Contents

Introduction

THERE ARE TWO REASONS why a study of early Canadian lighting is appropriate at this time. First, the development of artificial lighting is an important part of our social history. Being a northern country, Canada has always been faced with the prospect of many hours of darkness during the winter months. Lamps and other lighting devices have had a special significance, although this fact has been little recognized by the chroniclers of the past. Newspapers and books made only passing reference to the subject, even when great changes were in progress; and if the contemporary writers saw little of the impact of increasing resources of light, later historians have been even less impressed. One can find some references in the excellent works of Guillet,[1] and four pages of lucid drawings in the *Picture Gallery* of Jefferys. But most Canadian historians say so little of the material background against which the great drama was unfolding that one almost comes to picture the actors in modern dress and setting.

Lighting is just one of the many branches of our material history that ought to be explored. Others equally deserving of study are domestic heating, the equipment of the kitchen, mechanical means of transportation, and the evolution of farming techniques. The present study was undertaken as a kind of experiment to see whether or not the resources of libraries and collections are sufficient to permit reconstruction of both the technological developments and the social changes for which these developments were in part responsible.

The second reason for this study is the rising interest in Canadian antiquities, stimulated by the Centenary of Canadian Confederation. Museums and individuals are expanding collections at an increasing rate. Old-time interiors are being reconstructed in historic houses and museums, and reproduced for pageants and dramatic presentations. In such reconstructions it is most important that the objects selected be appropriate to the period and to each other. Bad mistakes have been made, and some of the most conspicuous involve lighting. But as Canadians are more and more exposed to these interpretations, they will become increasingly knowledgeable and thus less tolerant of anachronisms and other errors.

The investigation of early lighting, like other forms of historical research, is frustrating in that every fact brought to light seems to cast a shadow of questions that demand further research. The task can never be completed, but that is a challenge as well as a frustration. I say this to explain why there can be no pretence that the present work gives all the answers. It is also the reason why the survey has not been restricted to the British North American provinces, even though the main interest is there. The settlers of this country brought with them the lighting devices of France, and later those of England through the American colonies. During the first half of the nineteenth century the territories that are now Canada were almost completely dependent for lamps on the northeastern United States. Later some lamps of Canadian manufacture appeared, especially with the growth of the glass industry in Canada, but they were a minor trickle in the flood of lamps from Philadelphia, Boston, and Pittsburgh. The knowledge that a particular lighting device was made or used in the northern United States, and especially in the border areas, makes it necessary to consider the possibility that it was imported and used in the adjacent parts of Canada.

SOURCES

Sources for the study of technological history are both documentary and material. In using documents for this purpose I have adopted the general principle of relying as far as possible on the contemporary records of the period in preference to the accounts of modern students of the subject, even when the latter are acknowledged authorities. The contemporary records, of course, must be used with consideration of their nature. Some writers were incompletely informed on the developments of their own times, while others had personal bias, but these defects can usually be recognized.

The works consulted in the preparation of this account are listed in the bibliography and cited frequently in the text. Among the more important are the journals and letters of pioneers and the slightly less reliable memoirs that some of them published. Good examples which appear in the bibiliography are the books of Mrs. Moodie and her brother, Major Strickland, and the letters and journals of Anne and John Langton. But one must be prepared to read many pages of irrelevant matter for one brief reference to the subject at hand. Much the same applies to the newspapers of the day. How unimportant to us now seem the serial romances that filled pages of those journals and magazines. The columns of European despatches and commentaries on current events, starting with half a column of headlines, are immensely fascinating but lead the search into by-ways. Most rewarding are the advertisements, but even with these there must be caution, as publishers of newspapers had stock cuts of ships and trains and lamps as well.

City directories for both Canada and the United States have been consulted with profit. They provide names and addresses of companies, dates of establishment and disappearance, and names of directors and staff. The advertisements, too, are often very informative.

One of the most productive sources has been the volumes of the *Scientific American*. As a journal of science and invention it began publication on August 28, 1845, with a new series starting from July 2, 1859. For years each weekly issue carried lists of patents and descriptions of inventions. The illustrations that accompany the latter often have more information than would be essential to a simple patent drawing: the cut of a new burner may also show the style of lamp then in use. Some issues carry summary articles reviewing the history of a technological development such as the friction match or the petroleum industry. For the period covered this publication is probably the world's richest record of technological history.

The Canadian Patent Office Record and Mechanics Magazine, started in 1873, was patterned after the *Scientific American*, and in fact some volumes are called *The Scientific Canadian*. But it proved less useful than its American model. Its editors emphasized the great engineering feats of the day, to the neglect of the lesser technologies. However, the summaries of patents are a valuable source of quick reference for Canadian inventions.

Extensive use was made of the records of the Canadian and United States patent offices. At Washington the early "name and date" patents were consulted in the National Archives. Helpful information was found in both the Canadian and American registries of trade names, which are associated with the respective patent offices. Many British patents were examined, either in the *Abridgements* or as copies of the original. In Boston I was able to consult the early *Brevets* of France. Using patents in historical research also requires caution. The fact that a patent was issued is no guarantee that the article was ever available to the public, and while a device with a patent date cannot be older than that date, it may be of much later manufacture. Nevertheless, the combination of the actual device and its patent is almost ideal as a historical source.

In more recent times some of the writings on the subject of lighting have already become classics. First place must go to the pioneer study of Walter Hough on the heating and lighting utensils in the United States National Museum. Somewhat earlier appeared the chatty but very useful *Colonial Lighting* of Hayward. Long out of print, it is now available as a paperback reprint. *Flickering Flames*, by Leroy Thwing, is the most straightforward account, and is beautifully illustrated. Yet the scope of these works is either world-wide or purely American, and in both cases there is little reference to Canada. For late nineteenth-century lighting the only reference work is Freeman's *Light on Old Lamps*. It contains much valuable information, but the illustrations vary in quality, and the correlation between text and illustrations is deplorable.

From England, *The Social History of Lighting*, by O'Dea, is an excellent and attractive summary of developments, especially in gas and electricity. On a more technical level the *Chemical Technology* of Groves and Thorp admirably summarizes late nineteenth-century knowledge of both lamps and fuels. In France, d'Allemangne's *Histoire du luminaire* is especially good on the developments of the late eighteenth and early nineteenth centuries.

Probably the richest source of information on early lighting, and not exclusively North American, is *The Rushlight*, issued quarterly by The Rushlight Club, of Cambridge, Mass. Formed in 1932, this club is the oldest organization devoted exclusively to the study of early lighting. Its publication first appeared in 1934. Although much of its contents was summarized in *Flickering Flames*, this modest magazine is required reading for all serious students of lighting, containing as it does many articles by Leroy Thwing, Edward A. Rushford, Arthur Hayward, Mrs. Lura A. Watkins, Edwin B. Rollins, and other authorities on the subject. I have been fortunate in having access to a nearly complete file of back numbers. Another periodical, the magazine *Antiques*, has included equally good articles on old-time lighting, but these are scattered through many volumes.

The actual specimens of antique lighting devices complement and substantiate the written record. The best collection of such material with a distinctly Canadian orientation is in the National Museum of Canada, part of the great Canadiana collection begun by Dr. Marius Barbeau and expanded to its present form by the writer. Over three hundred catalogued items pertaining to lighting, from all parts of Canada, may be studied here. Specimens in this collection, where referred to in the following chapters, have their catalogue numbers prefixed by the letters NMC. Other public museums with significant lighting collections are the Nova Scotia Museum at Halifax, the New Brunswick Museum at Saint John, Upper Canada Village at Morrisburg, Ont., Black Creek Pioneer Village near Toronto, and the Oil Museum of Canada at Oil Springs, Ont. Special mention should be made of the Hastings County Museum at Belleville, Ont., which recently acquired the private collection of Dr. W. A. Paul, now of Napanee. This includes some very important pre-kerosene lamps not represented in other Canadian collections. Mention should also be made of the great collection of early electrical devices assembled in Toronto by the Hydro-Electric Power Commission of Ontario. Although not yet on public display, it is readily accessible to serious students, and its fine series of nineteenth- and early twentieth-century electric lighting devices was very valuable to the present study.

A number of private collections of lighting devices in Canada have been examined, and the pertinent items described and photographed, as noted at the appropriate places in the succeeding chapters. The writer's own collection was assembled at first to supplement that of the National Museum of Canada, but it has grown to include over four hundred catalogued items, and is particularly rich in the patented burners of the late nineteenth century, an area that has been neglected. Catalogue numbers in this collection are prefixed by the letters LSR.

There are many important collections of lighting devices in the United States. That of the Museum of History and Technology, U.S. National Museum, must be given priority, not that it is the largest, but because it includes many items of historical interest and many of the models submitted by inventors along with their applications for patents. Probably the largest collection is that of the Ford Museum at Dearborn, Mich. This is rich in large series of various lamps, which happily for the serious student are nearly all on display. It is said that a portion of this collection came from adjacent parts of Ontario, but how much, if any, I have not been able to determine. Other important public collections are at Old Sturbridge Village in Massachusetts, the Detroit Historical Museum in Michigan, and the Otis House Museum in Boston. There are hundreds of important private collections of lighting devices in the United States, especially in New England. I have had time to see only a few of these. Those from which I learned most are the collections of Mr. Stratford Lee Morton, of the Academy of Science of St. Louis, Mo., and Mr. William A. O'Connell of Quincy, Mass.

ACKNOWLEDGEMENTS

My thanks are especially due to the Centennial Commission of Canada for a generous and timely grant, which made it possible for me to visit collections and archives, and so condense a programme of research that might have taken a number of years on my own resources.

Continued study of the extensive lighting collection of the National Museum of Canada and publication of photographs of specimens in this collection were made possible by the permission of Dr. Richard M. Glover, the then Director of the Human History Branch, and Mr. F. J. Thorpe, the Chief Historian. The privilege of examining and photographing lighting devices under their respective care was granted by Mr. George McLaren of the Nova Scotia Museum, Halifax; Mr. Lloyd Muir of the New Brunswick Museum, Saint John; Mrs. J. W. Sargent of the Hastings County Museum, Belleville, Ont.; Brigadier J. A. McGinnis of the Toronto Historical Board (Mackenzie House), Toronto; Dr. H. J. Newman of the County of Halton Museum, Milton, Ont.; Miss Olive Newcombe of the Dundas Historical Society Museum, Dundas, Ont.; Mrs. Beatrice MacLachlan of the Oil Museum of Canada, Oil Springs, Ont.; and Mrs. Margaret Philip, Markham, Ont. Mr. G. E. Davison and Mr. Arthur Plumpton, of the Ontario Hydro Museum, Toronto, not only permitted use of material in their care but also provided essential information on the early history of lighting in Canada. Mr. W. A. Landon, of the Consumers' Gas Company, Toronto, was most helpful in the study of early gas-burning devices.

In the United States I enjoyed access to the National Museum reserve collection of lighting devices through the courtesy of Mr. C. Malcolm Watkins, Curator of the Division of Cultural History, U.S. National Museum, Washington. At the Ford Museum at Dearborn, Mich., Dr. G. O. Bird and Mr. Carleton Brown made it possible for me to examine and photograph lamps, many of which had to be removed from the exhibition cases. Mr. Stratford Lee Morton, President of the St. Louis Academy of Science, St. Louis, Mo., not only allowed me to use his excellent collection but also provided generous hospitality during my visit. At the Science Museum in South Kensington, London, England, I had a useful discussion with Mr. William T. O'Dea, and was greatly helped in the use of the collections and records by Mr. G. M. Lane.

The privilege of access to books and documents in provincial archives was given by Mr. A. M. Fraser of the Newfoundland Archives, Mr. C. Bruce Fergusson of the Nova Scotia Public Archives, Dr. Douglas Boylen of the Confederation Centre Library, Charlottetown, P.E.I., and Mr. C. Antoine Pelletier of the Archives du Québec. Other libraries used extensively were those of the Canadian Patent Office, the National Museum of Canada, and the National Archives, Ottawa, the University of Toronto Library, the Royal Ontario Museum Library, the Toronto Public Library, the Great Library of Osgoode Hall, Toronto, and the Hamilton Public Library. The Lawson Memorial Library of the University of Western Ontario, through Dr. J. J. Talman, permitted access to the fabulous Barnett Collection of clippings, and Mr. Richard Phelps of the staff was most helpful in making this available.

The Boston Public Library proved to be a most valuable source of reference, as it has to many another member of the Rushlight Club. The fine series of French *Brevets* in its collection is stored in the New England Deposit Library, where I was courteously received. In the library of the Franklin Institute of Philadelphia I found much information on the early lamp manufacturers of that city, thanks to Dr. Joseph S. Hepburn. Old trade catalogues were consulted in the Print Department of the Metropolitan Museum of Art, New York City. At the Public Library of Rochester, N.Y., I was provided with the information on the famous "Rochester lamp" which I had failed to find elsewhere. In the library of the Museum of History and Technology in Washington I had access to the early volumes of the *Scientific American*. In London I made use of the

British Museum Library and the Library of the Science Museum. From Vienna Dr. Josef Nagler, Director of the Technisches Museum für Industrie und Gewerbe, kindly sent me information and photographs of the "Vienna burner."

In the work of building up the Canadiana collection of the National Museum of Canada, and later my own collection of lighting devices, I have had many contacts with the antique dealers of Canada, from Nova Scotia to British Columbia. The majority of these have been friendly, co-operative, and interested in the encouragement of antiquarian studies in Canada. Some of them are mentioned in the following pages in connection with the provenience of specimens, but to all of them I extend my sincere if collective thanks.

Miss Anne Liebeck, my secretary, not only has been a skilful amanuensis, but has helped in the search for data, and by her critical reading has eliminated many errors and discrepancies.

My wife, Grace Evelyn Russell, has been my constant companion in the search for the mementoes of Canada's past. Her encouragement has been a major factor in enabling me to complete what has been, at least in recent years, an after-hours project.

CHAPTER I   # From splint to candle

EVER SINCE MAN learned to make a campfire and then to set up a crude fireplace in his cave or hut, he has enjoyed the by-product of artificial light. The French and English settlers brought the hearth to Canada. In their homes along the St. Lawrence Valley, in the Maritimes, and along the shores of Lake Ontario, the fireplace was the domestic centre, the principal means of cooking and source of warmth. It also provided light, a yellow flickering light to be sure, but sufficient in a home where everyone worked hard from sunrise to sunset and went early to bed. Even after stoves came into use for heating late in the eighteenth century, the fireplace retained its importance for cooking, at least until the 1840s and even later in remote areas. It remained as well a source of light, and it is easy to picture the family gathered around it after the evening meal, perhaps to listen to a Bible reading, perhaps to sew or mend. As they added fuel from time to time they would observe that some woods gave a more luminous flame than others; faggots of pine or birch gave a bright blaze, and pieces of birch bark flared briefly in a fire that had died down. It was a simple step to take such materials out of the fireplace as independent illumination to brighten a dark corner or light the way to bed, and from that to fashion pieces of wood in advance for the purpose. So were born the torch and the splint. The torch in North America was usually an outdoor light, and hence falls beyond the scope of this book. The splint, in theory at least, was the ancestor of a large family of domestic lighting devices.

SPLINT AND RUSHLIGHT

A splint is just a sliver of wood, perhaps seven inches long and a quarter of an inch thick. The trick is to make it from wood that will burn with a bright flame away from a larger fire. For this purpose resinous woods are superior, and pine, with its good splitting properties, best of all. The New England colonists used the pitch-pine (*Pinus rigida*), whose wood seems saturated with resin, but which ranges only into the southern edge of Canada. Splints used in Canadian homes were much more likely to be made from the wood of the jack pine (*Pinus Banksiana*), a species that occurs from Nova Scotia to the Mackenzie Valley.

Splints are so simple to make that they were probably used to supplement fireplace illumination or to provide a quick source of portable light all through the period in which the cooking fireplace was in vogue. There is no evidence, however, that Canadians ever used holders specifically made for these lights. Splint holders are either simple vices or arms with slots into which the splint is squeezed. There is even doubt that such special splint holders were ever used in New England.[1] On the other hand, it may well be that many of the conventional rushlight holders were commonly used to support splints.

The rushlight required more elaborate preparation—a process that is well understood today thanks to explicit directions handed

down to us and the experiments of modern antiquarians.[2] It used the so-called soft rush (*Juncus effusus*), which grows in wet areas, usually adjacent to streams. Unlike the more familiar bulrush, the soft rush has flowers and seeds in a loose cluster below the top of its stalk. In southern Canada the rush reaches maturity in late August. The thicker stems are selected and cut into convenient lengths of eight or ten inches. Authorities differ as to whether the stems should be peeled at once or first soaked in water for a few hours. In either case, peeling is an operation that requires a little practice to do well. Strips of the outer, fibrous layer are freed with the finger nails and pulled off, leaving just enough in one last strip to hold the fragile pith in one piece.

The peeled rush pieces are impregnated with some flammable fatty substance – lard or tallow or today, if one is willing to cheat, paraffin wax. In the old days the impregnation was done in a special ladle known as a grisette, which had an oval bowl in which fat could be melted and the rush stems drawn through. No examples of this device are known from Canada and it seems likely that most people impregnated the rushes in any available pot or pan.

The burning section of rush was normally held in the holder at an angle of about 45°, which seems to be the optimum position to combine good burning with little drip. The rush light is an interesting device closely linked to the British Isles. If we knew more about its importation and use in Canada it might shed light on the places of origin of some of our folk crafts and practices.

The rush light and its holder are such characteristic lighting devices that it is surprising to find in the pages of *The Rushlight* magazine a continuing debate as to whether or not they were actually used as such in New England.[3] Until recently evidence for their use in what is now Canada appeared to be even more tenuous. Typical rushlight holders occasionally appear in Canadian antique shops, but the possibility that they have been imported from England or the United States has not been ruled out. Recently there appeared in the Halton County Museum at Milton, Ont., a rushlight holder typical in every way except that it is made of brass instead of iron. Bearing in mind this difference, a description of it will serve as a standard for comparison with other examples.[4]

The holder was presented to the Halton County Museum by Mrs. Keith Barber of Georgetown, Ont., and is known to have been made locally. The metal parts are of brass, and remembering that this alloy has to be worked cold, one cannot but admire its workmanship. Basically the holder is a pincer device, with one fixed arm and one counter-balanced movable arm. The fixed arm is an upright from the base and is made of a piece of brass about ¼-inch square in cross-section. Near the upper end it has been formed into a disc-shaped expansion, perforated for the hinge rivet, and above this the piece extends as one of a pair of jaws. The movable piece is U-shaped; the jaw is similar to that of the fixed piece. The two are pivoted on each other by a rivet which is loose enough to permit free movement. The curved portion of the movable arm was given a complete twist before being bent, producing an orna-mental effect and also adding rigidity. The free end of the "U" has been beaten out and shaped into an inverted cone. Such an addition to a rush-light holder is generally assumed to be for holding a candle; but that would be redundant, and its shape seems wrong. It may have been an extinguisher for the lighted rush. The base of the holder is a turned wooden cylinder, conoid above, with a flat top, and has been painted a dark chocolate brown. Over-all height of the holder is 9³⁄₁₆ inches.

The presence of an authentic rushlight holder in Ontario does not prove that it was used for burning rushes, but the probability is strong that it was. A faithful copy of the traditional form seems likely only if it was intended for the traditional purpose. Besides, the rush that was used to make the light grows in Halton County.

There are three rushlight holders in the collection of the National Museum of Canada, all made of wrought iron. One of these (NMC

2
Brass rushlight holder
Halton County Museum

D-276) is similar to the Halton County example described above, but the "candle socket" is not as high as the pincer jaws, and the base is a large conoid piece of cork. A second holder (NMC D-277) lacks the socket, and has the free end of the movable arm coiled into an ornamental spiral; the base is a tall, rectangular block of wood. In both of these there is some twisting of the metal. The third example (NMC D-275; figure 1) is not twisted. The movable arm terminates in a disc-shaped counterweight, and the fixed part is relatively tall and has a decoration of two annular "beads" on its lower part. Below this it expands to join the three curved legs that make up the base. This is the traditional form of rushlight holder, similar to that used in the crest of the Rushlight Club. All three holders were purchased from Mr. J. E. Flanigan of Brockville, Ont.

CANDLES

The candle's early history is uncertain and controversial, but it is generally agreed that it developed gradually from the taper, a rope impregnated with grease, wax, or bitumen. The taper was certainly used in Roman times, but whether the *candela* mentioned in Latin writings was a candle in our sense (that is, a self-supporting column of solid fuel with an internal wick) or some form of lamp is a matter of dispute.[5] By about the seventh century candles of essentially modern form existed, and the celebrated time-candles of King Alfred were certainly true candles. Early candles were made by pouring the melted fuel over the wick or by repeated dipping of the wick in the fuel; casting in a tubular mould was introduced in the fourteenth century.[6] By the time Europeans settled in North America in the sixteenth and seventeenth centuries, they were using candles that, except for the material, were essentially the same as we know today.

The substance almost exclusively used for candle-making in pioneer days was tallow rendered from the fat of sheep or cattle. Beeswax was also available, and was used to make candles for religious ceremonies, but it was too expensive for ordinary domestic use. Sometimes, however, it was added to the tallow for greater stiffness. Wicks were of twisted cotton string.

Tallow candles had a number of disadvantages. The biggest probably was a tendency to bend or collapse in warm weather. Various substances were added to stiffen the tallow and improve the light. The following is a recipe of 1839: "Melt together ten ounces of mutton tallow, a quarter of an ounce of camphor, four ounces of beeswax, and two ounces of alum. Candles made of these materials burn with a very clear light."[7] The same writer recommends steeping the wicks in lime-water (calcium hydroxide) and saltpetre (potassium nitrate). Candles made from tallow, camphor, beeswax, and alum were later manufactured commercially under the name of adamantine candles.[8] A letter in the New Brunswick Museum Archives dated June 11, 1844, and signed by John Ward & Sons of Saint John, acknowledges receipt of forty boxes of "Adamantine Candles" from Messrs. Hancock & Mann of Boston.

Guttering was another problem. Any irregularity, such as a bit of carbon from the wick, could melt a channel into the edge of the candle, through which liquid tallow would run off before it could be burned. The early wicks of twisted cotton particularly tended to form unburned ends of carbon. This problem was partly overcome by the invention, about 1820, of the plaited wick, which splayed out during combustion so that the separate ends were completely consumed.[9]

Finally, tallow candles, being made of animal fat, were likely to be eaten by mice and rats. For this reason they had to be kept in a tightly covered box or "candle safe." One type of container made for this purpose was of sheet metal, about eighteen inches long, and cylindrical in shape. It had a hinged lid in the middle and a loop at each end so that it could be hung on the wall. Examples are known from Nova Scotia and Ontario.

If itinerant candle-makers plied their trade in the British colonies, as they did in the United States, they left little record of their passage. Candle-making seems to have been shared by the sophisticated manufacturers in the towns and the housewives on the farms. The advertisement gives an idea of the wares available in 1825 from professional candle-makers. But local manufacturers could not meet the demand

Novascotian, *Halifax, January* 26, 1825

F. W. CLARK,
MANUFACTERER, OF SOAP AND CANDLES.
UPPER WATER STREET.
WHOLESALE AND FOR EXPORTATION.

BEGS leave most respectfully to return his sincere thanks to the gentlemen of the Army, Navy, and his friends in general, for that pr ference (of Public favour) which he has experienced during the last 11 years ; and having spared neither expense nor exertion to render his Manufacture equal to any that can be imported, he trusts by a course of unremitting attention to merit a continuance of their patronage.

N. B. Families can be supplied with pure Tallow Candles with Wax'd wicks if ordered.—Also Turpentine Soap put up in small boxes. *Fiat Candles made to order.*

A piece of soap of Mr. Clark's Manufacture has been left at our office for public inspection. We have submitted it to some Judges, who think it of superior quality.

January 26———faw.

WATCH STOPPED.

STOPPED yesterday at the Police office, supposed, to have been Stolen, a SILVER WATCH, which has been Remired by Joseph Henderson at Windsor,

and large lots of candles were imported from the United States. In 1826 "48 boxes of Dipt and Mould Candles" from Boston were offered for sale in Halifax, the same town where Mr. Clark, the candle-maker, was operating.[10] Later English manufacturers entered the market with both moulded and composite candles, the latter perhaps being the tallow and beeswax mixture.[11]

Domestic production of candles, like the commercial, was both by dipping and by casting in moulds, depending on the housewife. Anne Langton wrote in January, 1839: "We have latterly made dip candles in preference to moulds, it is much more agreeable to have one good making, and have done for a time, than to be filling your moulds every day."[12] But evidently things did not always go as well as she wished, for in December of the same year she wrote to her brother William in England: "I wish I could have an hour's conversation with a tallow-chandler. Can you procure me some hints concerning the business, as to the temperature of the room, temperature of the tallow, etc.; what can prevent a dip from being thicker at the bottom than at the top? Also look at one properly made and tell me how near the wick reaches to the bottom of the candle."[13] Evidently the reply was not too helpful, for in August 1840 she wrote:

Thank you for the information that you got for me. Part of it will be useful, but the plan of dipping by means of a pulley is scarcely applicable to my small scale of operations. More frequently I have a very small amount of tallow, so that a box to admit six or seven candles is all that I can well afford, as I have no means of keeping up the temperature but by replenishing from the fire. A small stick with six candles on it can be dipped by the hand as easy as any other way. What I have gained from your enquiries is that I ought to raise them from the tallow more slowly than I have been accustomed to do.[14]

Her brother John, however, took the suggestion about mechanical dipping more seriously, and eventually built for Anne an elaborate

revolving frame, like the stern paddle wheel of a river boat. Anne made a sketch of herself operating it. In April 1846, using this device, Anne was able to make forty-nine pounds of dipped candles.

Guillet[15] gives a very good account of candle-making by the dipping method. Sticks about two feet in length were used. To these five or six candle wicks were tied by one end, so that they hung down like a well-spaced fringe. The tallow was melted in a pot over the fire, usually with a little water added to prevent scorching. There is no record of the use of a double boiler, which is curious because this device was well known. Optimum temperature for dipping seems to be just at the melting point. Holding the ends of the stick, the candle-maker dipped the dangling wicks into the melt, then withdrew them and hung them to congeal, usually between the backs of two chairs. If there were a lot of sticks, then two long poles were stretched between the chair backs and the dipping sticks laid across these. After the first one or two dips it was advisable to pull the wicks straight while they were still semi-pliable.

In the dipping method it was more efficient to make a number of candles at once, because by the time the last set of wicks was dipped the first was ready to be dipped again. This principle was utilized in various rotary frames which enables the candle-maker to stay in one spot. The usual frame was made like a windlass, the spokes each supporting at the end a cluster of wicks on a stick or block of wood. Each cluster would be dipped, hung on the spoke, the wheel rotated to the next spoke, its cluster dipped, and so on. John Langton's device was more ingenious. Its axle was horizontal, with twelve radial spokes in a vertical plane at each end. From the end of each spoke a short piece of wood dangled from a loose swivel. This piece of wood had a hole to receive one end of a dipping stick. When set up, the device would have had twelve dipping sticks, each with eight dangling wicks. The looseness of the pivoted sticks kept the wicks hanging vertically in any position during rotation, yet allowed the operator to raise them and then lower them into the rectangular tallow holder.

Candle dipping was most successful in fall or spring, when the room could be cool even with a fire; the temperature of the tallow and of the surrounding air had to be right for good results. These and other variables led most housewives to prefer making their candles in moulds. This more common method also had the advantage that making a few candles was just as efficient as making a large batch, and it was therefore possible to use tallow as it became conveniently available. Mrs. Traill, in her famous *Guides*, devotes about two pages to candle-making with moulds but gives only passing reference to the dipping method.[16] In an earlier letter home she wrote:

Every one makes their own candles (i.e. if they have any materials to make them from). The great difficulty of making candles—and, as far as I see the only one, is procuring the tallow, which a bush-settler, until he begins to kill his own beef, sheep, and hogs, is rarely able to do, unless he buys; and a settler buys nothing that he can help. A cow, however, that is unprofitable, old, or unlikely to survive the severity of the coming winter, is often suffered to go dry during the summer, and get her own living, till she is fit to kill in the fall. Such an animal is often slaughtered very advantageously, especially if the settler have little fodder for his cattle. The beef is often excellent, and good store of candles and soap may be made from the inside fat. These candles, if made three parts beef and one part hogs'-lard, will burn better than any store-candles, and cost less than half price. The tallow is merely melted in a pot or pan, convenient for the purpose, and having run the cotton wicks into the moulds (tin or pewter moulds for six candles cost three shillings at the stores, and last many, many years), a stick or skewer is passed through the loops of your wicks, at the upper part of the stand, which serve the purpose of drawing the candles. The melted fat, not too hot, but in a fluid state, is then poured into the moulds till they are full; as the fat gets cold it shrinks, and leaves a hollow at the top of the mould; this requires filling up when quite cold. If the candles do not draw readily, plunge the mould for an instant into hot water, and the candles will come out easily. Many persons prefer making dip-candles for kitchen use; but for my own part I think the trouble quite as great, and give the preference, in point of neatness of look, to the moulds. It may be, my maid and I did not succeed so well in making the dips as the moulds.[17]

With apologies to the pioneers who practised the art of candle-making of necessity, I offer a couple of hints that they may have known but did not record. For one thing I have found it useful to stand the mould in a shallow pan of cold water while pouring. This congeals the tallow at the wick tip before it can run out around the knotted wick end. Keeping the wick tight and therefore straight did not seem to worry the pioneers, but it did me, so I tied the wicks to the "skewer," and twisted the latter enough to take up any slack. Another way is to tie the string to the stick with a "clove-hitch" knot, which can be pulled tight from the free end.[18]

Candle moulds, whatever their relative popularity, must have been used in a great many kitchens, for they continue to appear in Canadian antique shops and shows.

A typical example (LSR 4) was purchased from Mr. C. L. Graham of Napanee, Ont. It is of sheet metal, now painted black, and consists of 6 slightly tapering tubes. These are open at the upper end, and closed at the lower with a conical cap except for a small hole for the wick. The 6 tubes are held together by a rectangular pan at the top and an inverted pan at the bottom with holes into which the conical points are set. There is a curved handle for carrying and a wire ring for hanging. Height of the mold to top of handle is 11½ inches. Candles made in this mould are a little over-size in diameter for most candle holders. Similar moulds are known from Quebec.

There are many variants in candle moulds. The number of tubes may be greater or less than six; single-tube moulds and also sets of twenty-four are known. Many moulds have no base and are not self-supporting. Presumably they were held in a wooden stand. In some examples the tubes are arranged in a circle, as that (LSR 318) shown in figure 4, which was purchased from Garrett's Antiques of New Glasgow, N.S. There may have been some slight advantage to this arrangement for convenience in pouring.

3
Six-tube candle mould
Napanee, Ont. LSR 4

4
Six-tube circular candle mould
New Glasgow, N.S. LSR 318. ROM *photo*

In the coastal areas of New England the settlers discovered that an excellent candle wax could be obtained by boiling the berries of the wax myrtle (*Myrica cerifera*). This "bayberry" wax produces candles that are firm, give a good light, and have an attractive grey-green colour, which, however, fades on extended exposure to daylight. On being extinguished, they give off a smoke with a pleasant aromatic odour. Bayberry candles may have been made in Nova Scotia or New Brunswick, where many of the early settlers came from New England and brought with them their domestic lore and customs.

Late in the eighteenth century a new substance for candles was introduced, spermaceti, the waxy fat from the head of the sperm whale. It became popular early in the nineteenth century with wealthier people because it gave a bright steady flame with no odour or running, but it was much too expensive for ordinary folk to buy, either as raw material or finished candle.[19]

After 1831, stores began selling candles made from stearine, a material which quickly proved superior to tallow, yet was cheaper than beeswax or spermaceti. Stearine is a solid mixture of stearic, oleic, and palmitic acids. It is made by converting animal and vegetable fats into soap, thus eliminating the glycerine, and then treating the soap with sulphuric acid. Stearine candles could be made in mechanically operated moulds on an assembly-line basis, with the result that candle manufacture by the 1850s passed mostly into the hands of large commercial companies, such as those of Price and Field in London, England. Stearine candles are still available; they are hard and snowy white, and burn with a good flame.

The petroleum industry that began about 1860 soon made available a new candle substance, paraffin wax, which was just as good as stearine for large-scale manufacture and much less expensive. From that time on the paraffin candle has been almost the only kind available for both utilitarian and decorative purposes.[20] There is little record of its impact, because it was so small an innovation compared to the kerosene lamp that came in about the same time. But it has remained the backstop to that and other spectacular means of illumination, and has retained for the candle a place of honour on ceremonial occasions.

CANDLE HOLDERS

In my boyhood, paraffin candles were still an important auxiliary source of light, called upon when the kerosene was in short supply or the electricity failed. This did not happen often enough to make special candle holders seem necessary. We just dripped some molten wax from the lighted end onto a saucer and pressed the base of the candle into this while it was still sticky. In earlier times, however, when candles were the common, perhaps the commonest, means of lighting, candle holders of some sort were household necessities, both in the pioneer's cabin and the leading citizen's mansion. Candles can be held in two ways, either by being fitted into a socket, or by being impaled on a spike. The socket type came in many varieties, some of which are described below. The spike type is called a pricket, and in its simplest form is a nail projecting through a piece of wood. Very elaborate prickets are used to hold the ritual candles in the Catholic Church.

One of the basic types of socket candle holder (NMC D-519) is illustrated in figure 5. It consists of a short vertical tube of suitable inside diameter to receive the candle stem. At the top is a flaring lip to catch minor dripping. Bigger drips are caught in the saucer-shaped basal tray. There is a ring-shaped, decorated metal handle. This example is of tin, is brass plated, and stands about two inches high. Similar holders were made in iron, brass, or pewter. Variations are

5
BELOW: *Simple candle holder probably Quebec.* NMC D-519

mainly in the tray, which may be shallow or deep, or have the rim scalloped.

This type of holder is practical but by the time that the candle has burned down to the lip of the socket it has cemented itself into position and is difficult to remove. Many holders were therefore made with a piston on which the bottom of the candle rested. The piston could be raised or lowered by means of a finger grip projecting through a vertical slot on the side of the socket tube (figure 6). With this

6
Candle holder with piston
with burning tallow candle
Isle-aux-Coudres, Que. NMC A-125

7
RIGHT: *Springloaded candle holder*
Perth, Ont. NMC D-605

arrangement it was possible not only to eject the butt of the candle, but also to adjust the amount of candle projecting above the socket at all times. Many such holders had long tubes, and pistons that could be raised or lowered most of the length. Thus even a long candle needed to project only a few inches above the lip of the socket; as it burned down it could be raised, providing constant support for the tallow, and keeping the flame at about the same height above the table.

From this arrangement was developed the spring-loaded piston, which could raise the candle by itself (figure 7). To keep the candle in the holder the socket was capped with a short tube having a turned-in flange. This gripped the rim of the candle but left enough opening in the centre to permit combustion. The cap also prevented guttering and dripping. Candle holders of this sort, in brass, often bear the plate of Cornelius and Baker, Philadelphia, who operated from 1853 to 1869.

A curious variant of the common candle holder (NMC D-518) is

8
Candle holder with clamp
Norwich, Ont. NMC D-518
9
ABOVE: *"Hog-scraper" candle holder*
purchased at North Hatley, Que.
NMC A-1112

shown in figure 8. What appears to be a socket for the candle is in fact closed near the top. The candle is actually held by a spring-loaded clamp, which can be swivelled to the side. Such an arrangement permitted the candle to burn down almost to its last vestige, while allowing easy removal of the residue. This candle holder was presented to the National Museum of Canada by the late Merrill Kinsey, who stated that it had been in his family home in Norwich, Ont., for at least fifty years.

A very popular type of candle holder in the first half of the nineteenth century was that which came to be called the "hog-scraper" (figure 9; NMC A-1112). It had no handle, and in place of the conventional concave saucer tray had a narrow, convex base. A candle holder of this sort appears on the shelf over the fireplace in the sketch by Anne Langton of her brother's cabin in 1837. There is some disagreement as to how this type of candle holder got its name. Real hog-scrapers of this general form were made and used, but whether they were copied from the candle holder, or merely gave it their name, is uncertain. Knowing from personal experience that scraping a slaughtered pig is a messy job, I cannot imagine a real candle holder being used for that purpose.

Another type of adjustable candle holder is shown in figure 10. The socket is made by twisting a piece of strap iron in a spiral, leaving a space between adjacent turns. Inside is a flat piece of metal with a handle projecting out through the spiral slot. By moving this handle, the piece of metal (which forms the support for the bottom of the candle) can be raised or lowered. The same principle was also used to raise and lower the wick in certain oil and lard lamps. This type of candle holder is characteristically European, but those shown in figure 17 were purchased by Mr. Stratford Lee Morton in Yarmouth, N.S. There is another example in the Confederation Centre Museum at Charlottetown, P.E.I.

10
Spiral candle holders
Yarmouth, N.S.
Morton Collection, St. Louis, Mo.

The term candlestick, commonly applied to various holders, properly belongs to the pedestal type, such as shown in figure 11. These were usually tall and ornamental, and formed the central decoration of mantelpiece or table. The metals used were brass, pewter, and silver, and were made by casting or turning, or a combination of these methods. The example shown (NMC D-516) is one of a pair from Arnprior, Ont., and is of cast and turned brass. Candlesticks were also made of glass and, like other cast glass objects of the nineteenth century, appeared in a variety of patterns. As such candlesticks are still being made and sold, the pattern is the principal clue to date of manufacture; for illustrations and descriptions the reader should consult the standard works on pressed glass,[21] but in general it may be said that highly intricate patterns are likely to be the old ones. Even more indicative of age is a combination of blown glass with casting. Candlesticks used in Canada in the early nineteenth century came from England or from Massachusetts. Later, as a Canadian glass industry developed, one unique form made its appearance here. This was the mercury-glass blown candlestick made at the Napanee Glass House during its brief period of existence from 1881 to 1883.[22] Three examples are in the Canadiana Department of the Royal Ontario Museum and others are in the collection of Mr. J. Mooney of Napanee. They are of relatively thin, milky glass, with a distinct pontil mark on the base. The silvery appearance, popular in the late nineteenth century, was created by introducing a little metallic mercury to the interior of the hollow glass object while it was still warm. The glass-blower then shook the candlestick to spread the mercury uniformly in a film adhering to the inner surface. These candlesticks, according to oral tradition, were made from the residues of window-glass melts. Another story is that the somewhat cloudy glass produced by the Napanee Glass House, one of the reasons for its failure, had to be disguised by the mercury finish.

11
Brass candlestick
Arnprior, Ont. NMC D-516
12
BELOW: *Tin candle sconce*
Shannonville, Ont. NMC D-271

13
Tin scoop used as a
candle sconce
purchased at North Hatley, Que.
NMC A-1197

Candles can be supported on the wall by means of a sconce. A simple form is shown in figure 12. It is one of a number that are said to have been purchased about 1885 for a hotel in Shannonville, Ont., but were never used. It is made of black-painted tin, with a straight back, a nearly circular base, and a split candle socket. This type of sconce is represented in the National Museum of Canada collection by other examples of less sophisticated design, probably much older than 1885. Candle sconces, like lamp sconces, were often provided with reflectors, which could be a simple plate of shiny tin or a mosaic of mirror segments cut and fitted together to form a roughly parabolic surface.

The curious candle holder shown in figure 13 was evidently improvised from a small tin scoop. There is no socket for the candle, which had to be attached with melted wax. The curved surface of the scoop made a natural reflector. A small hole near the lip permitted hanging on a nail in the wall, while the scoop handle provided a convenient means of carrying. This example (NMC A-1197) came from Mrs. Frances Bowen of North Hatley, Que. Later, candle sconces were made deliberately in the shape of a scoop. The example (LSR

179) shown in figure 14 was purchased from Mr. Lee Phillips of Bruce Mines, Ont.; it has a decorative transfer representing flowers, indicating a late nineteenth-century or later manufacture. The candle fits into a doughnut-shaped cast-iron ring.

Sophisticated society had the elaborate hanging candle holders known as chandeliers. On ceremonial occasions the effect of dozens of candles glinting on hanging glass prisms was spectacular. Ordinary Canadian homes could not afford anything so magnificent, and even in churches and public halls the chandeliers were likely to be improvised by the local tinsmith. However, well-to-do householders might have owned a type of ornamental candle holder frequently mentioned in newspaper advertisements of the 1840s and 1850s, the girandole.

Reference to various dictionaries, English, American, and French, going back to 1884, shows a general agreement that the term girandole, as applied to a lighting device, means a branching or multiple candle holder, ornamented, and supported by a base or a wall bracket, in contrast to the chandelier which is suspended. Few antique dealers seem to know this term, but many use "girandelle" to refer to vase-shaped candle holders of glass or china, usually with a circle of pendants. The Oxford Dictionary of 1901 gives alternate, presumably erroneous, spellings of girandole as gironell, girondel, and girandel. Misspelled or not, the essential features are the branching frame and multiple sockets. The single-candle "girandelles" might better be called candle vases.

In spite of the frequent references to girandoles in old advertisements, examples of them are rare today. A good one is shown in figure 15 (LSR 329). It was purchased from Mr. Harold H. Johnson of Burlington, Ont., and is said to have been obtained east of Oshawa. Total height is 16 inches. It rests on a rectangular base of white marble, 6 × 3½ × 1 inches. The main part is an elaborate casting, secured

14
Metal candle sconce
made to resemble a scoop
Bruce Mines, Ont. LSR 179. ROM *photo*

15
Girandole
purchased in Burlington, Ont.
LSR 329. ROM *photo*

to the base by a bolt. The lower part is an open-work plaque, on which is represented in bas-relief a young girl in nineteenth-century costume, holding a bowl. Beside her, in expectant attitudes, are a poodle and a fawn. Behind her are hollyhocks, and above her is an arbor of grape vines. In the background is a balustrade with an urn-like pedestal. The other side of the plaque shows the design as a crude intaglio, indicating that the girandole was not intended to be seen from both sides, or in a mirror. At the top of the plaque is an inverted flower, from which 3 branches extend, one straight up, the other 2 in curves to the side. Each is ornamented with elaborately coiling branches, and each terminates in a small pedestal, into which a candle socket shaped like a lotus flower is screwed. Between socket and pedestal is secured the cross-arm of an oval band cut and pressed to simulate a ring of grape leaves. From each leaf a glass prism pendant with cut stars is suspended, 10 for each band or a total of 30 for the girandole. All of the metal parts have been gilded, in recent years judging from the fresh appearance and the careless way in which the paint has been allowed to seep onto the base. The girl's costume suggests a date of 1850 to 1855, according to Mrs. K. B. Brett, Curator of Textiles, Royal Ontario Museum. Significant features are the jacket with its flaring lower portion, the full but not flaring skirt with the lower third of lace or embroidery, the three-quarter, open sleeves, the low-cut neckline, and the hair, which appears combed from a middle part with hanging curls.

The style of ornamentation of this girandole suggests English manufacture, but in the headquarters of the Rochester Historical Society, Rochester, N.Y., there are two girandoles that are almost identical except for the plaques, which depict American frontier figures. So this type of girandole, at least, was evidently made in the United States.

The term candelabrum is somewhat overlapping in definition with girandole, but usage seems to restrict candelabrum to the multiple candle holder in which the sockets are arranged in line, either horizontally or inclined. Such candle holders resemble the traditional menorah of Hebrew ritual. They are often seen in Canadian antique shops, but I have no data on their history in this country.

CANDLE ACCESSORIES

The tallow candle with its wick of twisted cotton required constant attention. Incomplete combustion of the wick left carbon remnants called snuff which cut down the amount of light, and fell onto the edge of the candle to cause guttering. Without the frequent use of the instrument called a snuffer, there was a rapid decline in illumination and a wasteful consumption of the candle. The snuffer, therefore, was an important household necessity in the eighteenth and early nineteenth centuries.

A typical snuffer (figure 16) looks a little like a pair of scissors, but one of the blades bears a kind of box or pan, and the other a little door, as it were, for the box. When the wick was trimmed with the scissor blades, the burned portion was pushed into the box without falling onto the candle. The blade that carried the box was usually longer and pointed, and could be used to lift a fallen wick to permit trimming.

Snuffers were made of iron, brass, or silver. There was great variety in style and ornamentation, but the basic design did not usually differ

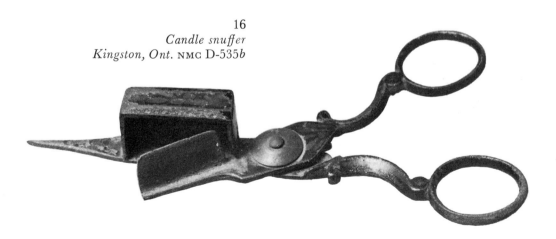

16
Candle snuffer
Kingston, Ont. NMC D-535*b*

much from that described.[23] An exception is shown in figure 17. Here the short blade merely presses the wick into the box, where a pivoted blade comes down to cut it neatly. This particular example (NMC B-29) was purchased from Mr. Fred L. Mayes of Saint John, N.B.

For some reason the expression "to snuff a candle" has come to mean to extinguish it. This, of course, is quite wrong. The snuffer was used to remove unburned wick or "snuff," and so actually increased the brilliance of the flame. The real extinguisher was usually of the type shown in figure 18 (NMC A-1053). It is a simple cone of tin with a metal-strip handle, and was purchased from the Misses Elliott of Danville, Que. Other models were made of brass or even silver, with or without ornamentation, but were essentially the same. Extinguishers were probably not as common as snuffers, as candles were usually put out by blowing on the flame, and then pinching out the last ember between thumb and finger.

17
Candle snuffer with cutting blade
purchased in Lancaster, N.B. NMC B-29

18
Candle extinguisher
purchased at Danville, Que. NMC A-1053

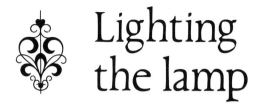

CHAPTER II

Lighting the lamp

BEFORE THE INVENTION of the electric lamp, where there was light there always had to be fire. Part of the history of lighting, therefore, is the record of how the kindling of flame was made progressively easier. Of course the basic reason for making fire was to obtain heat for warmth and cooking. Once logs were burning in the hearth it was simple to light a candle, or a tobacco pipe, by means of a blazing splinter. But until the days of the friction match, the initial ignition was a tricky, arduous job. Fire was carefully conserved, and if by ill chance the banked coals went dead over night, a hurried trip to a more fortunate neighbour might be necessary to get a small share of the remnants of yesterday's blaze.[1] Some people used a covered sheet-metal box with a handle for carrying live coals, but ordinarily a shovel would serve if the trip were short.

Primitive tribes had various friction devices, like the bow drill for making fire, but European man and his American offshoot had long depended on the sparks struck from iron by the impact of flint. The flint-and-steel outfit was one of the normal necessities of living. Such an outfit (LSR 270) is shown in figure 19. It was purchased from Mr. Ronald Bousfield of Hampton, N.H., but is similar to the tinder-box illustrated by Jefferys (p. 206) and described by other Canadian antiquarians. The main part is the container or tinder-box, a low, cylindrical can with a tight-fitting lid and ring-shaped handle. The lid bears a split tube to receive a candle. Of the contents of the box, the disc with handle is for extinguishing lighted tinder. The iron bar with handle is the strike-a-light or "steel." The pieces of "flint" are in this case chert, about the same thing mineralogically. The dark strips of fabric are pieces of scorched linen and are of recent manufacture, but some shreds of tinder did come with the box.

Let us hear from an actual user of flint and steel. The following are the recollections of a middle-aged man in the 1860s, telling of the conditions during his boyhood.[2] *In every house was a tin box, a round tin cup rising some inch-and-a-half at the sides, in which was a*

19

OPPOSITE: *Tinder box and accessories New Hampshire.* LSR 270. ROM *photo*

quantity of "tinder." On that was a plain disc as a cover, and over all
a lid which had on its upper surface a socket for a candle. A flint – a
common gun flint, much more common then than now – and an old
file. This was the fire-raising apparatus. The flint in the right hand,
the steel in the left, its point raised above and pointing to the "tinder,"
a few strokes of the flint against the steel and a faint spark is evoked
from the tinder. To make the spark a generating blaze, a slip of dry
pine wood, its end dipped in melted brimstone, sufficed. These splin-
ters of sulphur-tipped shavings were the originators of the present
lucifer match, and in our boyhood days we spent many an hour shav-
ing them from the block, a labor which, as a pastime, would have been
pleasant, but as a task was irksome.

This account is very graphic, but like so many of its kind, was written to tell how the writer did it, not how the reader might do it himself. In trying to recreate this and other early techniques, I have found that little tricks or refinements not mentioned in the old accounts help to make the desired result possible or at least easier to obtain. For instance, I have learned that for satisfactory tinder one should have a piece of old linen from which the size has long since been washed and which is then charred almost to a coal. I use the following method. Tear the linen into pieces about three inches long, and put them into a small coffee tin and close the lid. Then put the tin on a hot stove and wait until there is a strong odour of scorching linen, even with the lid shut. The cloth should be as nearly black as it can be and still hold together. Another suggested method is to place the linen pieces in an oven and heat them until at some point a red glow appears, which is then extinguished by pressing.[3]

Guillet[4] mentions punk from the sugar maple as the common tinder used by Canadian backwoodsmen. Presumably this was the dried interior of a rotted maple log, something not often seen today. Sometimes the tinder was primed with a pinch of loose gunpowder.

There seems, however, to be no record of tinder made by dipping linen in a solution of saltpetre (potassium nitrate). Cloth treated this way can be made to glow readily with sparks from the flint and steel. If it was never used it is a curious oversight, because the slow-match, a piece of rope impregnated with saltpetre, was long known to artillery-men and military engineers.

Another secret of success is to have a sharp edge on the "flint." True flint is rare in North America but any solid silica mineral will do: a quartz crystal, a piece of chert, chalcedony or agate, or even a solid piece of quartzite. The edge is struck with a downward glancing blow against the steel, causing sparks to fall on the tinder. Natural pyrite can be used as a substitute for the steel, but the sparks produced are less abundant.

On occasion the firing mechanism of a flint-lock gun or pistol was used to make fire by flashing it into tinder. From this came the flint-lock lighter or tinder pistol, the flint-bearing hammer of which struck sparks, not into a "pan" of gunpowder, but into a small box contain-ing scorched linen. The example (NMC F-108) shown in figure 20 is marked on the sides "MORTIMER" and "LONDON." It was purchased

20
Tinder pistol, English early nineteenth century purchased in Victoria, B.C. NMC F-108

from Mr. Robert Nichols of Victoria, B.C., who as far as known obtained it in the province. Note the small brass candle socket, analogous to that of the tinder-box. A version of the tinder pistol is made today as a cigarette lighter; it uses sparking alloy instead of flint and a naphtha-soaked wick as tinder.

Old-time accounts of making fire with flint and steel speak of blowing gently on the tinder after it has taken a glow from the spark to make it blaze. I have never been able to do this, but like the writer of the reminiscences, I have used the sulphur splint. I make these by splitting a six-inch piece of straight-grained pine into slips about $\frac{3}{8}$ inch wide and $\frac{1}{16}$ inch thick. The ends are trimmed to a blunt point. Melting powdered sulphur in a test tube over a Bunsen burner flame, I dip the points of the splint into the melt, repeating the action after a moment of cooling until a tip of solid sulphur has been built up at the end of the stick. Such sulphur matches once had many uses around the home, even after the friction match became available. In using them with flint and steel, one finds that the glow started by the spark on the tinder is expanded a bit by gentle blowing; then the sulphur tip of the splint is brought in contact with the ember; with a little more blowing the sulphur will break into flame. Be careful not to inhale at this moment, or you may get a choking whiff of sulphur dioxide.

The steel strike-a-light took many forms. A wide variety used by Canadian Indians are preserved in the ethnology collection of the National Museum of Canada. However, as our anonymous writer noted, an old file was probably the usual steel.

Various writers, including Charles Dickens, have commented on the difficulty and frustration of trying to make fire with flint and steel, especially on a cold or damp morning. Others apparently felt the same way and tried to find an easier method. In addition to the tinder pistols there were a number of mechanical devices, such as the tinder-box patented by I. Ives of Farrington, Conn.[5] This consisted of a little trough-like metal box in which flint and tinder were stored. A steel wheel mounted outside one end could be spun rapidly by pulling a string wound around its axle. The operator held the flint against the whirling wheel so as to direct the shower of sparks onto the tinder in the box. Two examples of this device have been described and illustrated by Christy (pp. 87, 229), who identified them as of English manufacture, but the invention is certainly American. No example has been reported as yet from Canada, but it should be watched for, especially in the Atlantic provinces.

Long after flint and steel had been abandoned and almost forgotten as a means of fire-making, chemical technology revived the idea in a different form. About the turn of the century the Austrian chemist, Karl Auer von Welsbach, discovered that soft iron alloyed with traces of certain "rare-earth" metals would give off showers of sparks when scratched vigorously. An alloy of iron and cerium proved most effective, and was produced under the name of Auer metal. A piece mounted on one end of a tweezer-like device so that it was scraped against a miniature file on the other tip when the "tweezers" were squeezed made a very good instrument for lighting gas jets, and examples are still sold today. The "flint" of a modern pocket lighter is also a form of Auer metal.

THE FRICTION MATCH

As physical science developed in the latter part of the eighteenth century, chemical methods of making fire were discovered. Most of these depended on the properties of potassium chlorate ($KClO_3$), which was first made in 1787 by the French chemist, Claude Louis Berthollet. This is a compound that is relatively unstable and gives up its oxygen readily. Mixed intimately with combustible substances and stimulated by friction or heat, potassium chlorate will burn or even explode. Berthollet found, for example, that a mixture of the compound with powdered sugar, when brought into contact with a drop of sulphuric acid, would immediately burst into flame.

This reaction is said to have been applied to practical fire-making by a Parisian named Chancel in 1805.[6] He made wooden splints with one end tipped with potassium chlorate and sulphur paste, and sold them in a kit that included a small jar containing an asbestos pad moistened with "oil of vitriol" (sulphuric acid). The splint was ignited by touching the tip to the acid and quickly withdrawing it from the jar. In some versions of the Chancel match the paste of potassium chlorate and sugar was a coating over a sulphur head, ensuring certain ignition of the match stick.

It is easy to make Chancel matches. Old accounts speak of carefully mixing the ingredients as dry powders, but this is dangerous for friction can ignite potassium chlorate. The risk can be avoided by adding the two substances in equal quantity to water to make a thin paste which can be stirred without danger. I add a few drops of water-soluble glue; this is not necessary, but it makes a stronger, more tenacious head, and delays the ignition until the match is well out of the jar. I use a small, wide-mouth bottle with a plain cork and a circular pad of asbestos at the bottom. Strong sulphuric acid, a very corrosive liquid, is poured over the pad, sufficient to leave a slight excess of liquid. The jar must be kept tightly corked when not in use because concentrated sulphuric acid is very hygroscopic and will absorb moisture from the atmosphere until it has diluted itself to an ineffectual weakness. This was one of the complaints about the Chancel match.

These matches are said to have been introduced into England about 1815 by one Mr. Heurtner, who had a shop on the Strand.[7]

The kits were sold under the name of "Instantaneous Light Box."[8] An improvement was introduced in 1828 by Samuel Jones of London. His "Promethean Match"[9] had a tiny glass globule of sulphuric acid embedded in the potassium chlorate head, and was lighted by crushing the head with a little pair of pliers.[10] All Chancel-type matches were expensive, inconvenient, and potentially dangerous, but they were so superior to flint and steel as a fire-maker that they had a wide use for about twenty years. A manufacturer in Tübingen is said to have produced sets in large quantities.[11] Similar kits were used, and presumably made, in North America. In figure 21 one of these (LSR 160) is shown; the case is not unlike that of some modern pocket lighters, but inside is a small socket for the sulphuric acid bottle and space for a number of matches. This example was purchased from Mr. Miner J. Cooper of Windsor, N.Y., who obtained it in Connecticut. If such kits were widely used in New England during the 1830s, some were likely brought into the British colonies, for many novelties and amenities in those days came from Boston.

The next step in the evolution of the match was to eliminate the

21
Instantaneous light box, American cover, sulphuric acid bottle main part of box. LSR 160

sulphuric acid bottle. It has been noted that potassium chlorate in mixtures with combustible substances may be inadvertently ignited by friction. The deliberate use of this property was the objective of an English inventor, John Walker of Stockton-on-Tees, Durham,[12] who produced a dry match in 1826 by coating the sulphur head of a splint with a mixture of potassium chlorate and "black antimony" (antimony sulphide). Walker marketed his invention under the name of "friction-light" but refused to patent it, and it was soon being made by others, including Samuel Jones, the inventor of the "Promethean." Many were sold under the name "Lucifer," a term that was carried over to later developments as a synonym of "match." The Lucifer match was usually a flat splint, and came in a rectangular cardboard box, the prototype of the familiar match box. With these matches was a piece of sandpaper; to ignite the match the head was pinched in a fold of the paper and drawn out quickly. Sometimes it did not ignite and sometimes the flaming head came off in the paper.

The modern friction match, which can be struck on any rough surface, appeared in Vienna in 1833, the product of the firm of Romer and Preshel.[13] In these matches white phosphorus was substituted for part or all of the potassium chlorate. In spite of the evidence of Austrian origin, English manufacturers named them Congreve matches and fostered the legend that they were invented by Sir William Congreve, of military rocket fame, who in truth had died several years before they appeared. Whatever their origin, they at once achieved a widespread popularity. Unfortunately the poisonous nature of white phosphorus was not at first fully recognized, and the men and women who made the matches often became the victims of phosphorus disease, suffering a mutilating decay of the jaw bones. Improvements and precautions eventually eliminated this hazard, and by 1860 the "strike-anywhere" match was in almost universal use throughout Europe and North America.

22
Brass match box, with "Congreve" matches
formerly the property
of Bishop John Strachan
University College, University of Toronto
courtesy Prof. H. N. Milnes. ROM *photo*

Typical "Congreve" matches and a characteristic container of the 1840s are shown in figure 22. They are said to have belonged to Bishop John Strachan (1778–1867), and were presented to University College, University of Toronto, by Mrs. G. Bagnani.

The container is a brass cylinder, with a dome-shaped cap fitting over the rim. At the apex of the cap is a small turned brass socket, suitable for a miniature candle. Another socket, of very small size, projects at an angle from the shoulder of the cap. Height of the match box to top of socket is $3\frac{1}{4}$ inches and diameter at the base is $1\frac{9}{16}$ inches. There are 32 matches preserved with the box, each a slender rounded splint $1\frac{7}{8}$ inches long and about $\frac{3}{32}$ inches in diameter. The heads are very small, in keeping with the danger of accidental ignition. Four different colours of head are represented: red, yellow, blue, and brown. Christy (p. 116) has described such varicoloured Congreve matches in the Bryant and May collection as of Austrian origin. Cylindrical brass match boxes with candle and match sockets have also been described and illustrated by Christy (pp. 280, 291). They date from between 1840 and 1850 and apparently were intended for "Vesta" matches, a wax-impregnated match that could be inserted in the tiny slanting socket and used briefly as a candle. However, the Congreve matches that came with the box also fit the socket nicely.

John Strachan was a Scot who came to Canada in 1799, was ordained in the Church of England, and eventually became the first bishop of Toronto and head of the church in Upper Canada (modern Ontario). During the War of 1812 he rallied Canadian patriotism, and he later contributed much to the development of Upper Canada. Unfortunately, his reactionary policies favouring dominance of the "established" church in politics and education made him a controversial figure in his time and an object of strong criticism by later historians. He was one of the founders of King's College which later became the University of Toronto, but here again his efforts to prevent its secularization by the legislature brought him into conflict with others, including the first vice-chancellor, the John Langton mentioned in chapter 1. In spite of our qualified admiration of this famous Canadian, it is fitting that mementoes of his life should be preserved in the University that he helped to establish.

The final step in the history of chemical fire-making was the invention of the safety match. The friction match, igniting on any rough surface, could be set off by accident or by the innocent playing of children. The remedy was to separate the igniting ingredients, putting part on the match head and part on the side of the match holder (figure 23). The first practical safety match is said to have been invented by J. E. Lundstrom of Jönköping, Sweden, in 1855.[14] The first American patent was taken out by T. W. Hjerpe in 1863.[15] In a way the safety match is a combination of the Chancel match and the Walker match. The match head is too inert to be ignited by simple friction but active enough to react to friction in contact with a stimulating chemical such as antimony sulphide. Although not as convenient as the friction match, the Swedish or safety match became popular as a pocket match for smokers, and survives today in the ubiquitous paper-match folder.

During the first half of the nineteenth century such matches as were available in Canada were imported from the United States or Europe. In 1856 Ezra Butler Eddy of Vermont settled in Hull, Que., across the Ottawa River from Bytown, the future city of Ottawa, and in rented space began making safety matches. Ten years later he had expanded into general lumber production, and by the 1870s he was mayor of Hull and member of the Quebec Legislature. Besides meeting most Canadian needs for matches, the E. B. Eddy Company exported them to many parts of the world.[16]

An unusual lighting device employing the friction match was patented by James S. Foley of Chicago, Ill.[17] The patent describes a tubular mechanism containing match heads which are forced by a

23
Safety-match container and matches North Hatley, Que. LSR 294

plunger out between two spring-metal claws and so ignited. An example of this device (LSR 267) is shown in figure 24. It was purchased from Mr. D. H. Kennedy of Weston, Ont. It consists of three parallel metal tubes, the middle one being for the plunger and the two outer ones for the match heads. These are introduced by rotating the common lid piece of the two outer tubes. An oval lever at the lower end of the device permits moving a match head into position from either tube. The lever has to be returned to mid-line before the plunger can be pushed down, and there is a covering for the opening when the device is not in use. The surface of the lever is inscribed "FOLEY & RUSE / TORONTO, ONT. / PAT$^{\underline{D}}$ 1887." I have tried this device with heads cut from wooden matches and have made it work only once, when the match head went off like a rocket. Probably the match heads were made specially for it.

24
Foley patent match lighter
Toronto, 1887. LSR 267

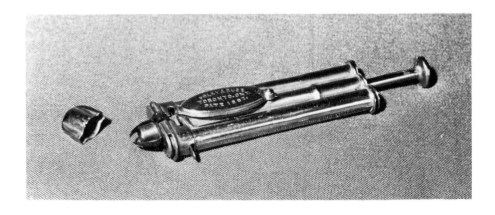

25
Iron double crusie, burning grease
Quebec City. LSR 263. ROM *photo*

CHAPTER III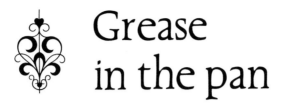

Grease in the pan

TALLOW is one of the few natural fats or waxes that is solid enough at normal temperatures to support itself and so provide the material for candles. But there are many other animal and vegetable fats, liquid or semi-liquid, that will burn with a luminous flame when conducted through a wick. The simplest way to use them for lighting is to place them in a shallow container, add some fibre as a wick, and apply a flame. So we have the primitive lamp, which has been invented many times in human history. Palaeolithic man scooped a hollow in a sandstone slab and made a lamp to illuminate his cave. Along the sea coast, half a clam shell served as a vessel for fish oil. In the Arctic the Eskimo carved a flat, half-oval dish from soapstone, added a piece of seal fat for fuel and a row of "Arctic cotton" fibres along the straight side of the dish for a wick. This device is as much a stove as a lamp.

In the ancient Mediterranean world, where western civilization began, early lamps were made of baked clay. Saucer-shaped at first, they progressed through pitcher shape to the classical design with its teapot-like spout. The fuel was olive oil and the wick was twisted cotton. The same form was also made in bronze, often with two or more wick spouts. During the Middle Ages, lamps of wrought iron appeared in central and northern Europe. They had two advantages over those of clay. They were almost unbreakable, and the metal body transmitted heat from flame to fuel. Because of the latter characteristic they could use solid fat in place of liquid oil. As olive oil was not produced in these regions, this was particularly important. Many different shapes of these grease lamps were evolved. The simplest was a shallow, rounded saucer without any special place for the wick. Then came square and triangular shapes with corners, where the wick could be conveniently located. It was an easy step next to exaggerate one of the corners into a wick channel and so produce the crusie lamp.

CRUSIE LAMPS

Crusies had been in use for many years before the colonization of North America began. The word "crusie" is of Scottish origin and seems to have been derived from "cruse," a vessel for oil. Most of the crusies that have been preserved from colonial times in New England or eastern Canada are similar to those that were used in the Scottish highlands. They consist of an iron pan roughly circular in the main part but with one side drawn out into a pointed channel for the wick. Opposite this channel the handle is attached, a strip of iron extending upward and forward, with a perforation near the upper end. To this end is attached, by a wire link, an iron spike shaped like a boat-hook. The hook could be caught on the edge of a shelf or mantle, or the point driven into a chink in the wall.

Crusies work well with tallow or lard, but the usual fuel in Canada was simply a piece of fat, from which the oil would be rendered by the heat of the flame. The first time that the fuel was introduced, or when the wick was replaced, it might be necessary to hold the lamp over the fire briefly to melt some of the fat; after that there would

26
ABOVE: *Iron two-wick crusie drip pan said to be from Quebec.* NMC D-258
27
RIGHT: *Iron covered crusie said to be from Barnston, Que.* LSR 35

always be enough residue, either melted or congealed, to get the flame started. The wick was a piece of twisted cotton cloth, and there was an optimum position for it in the pan, slightly draped over the lip of the channel. A small iron spike, the wick pick, was used to move the wick up or down. Often it was attached to the upper end of the lamp handle by a short length of chain. To catch any drip from the over-hanging wick, crusies were usually made double. The lower pan or drip catcher was of the same shape as the upper, but with a slightly longer front end. The handle was attached to the lower pan, and the upper or fuel pan was suspended just over the lower by a short handle hung over a hook on the main handle. The arrangement can be understood better by studying the illustrations.

The double crusie (LSR 263) shown in figure 25 was obtained in the Quebec City area by Mr. Godfrey Moore of St. Catharines, Ont., from whom it was purchased. Most Canadian crusies come from Quebec Province, the only exceptions known to me being two from Markham Township, Ont. Whether the "Scottish" crusie was brought over by the early French settlers or whether it was introduced by the Scottish immigrants to Canada is not known. Similar crusies, known as crassets, were used in the Channel Islands.[1] An example (NMC E-II-2b) from the Island of Guernsey is almost identical with the Quebec crusie of figure 25.

Naturally there were variants of the typical form. The crusie shown in figure 26 (NMC D-258) has two wick spouts, but it is evidently only the drip pan, and the fuel pan is missing. It was purchased from Mr. Phillip Shackleton of Manotick, Ont., but is said to have come from Quebec. Covered crusies are rare; one is illustrated by Thwing (p. 31). The example shown in figure 27 (LSR 35) was purchased from Mrs. Fern Brook of Simcoe, Ont., who obtained it at Barnston, Que. Although the iron is pitted, as if very old, the lid is of sophisti-cated design. It is attached to the top of the pan by means of a turned-

in rim, which can be sprung in or out of place. What appears to be a rivet in the centre of the lid is the broken pivot of a small plate, now missing, which could be swung to cover or expose the interior of the pan near the wick. A similar lid appears on a lamp illustrated by Thwing (p. 37) but this has a separate wick trough, no trace of which is evident on my example.

BETTY LAMPS

Some unknown genius, perhaps in the fifteenth century, figured out how to obtain the advantages of the double crusie in a single-pan lamp. He introduced a separate, sloping trough for the wick, inside the rim of the pan. Any drip from the wick would fall back into the pan. Perhaps this device was invented more than once, for two different versions were brought to America.

One form made of sheet metal ("tin") is associated with the German settlers of southeastern Pennsylvania, the so-called Pennsylvania Dutch. A good example (LSR 29) is shown in figure 28; it was purchased from Mr. C. F. McDougal of Ridgeway, Ont., and is said to have been used in the Port Colborne district. The sides of the pan are vertical and the front rounded, the outline suggesting a trefoil. Most of the top is covered by a two-part lid, the posterior part being fixed in place and the anterior part joined to it by a transverse hinge, so as to be swung back to expose the wick trough and part of the fuel cavity. The front end of the hinged lid is cut away in a rounded notch, so as to leave clear the tip of the wick trough. Lamps of this type are the traditional betty lamps, although the name may be extended to include all grease lamps with a separate wick trough.

Many suggestions as to the origin of the name "betty" have been noted by Thwing (p. 34). That author favours derivation from the

28
Tin betty lamp
Port Colborne, Ont. LSR 29

29
Iron betty lamp
Belleville, Ont. NMC D-274

German *besser*, meaning better. To these I would add the suggestion that it may have come from the German *Bette*, the old form of the word for bed. A dripless grease lamp could be used to light one's way to bed, or in other domestic activities not immediately adjacent to the fireplace. In a predominantly English-speaking society, "Bette" would inevitably come to be pronounced "betty."

Betty lamps came to Upper Canada with the immigration of settlers from Pennsylvania after the American revolution. They thus took the place that might have been occupied by crusies if the western province had been settled from Lower Canada. True crusies with an Ontario provenience are rare, but Pennsylvania-type betties are known from the Niagara Peninsula and from Waterloo and Oxford counties. An example from Beamsville had dried vestiges of the fuel still in it when purchased. Tradition has it that betty lamps were used in the Port Colborne area up to about 1840. Two examples from there have been covered at some relatively recent date with aluminum paint.

The betty lamp shown in figure 29 (NMC D-274) is of very different design. Like the typical crusie, the general shape of which it follows, it is made of wrought iron. A portion of the lid, in outline like a miniature of the pan, is hinged so as to swing and expose the wick trough and enough of the interior to permit refilling. There is a little flat finger grip on the hinged cover. This style of lamp was used in New England and was probably brought to Canada by United Empire Loyalists. The lamp illustrated was purchased from Mr. T. G. Wrightmeyer of Bath, formerly of Belleville, Ont.

Figure 30 illustrates an open betty lamp (NMC A-278) which is representative of a number of examples from Quebec Province. It is made of cast bronze, and the wick trough is riveted to the bottom of the pan. There are a relatively large number of these lamps in collections, identical in shape and design and presumably cast from the same mould. They appear to have been of rather late manufacture and may have been intended as trade goods.

In the United States there are other shapes and designs of betty lamps, even some made of pewter.[2] In Canada the majority of examples that have survived are of the Pennsylvania sheet-metal type, the only important variation being in size.

Crusie and betty lamps seem to have lost popularity well before the appearance of the kerosene lamp. Perhaps the trouble-free stearine candle displaced them. These lamps had certain advantages over the tallow candle: no elaborate preparation or constant care, and the possibility of being used to cast light downward without spilling grease. Early nineteenth-century newspapers and personal journals make little or no reference to them, but the number of examples that have survived suggests that in some areas, such as the vicinity of Quebec City, or the German-American settlements of southwestern Ontario, the crusie or betty once rivalled the candle as the principal source of domestic illumination.

30
*Bronze open betty lamp
said to be from Quebec.* NMC A-278

CHAPTER IV

When whale oil was king

THE LAMP SHOWN in figure 31 is burning whale oil. Compared with some whale-oil lamps it is of plain design, and might have been used in a kitchen or bedroom. The burner consists of two short wick tubes projecting through a metal disc, which is screwed into the collar of the font. Some whale-oil lamps were even simpler, while others were much more complicated in both body and burner, but for the first forty years of the nineteenth century, whale-oil lamps were the most sophisticated lighting device generally available.

The great demand for whale oil as a lamp fuel was the basis of the celebrated whaling industry of the eighteenth and nineteenth centuries. In northern countries, where olive oil was not available, man must have used animal fat as an illuminant from early times. Along the coasts, the occasional stranded whale would have provided an unforgettable abundance of fuel and food. As people learned how to make better weapons, and to build and handle sea-going craft, they were able to carry the search for whale meat and oil into the natural environment of their prey. By Viking times, the first to twelfth centuries A.D., they were hunting the larger species. The whaling industry spread from Scandinavia to the Bay of Biscay in the twelfth century, probably as a result of the Norman conquests. By the seventeenth

31
Glass hand lamp
with screw-in burner, burning whale oil
Philadelphia, Pa. LSR 259. ROM *photo*

century large-scale whaling was being carried out in Arctic waters, mostly by ships from the Netherlands. They were displaced in the mid-eighteenth century by British vessels aided by government subsidies. Principal areas of the hunt were the Norwegian Sea and Baffin Bay.

New England colonists joined the whaling operations in the western Arctic, and the industry continued to develop after the establishment of the independent United States of America. In many Massachusetts ports, especially those on the Island of Nantucket and in the New Bedford area, whaling became the way of life. Ships became progressively larger, and the pursuit became better organized and more widespread. As Arctic whaling declined, attention turned to the southern seas, where the whales produced a superior form of oil. Soon New Bedford became the whaling capital of the world. In 1830 the American whaling fleet brought in 106,800 barrels of sperm oil, 115,000 barrels of common whale oil, and 120,000 pounds of whale bone.[1]

In spite of a strong maritime tradition and close links with New England, the Atlantic colonies of British North America never really got into the whaling business. An attempt to set up a whaling station at Dartmouth, N.S., in the eighteenth century is said to have been discouraged by British authorities. A later effort may be recorded by a Halifax advertisement of 1829 calling for "FIFTEEN or EIGHTEEN active and enterprising YOUNG MEN (and a good COOPER)" to man a "Ship about to be fitted for the Brazil Bank WHALE FISHERY."[2] Newfoundland was a base for whaling vessels from early times, and even today some coast whaling is practised out of Fogo to provide meat for mink ranches, but the adventurous spirit of the Newfoundlanders was channelled into the great annual seal hunt.

In a way it is incorrect to say that the whaling industry declined. It is vigorously pursued today by highly organized fleets, the largest

being those of Norway and the Soviet Union. But the period celebrated by Melville, when the sailing ships out of Scotland and Massachusetts roamed the southern seas reaping fortune or disaster, drew to
a close about 1850 as steam-driven vessels and mechanized equipment
became available. About the same time there was increasing demand
for whale oils as lubricants and industrial ingredients. The supply of
whales began to dwindle and the price of oil to rise. From data provided by Brandt I have calculated that the price paid by wholesalers
for a U.S. gallon of whale oil between 1827 and 1831 was 30 cents,
and of sperm oil 66 cents, whereas between 1852 and 1856 the corresponding prices were 67 cents and $1.50.[3] Then during the American
Civil War the New England whaling fleet was pressed into Union
service and almost destroyed by Confederate commerce raiders. According to Brandt the price of sperm oil never fell below $1.00 per
gallon between 1847 and 1877, and reached $2.55 in 1866 after the
war. Undoubtedly the introduction of other lamp fuels was stimulated by the cost of whale oil, which was forced beyond the budget of
ordinary homes.

THE WHALES

The prime target of the seventeenth- and eighteenth-century whalers
was the right whale (*Balaena mysticetus*), the popular name indicating its greater desirability. This species was once abundant both east
and west of Greenland, where it could find sufficient concentration of
the minute marine life on which it fed. Not the largest of whales, it
might reach a length of sixty feet. It was prized for the thickness of
its blubber, the layer of fat beneath the skin from which oil is derived.
It also provided whalebone or baleen, an elastic material which grew
in large, overlapping blades alongside the creature's toothless jaws,

and served to strain the tiny organisms from mouthfuls of sea-water. The springy nature of whalebone made it useful as a support where strength and flexibility were needed. It may be that the elaborate supporting garments used by the ladies of the 1860s and later, and the female figure they produced, would not have been fashionable had such an ideal reinforcement been unavailable. The invention of the steel corset stay may have contributed in a small way to the decline of whaling.

Less desirable were the various species of rorqual or finned whales, so called because of their vertical dorsal fin. One species, the blue whale (*Balaenoptera musculus*), is the largest of all known animals, reaching lengths of between eighty and one hundred feet. Although rorqual blubber is not as thick as that of the right whales, nor the baleen of as good quality, a big "finner" was not to be neglected by old-time whalers.

Sperm whales belong to a different family of cetaceans which have no baleen, but have teeth in the lower jaws. The species most sought, *Physeter macrocephalus*, reaches lengths of sixty to eighty feet. At one time it was widespread in the southern oceans and the mainstay of the nineteenth-century whaling industry. The blubber of sperm whales is much less voluminous than that of right whales, but it yields an oil superior both as an illuminant and as a lubricant. The real prize, however, is found elsewhere. The peculiar high, flat head of the sperm

Sperm whale   whale encloses a cavity between the hide and the upper surface of the

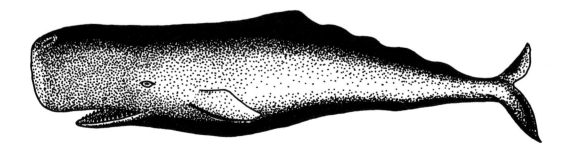

skull. Within this "case" is an oil from which is produced the spermaceti of commerce, the most valuable of all whale products. An average
sperm whale yielded up to three hundred gallons of spermaceti oil.

WHALE HUNTING

Hunting for whales of any species was an activity that took courage
and endurance. The pursuit of the right whale led to many geographi-
cal discoveries in the frigid waters of the Greenland Sea and Baffin
Bay, and following the sperm whales to the South Pacific was no less
of an adventure; both have been the subject of many thrilling books
and stories. Home lighting in those days depended on the hardships,
sufferings, and dangers of long cruises under sail. The greatest peril
came at the actual kill, made with the old methods and equipment
which persisted during most of the period of the whale-oil lamp.

When the lookout in the crows-nest, high up in the mast-head,
spotted the fountain-like plume of vapour and water from the spout-
ing whale and called out the traditional "There she blows!" the
captain manœuvred the ship close to the spot where the whale could
be expected to reappear. Then the boats were lowered, each manned
by half a dozen oarsmen, a helmsman, and a harpooner in the bow.
The harpoon was a barbed steel spear about three feet long, attached
to a six-foot wooden pole as a handle. To the head was secured about
five hundred feet of heavy line, coiled in tubs so it would play out
readily.

The boats waited, as close as possible, for the whale to surface.
Once within range, the harpooner drove his weapon into the great
back, preferably just behind the head. The whale would usually dive
in his efforts to escape, carrying with him the harpoon and line. This

was the moment of greatest danger. The line ran out so fast that pails of sea-water had to be thrown on the wood over which it passed to keep it from burning. When possible, the sailors tried to slow it by snubbing it round a post at the stern, but if it were checked too heavily or snagged, the whale would pull the whole boat and crew under with him. With luck, the whale would end its dive before all the line was played out. Eventually it would have to come to the surface where its enemies would be waiting with more harpoons. Finally, exhausted by exertion and loss of blood, it would lie motionless in the water. The harpooner would approach once more and drive the killing weapon, a six-foot, unbarbed lance, into the whale's heart. With death, the creature would roll over on its side or back. The carcass might be marked temporarily with a flag, but eventually it would be towed to the ship and secured alongside.

There the skin was stripped away, and the blubber cut out in manageable slabs with long, chisel-shaped tools called spades. The slabs, hauled aboard by pulley and winch, were cut into smaller pieces in the hold. The whalebone, if it was a right whale, was chopped out of the head. If it was a sperm whale the top of the head was cut open to expose the "case," from which the spermaceti oil could be bailed in buckets. This could be stored as it came, but the blubber had to be boiled with water to separate oil from tissue. In the old days this was done at whaling stations, but later on board the larger vessels.

During the peak of the right-whale period, the first two decades of the nineteenth century, British whalers averaged about one hundred tons of oil per vessel. As the Arctic whaling declined from 1821 on, the sperm-whale hunting as practised by the New England whalers increased in importance. Sperm whales were still abundant and sperm oil had other important uses besides providing fuel for lamps. The year 1834 was a good one for American whalers, who brought home a total of 128,000 barrels of sperm oil.[4] From this peak the harvest began to fall off. The introduction of the bomb-lance and the harpoon gun in the middle of the century made whaling more efficient, but this only helped to hasten the decrease in the number of whales.

TREATMENT OF WHALE OIL

Crude whale oil, extracted by the initial boiling of the blubber, was full of impurities, and had an unpleasant odour due to decomposition of the blubber tissue. The first step in refining was to reheat it to the temperature of boiling water, thus driving off the volatile impurities. Then it was left to stand; the solid matter settled out and the clarified oil was drawn off. Whale oil was sold under a variety of names. That of the right whale was called black oil, train oil, or simply whale oil. The term sperm oil was sometimes used for all oil extracted from the sperm whale, sometimes restricted to that from the head after the spermaceti had settled out.

Sperm oil for lamps was further separated into grades. As winter approached the oil was boiled again and allowed to stand exposed to the outside temperature. A large part would settle as a granular solid. The mixture was placed in bags and pressed, and the liquid exuded was the winter-strained sperm oil, the best grade of lamp fuel because it was the lowest in viscosity. A grade of lesser value was the spring-strained oil, produced by pressing the residue in moderately cool weather. Cheapest was the summer-strained oil, which might be satisfactory in warm weather but would be useless in winter, the very time when lighting was most needed. Ordinary whale oil or train oil was also graded in this way, but by boiling and straining without pressure; again the winter-refined oil was the most valuable, although not in a class with sperm oil. Spermacetti was refined by pressure, but it was the solid residue that was the valuable part, and the extracted liquid was either used separately as a lubricant for fine machinery or mixed with ordinary sperm oil.

Long after it had ceased to be used as a lamp fuel in home and factory, sperm oil supplied the light in lighthouses. An advertisement of 1865 called for tenders to supply "850 GALLONS of the best quality winter pressed SPERM OIL FOR THE PROVINCIAL LIGHT HOUSES ABOVE LACHINE. One third of which must be from head matter which will stand limpid at 30° Fahrenheit, and the other two thirds at about 34°, subject to inspection and test before acceptance, and if required, to be measured out. The whole to be furnished in iron bound casks, containing fifty gallons each, in the best order, and to be delivered at the Contractor's risk, on such wharf near the Lachine Canal Basin at Montreal, and on such day on or about the first day of July next, as may be specified in the contract."[5] But the advertisement went on to invite other tenders for "6,500 GALLONS of the best quality of NON-EXPLOSIVE COAL OIL." Whale-oil lamps, although inferior in light emission, required less tending than kerosene lamps.

SEALING AND SEAL OIL

If British North America did not participate in the great whale hunts of the nineteenth century, it had its own enterprise as daring and spectacular as any that yielded fuel oil from the sea. This was the Newfoundland seal "fishery." The "swilers" never had a Melville, but they had a sympathetic observer and reporter in George Allan England, whose *Vikings of the Ice* is not only a vivid account but also a reliable record, of an adventurous enterprise now almost abandoned.

The Newfoundland sealing was based on the annual migration of two species, the harp seal, *Phoca groenlandica*, and the hooded seal,

Cystophora cristata. Each year, from their summer waters of Baffin Bay, they swim down along the Labrador and Greenland coasts and around Newfoundland to winter in the Gulf of St. Lawrence and on the Grand Banks. Just before spring they start north again, and in late February or early March the females bear the young on the floe ice north of Newfoundland. While the "pups" are still helpless and the mother still in attendance, the seals are vulnerable to the hunters.

Sealing began in Newfoundland in the eighteenth century, using fixed nets just off shore. Later men went out on the ice, at first on foot, then in skiffs, and finally in small sailing ships. More and more the hunt became big business, and by 1840 some 631 vessels were going to the ice fields. The maximum catch was in 1884, when 685,530 seal skins were brought back. Steam vessels were first used in 1863 and by 1894 were twenty-one in number.

With the decline in the demand for seal oil and hides there has been a shift to a market for the furry pelts of the young pups. Much of the hunt is now centred in the Gulf of St. Lawrence and is a return to the old land-based operations, modernized by the use of airplanes and helicopters. But ships still go to the northern ice, including at least one from Bowring Brothers of St. Johns, the firm that has been to sealing what the Hudson's Bay Company was to the fur trade, and which, like its counterpart, understands the importance of tradition.

Actual killing of the seals is perhaps no more cruel than the harpooning of whales, but it is a spectacularly sanguinary operation, and has drawn so much unfavourable comment that it is now strictly regulated. In the old days sealing ships carried crews of over a hundred men, most of whom were there just to kill the seals. On sighting a herd they would go over the side onto the ice, equipped with rope, skinning knife, compass, and either a long wooden pole armed with spike and hook (the gaff) or a rifle. The placid harp seal could be killed by blows but the more pugnacious "hood" had to be shot.

The dead seals were skinned, either on the ice or back at the ship, leaving the thick layer of fat attached to the hide. Also saved might be the front limb, called the flipper; its meat is a Newfoundland delicacy, tender and very dark, with a slightly fishy taste.

Back at port the fat-laden skins, called sculps, were scraped and the hide used to make fine leather. The oil was rendered out of the fat in heated vats. In the old days it was then stored in glass-covered tanks, in which sunlight bleached it to the "pale seal oil" of commerce. Today seal oil is no longer bleached, but would probably be just as good a lamp fuel as ever, if it were needed.

Like whale oil, seal oil continued to be a desirable lamp fuel for lighthouses after it had been displaced in the home. A Newfoundland Government notice of 1858 called for sealed tenders for 2,700 gallons of pale seal oil warranted to be the produce of young harp seals.[6] Seal oil as a lamp fuel was naturally more commonly used in the Atlantic colonies, but was being sold in Montreal in 1858.[7]

OTHER ORGANIC OIL FUELS

Most fishes are provided with some oil in their bodies, and the menhaden (*Elosa menhaden*) has so much that dried bodies will burn like torches. Even the common herring (*Clupea herrengis*) will yield valuable amounts of oil if boiled and pressed in quantity. Fish oil has about the same specific gravity as whale oil, and probably would function about as well in a lamp except that it is said to give off an unpleasant odour while burning.

There is a strong presumption but no absolute proof that fish oil was used as a lamp fuel in New Brunswick and Nova Scotia. Not uncommon from this region is a peculiar lamp of New England origin called a kyal or Cape Cod lamp. It appears to be derived from the Flemish spout lamp. A kyal from Mahone Bay, N.S., has been described;[8] it has a hood-like chimney to carry off the smoke. Several other examples are in the Nova Scotia Museum at Halifax. Kyals are traditionally supposed to have been used with fish oil as fuel.

An example in the National Museum of Canada (NMC B-27; fig. 32) is mostly of tin, and consists of an upper font that fits into a lower pail with wire handle. A curved copper wick tube extends outward and upward from the lower part of the font, and beneath this is a sloping tin trough leading to the pail. This trough served to catch the drip of unburned oil from the wick tube above it. Height of the lamp to top of handle is 9½ inches. It was purchased from Mrs. Audrey Griffith of Jordan, Ont., who obtained it on the south shore of Nova Scotia.

The use of olive oil as a lamp fuel in southern Europe has been noted. It never had much use for this purpose in North America, but it was offered for sale, along with whale oil, seal oil, and lard, by William Lyman & Co. of Montreal in 1855.[9]

Colza oil was the name given to oil pressed from the seeds of various plants of the cabbage genus (*Brassica*), the kind most commonly used being those of the rape (*B. campestris rapus*). This oil is used today in industry, but in the early part of the nineteenth century it had some favour as a lamp fuel. Michael Faraday recommended it for lighthouses. Its relatively high viscosity made it unsatisfactory for ordinary lamps, however. A lamp developed for it by Carcel in 1798[10] had three built-in, spring-operated pumps to maintain a uniform flow of oil up to the wick. Carcel lamps, because of their steady light, survived as laboratory standards of luminosity long after the end of their domestic popularity. Very few were used in America, and none has been found with a Canadian provenience, but rape oil along with other fuel oils was offered for sale in Toronto in 1844.[11] The Science Museum in London has a Carcel lamp in working condition, and a photograph of it in action has been published several times.[12]

32
Kyal or Cape Cod lamp, south shore Nova Scotia. NMC B-27

33
Blown glass whale-oil lamp
for drop burner
purchased in North Hatley, Que.
NMC A-1171. ROM *photo*

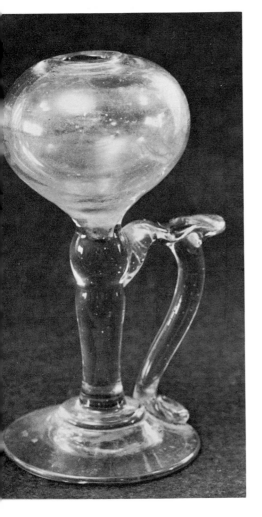

All these oils except colza oil will burn quite well in any of the lamps to be described in the remainder of this chapter, but I shall call these latter whale-oil lamps because that was the fuel most commonly used.

Little seems to be known about the lamps used by the early Norse, but they were probably like those of the Eskimo though using whale blubber for fuel. In the Bay of Biscay region whaling was practised by people who knew the pottery spout lamp. Probably they quickly substituted whale oil for the imported olive oil, and soon began designing lamps that were better adapted to this new fuel. The Flemish spout lamp, which reappears in North America as the kyal or Cape Cod lamp, marked the period when the Netherlands dominated the whaling industry.

About this time an unknown inventor threaded some twisted candle wick through a hole in a stopper and set it in a bottle with whale oil. So may have begun the long sequence of vertical-wick lamps. By the latter part of the eighteenth century this arrangement, using a metallic wick tube set in a metal disc, was the most widely used form of whale-oil lamp, and the word lamp usually meant just this sort of lighting device.

The simple whale-oil lamp persisted well into the nineteenth century, but the glass body became very handsome, some free-blown, some moulded, some a combination of the two. Fine examples are illustrated in standard works on pressed glass[13] and early lighting.[14] Figure 33 shows an entirely free-blown lamp (NMC A-1171), purchased from Mrs. Anne Beaulieu of North Hatley, Que. The bulbous font rests on a shaped cylindrical stem and a discoid base with pontil mark. There is no collar on the opening into the font. Lamps of this type used the so-called drop burner, a metallic disc perforated by one or two wick tubes, which simply rested on the opening into the font. In some burners of this type the disc is extended laterally as a tab, by means of which the burner can be lifted off the lamp. This lamp is probably of European origin, as those made in New England had raised collars around the font opening to receive a cork-sheathed burner.

The composite whale-oil lamp (LSR 262) shown in figure 34 is using the cork-mounted burner. The tall font is free-blown, and is shaped like a narrow inverted cone capped by a low cone. The collar around the font opening is about ¼ inch high. The combined base and stem is of pressed glass, with a squarish bottom and an elaborate ornamentation of steps and fluting. Height of the lamp to top of font is 10⅛ inches. It was purchased from Mr. D. McLeish of Toronto, and is said to be from a large private collection of Canadiana. A very similar lamp has been illustrated by Mrs. Lee[15] and ascribed to the Boston and Sandwich Glass Company. Watkins also shows such a lamp and dates it as somewhat later than 1830.[16]

The lamp shown in figure 31 (LSR 259) is of more plebeian design. With its broad, stemless base and generous handle it is the kind of lamp that one might use to light one's way to bed. The font is a simple, moulded conoid with a free-formed handle attached. The threaded collar for attachment of the burner is derived from the Miles lamp, described below. This example was purchased in Philadelphia, Pa. A similarly shaped lamp, but with a pressed pattern on the font, is illustrated by Hayward.[17] From indirect evidence, such as the form of the collar, such lamps may be assigned a date of 1830 or later.

TYPICAL WHALE-OIL BURNERS

The early whale-oil burners simply sat on the font opening, and later were provided with a tight-fitting cork. By 1830 they had evolved into the threaded form shown in figure 31. The base of the burner is a brass or tin disc, pressed into a saucer shape. The vertical part of

34
Blown and pressed glass whale-oil lamp with cork-stopper burner probably used in Ontario. LSR 262

the rim is threaded on the outside to screw into the collar of the lamp. There might be one or two wick tubes, depending on the model, ¼ to ⅜ inch in diameter. Usually they taper from bottom to top. The length of the wick tube projecting above the base is much less than that below. The upper part of the tube has a vertical slot, through which the wick can be raised or lowered by means of a little metal spike, the wick-pick, and the lower part is perforated to increase the area of contact between oil and wick. Burners of this type continued to be made long after the whale-oil period, and even appear in a Plume & Atwood catalogue of about 1908 as "lard oil lantern burners."

The use of two wicks in one burner goes back, according to legend, to a discovery by Benjamin Franklin that two candle flames close together emit more light than the same two candles well separated.[18] There is some doubt whether Franklin did make this discovery,[19] but the observation is correct. Modern photometric studies have shown that the luminosity of two adjacent flames is greater than twice that of a single flame, and that three adjacent flames give nearly four times as much light as one flame.[20] The effect results from the geometric increase in air draft when two or more flames are near each other.

METAL WHALE-OIL LAMPS

Figure 35 shows a tin lamp designed to burn whale oil, but made to resemble the familiar candle holder (NMC H-9).

The tube, instead of being open to receive a candle, is topped by a conoid oil font, with separate filler opening on the side. The burner has a single wick and screws into the collar of the font. This lamp was purchased from Mrs. Eva Boire of Mooers, N.Y. A very similar tin lamp in the Ford Museum collection is illustrated by Hayward.[21]

35

Tin whale-oil lamp with drop burner originally from Malone, N.Y. NMC H-9

Metal whale-oil lamps came in many shapes. A Halifax advertisement of 1827[22] announcing an auction sale by DeBlois & Mitchell mentioned "a bronzed 12 inch Grecian 2 Light Lamp with tin shade, two bronzed one light swelling reading Telescope Lamps with Japaned shades." To the modern reader the description is not entirely clear, but apparently it refers to two-wick and one-wick whale-oil lamps, of tin with bronze coating. "Telescope" may refer to a focusing lens. The shades would be low and conoid, with an enamel finish, supported by one or two wires from the lamp.

Whale-oil lamps of pewter were particularly characteristic of New England, and many were of graceful form and proportions.[23] I have not seen examples with a Canadian provenience, but it seems likely that some found their way into Nova Scotia or New Brunswick. Brass whale-oil lamps were also made, usually tall, with an annular ornamentation like that of brass candlesticks.

An example that appears to have been used in Canada is shown in figure 36 (NMC D-959). It was purchased in Ontario, but similar lamps have been seen with dealers in North Hatley, Que. The base and stem resemble those of brass whale-oil lamps from New England, but the font, with its overhanging conical top, is quite different from the characteristic, American egg shape. More distinctive still is the presence of a wheel to raise and lower the wick. A similar mechanism appears on two brass lamps of a different shape illustrated by Thwing.[24] The oldest American wick raiser of this sort is in the Samuel Rust lamp (see p. 74), but that has a flat, rather than cylindrical, wick tube. It may be that brass lamps of this sort are of European manufacture.

THE FLOAT LAMP

This is an ancient but ingenious variation of the oil lamp.[25] Its wick tube is supported by a small platform, such as a cork, which floats on

36
Brass whale-oil lamp, probably Quebec
NMC D-959

the surface of the oil in a drinking glass or similar vessel. Often the glass was partly filled with water before the layer of oil was added. Such lamps were commonly used as night lights, because they would put themselves out when the oil was consumed, and if the lamp were spilled, the water would probably extinguish the flame. One disadvantage was a tendency for the burner, because of surface tension, to drift to the wall of the vessel, where the heat of the flame might crack the glass. This was prevented in the "Victoria Night light"[26] by a U-shaped wire frame on which the burner platform rode up and down, but could not move sideways. As Thwing points out, antique examples of the float lamp are likely to be rare, as there is not much to be preserved. However, the Victoria night light is distinctive, and should be watched for in collections.

MILES PATENT LAMP

Spilling was always a danger with early whale-oil lamps. At the very least an upset lamp meant waste and a sticky mess of sometimes malodorous oil to be mopped up, but at that the owner would be lucky for if the flame were not put out by the accident it could set the escaped fuel afire and start an extensive blaze. In 1787 an Englishman, John Miles, of Birmingham, patented a lamp that could be knocked over without spilling its oil.[27]

The Miles "agitable" lamp was an improvement on, rather than a departure from, the whale-oil lamps already described. It was not the first patented lamp, but the patent specifications are unusual, because they give detailed directions on how to make a simplified version of the invention. Using them, as clarified by Thwing,[28] it would be easy to make a demonstration model. The chief difference from the simple whale-oil lamp is that the wick tube is set in a metal cap, which fits snugly over a raised collar on the opening of the font. Outside it is a second collar, with a turned-in edge. This is the "preserver" and its function was to catch any oil seeping out via the wick tube. A metal cap fitting onto the outside collar gave further protection against spillage. A small hole on the side of the wick tube served to drain excess oil from the wick and another minute perforation on the top of the font inside the preserver ring permitted equalization of air pressure and the return of spilled oil to the font. Miles also suggested two-burner models, and an "air-burner" in which a vertical tube through the font brought additional draft to the one or two flames at the top.

Miles described a simple cylindrical font, but actual lamps with the Miles burner are more like the tall metal whale-oil lamps described above. However, the presence of the preserver collar is distinctive. Some Miles lamps have been found in the United States but none is known to me from Canada. The importance of the Miles patent is that it showed how a burner could be made that kept the font almost air-tight and would still function satisfactorily. Oil lamps with screw-in burners were derived from the Miles invention, and the principle was passed on to burning-fluid and kerosene lamps.

THE RUMFORD LAMP

Sir Benjamin Thompson, Count Rumford, was one of the most distinguished scientists of the late eighteenth century, but his military and political careers were equally remarkable. Born in Woburn, Mass., in 1753, he took part in some of the early opposition to British taxation; but with the outbreak of the Revolution he remained a loyalist (i.e. "Tory") and rose to senior military rank. Sent to England, he became for a time Under-Secretary of State, for which service he was knighted. At the same time he gained prominence for scientific

37
Rumford lamp, New Brunswick Museum Saint John, N.B.
38
Close-up of burner, Rumford lamp New Brunswick Museum

activities and was elected a Fellow of the Royal Society of London. Subsequently he joined the court of the Elector of Bavaria and achieved high office, his administration being noted for many social improvements, such as the introduction of the potato and of the cooking stove. It was at this time that he determined the mechanical equivalent of heat. During the Napoleonic period he returned to London and founded the Royal Institution in 1800. The later years of his life were spent in France.

Rumford was a very practical scientist, and many of his investigations were aimed towards useful innovations or improvements. A thorough humanitarian, he believed it to be unethical for a scientist to patent an invention. As a result his numerous suggestions for the improvement of lighting were given freely to the world for anyone to use. The most notable was the lamp that bears his name.

There are, perhaps, ten or twelve well-preserved Rumford lamps in American collections, notably that of the Ford Museum, but there is only one known in Canada. It is in the New Brunswick Museum, Saint John, and is shown in figures 37 and 38. It is part of the collection that came from the estate of Miss Mary K. Odell, who died in 1937, the last descendant of Jonathan Odell, first Provincial Secretary of New Brunswick, and Jonathan Bliss, the first Attorney-General. As Rumford lamps date from the beginning of the nineteenth century, this one must have been in the household of one or other of these distinguished founders of the province.

The lamp is in good condition, lacking only the glass chimney. The base and stem, of green-painted metal, are obviously intended to resemble a candle holder. The cylindrical font that rises from the stem is painted white, to suggest the candle. From it emerges the wick tube, which as in all Rumford lamps is T-shaped in cross-section. What corresponds to the vertical arm of the letter "T" projects from the font as a narrow extension (see figure 38), and supports the wick-raising mechanism. This consists of a vertical toothed rack engaged by a pinion which is turned by a thumb wheel. Could the lamp be dissected, it would be seen that the lower end of the rack is connected to a stiff wire which extends down, then back up to connect with the wick support. Thus turning the thumb wheel to raise and lower the rack transmits the same motion to the wick. Notice that the wick was a flat ribbon; this was one of the first lamps to employ such a shape.

The reservoir is a more or less rectangular box, slightly narrower on the side next to the burner. It is connected to the font by a tube sloping at about 45°. The shade is of sheet metal, and is conical with a cylindrical, ornamentally perforated rim at the top. The shade is connected to the reservoir by a hinge, by which it can be swung back. A double wire, extending up from the wick raiser, forms a loop, which supported a tubular chimney.

Other Rumford lamps differ little from the New Brunswick example, the main variation being in the shape of the reservoir.[29] This lamp, with its flat wick and rack-and-pinion adjustment, was too much ahead of its time, but it was a notable inventive achievement and it is fortunate that such a fine example is preserved in a Canadian museum.

THE SAMUEL RUST LAMP

The Rumford lamp represents a temporary dead end in the development of lighting. The Samuel Rust lamp is more in the main stream of evolution and deserves mention, even though no example has yet been found in Canada. Samuel Rust, of New York City, obtained a patent on December 16, 1835, for a lamp with a new wick-raising mechanism. This was before the U.S. Patent Office assigned numbers to patents, and these early issues, many of which were destroyed in the fire of 1836, are known colloquially as name-and-date patents. The essential feature of the Rust lamp is the flat wick tube, in which is mounted a horizontal roller having a rough or toothed surface. This roller is connected to an external shaft and thumb wheel. From such an arrangement it was only a step to the toothed wick wheel which appears in all flat-wick kerosene burners.

The patent model of this lamp is in the U.S. National Museum. Rust sold his rights to William Rowe of Fishkill, so it may be presumed that there was some commercial production. Later Rust obtained several patents for minor improvements. It is doubtful that his inventions were ever used in Canada, but a watch should nevertheless be maintained for Canadian examples of this important stage in lamp development.

THE ARGAND LAMP

Chronologically the Argand lamp comes before those of Miles, Rumford, or Rust; but as it is the beginning of a long line of developments, it seemed best to discuss it after having dealt with the more aberrant devices.

Ami Argand, the father of scientific lighting, was born in Geneva, Switzerland, in 1750. He studied physics under de Sassure and chemistry under Lavoisier. In 1780 he was invited to Montpelier to advise the vintners on a new distillation process. Inadequate light for his studies set him thinking about improving his lamp, and he devised a burner having a tubular wick held between two metal tubes, the inner tube being open at the bottom to permit entry of air. By this means a draft was supplied to the inside as well as to the outside of the flame. The result was a spectacular increase in the amount of light, and the first scientific design in artificial illumination.

Argand took his invention to Paris, hoping to obtain financial support for its commercial manufacture. He failed to find backing but in the attempt he demonstrated his lamp to a number of people. He also discovered at this time, some say by accident, that an open glass cylinder enclosing the flame would increase the draft and further improve luminosity. Discouraged by lack of interest in France, Argand went to London in 1784 and there received encouragement and a patent.[30] Modern illumination may be said to date from that event.

Meanwhile in Paris an apothecary named Quinquet had duplicated the Argand lamp after seeing the original, and with a distiller named Lange began making them. Argand was never able to obtain a French patent, for France was already racked by the political disorders that culminated in the Revolution. He died on October 13, 1803, without having obtained the reward his inventive genius deserved. Even the credit was denied him in France, where his lamp was ungratefully known as the Quinquet. But in England his fame was secured by the manufacture, beginning in 1784, of properly designated Argand lamps.[31]

The early Argand lamps were of rather crude construction, such as any skilled tinsmith could produce.[32] None has been found in Canada but there are good examples in the Ford Museum. Their characteristic feature, apart from the centre-draft burner, is the arrangement of the oil reservoir; it is incorporated in the lamp support, and not offset as in the Rumford lamp. The fuel is fed to the small font through a horizontal or slightly inclined tube. Regulation of the flow is by the "bird-bath" principle, said to have been applied to lamps by Cardan in the sixteenth century. The same principle appears in the Rumford lamp and many later lighting devices. The accompanying diagram shows how it works. The reservoir A is filled with fluid after the stop-cock on the tube B is closed. The filler opening of A is then closed to make it air-tight, and the stop-cock in B is opened. Fluid passes through the tube B into the font C until the latter is filled to the level of B. Then no more air can enter A to fill the space vacated by the

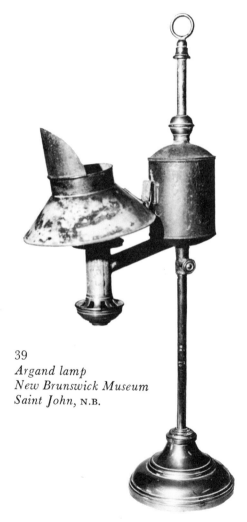

39
Argand lamp
New Brunswick Museum
Saint John, N.B.

fluid and the flow stops. But as the burning wick consumes the fuel, the level in c falls, and soon air can pass through b, displacing fluid which can flow into c until the air is again cut off. The refilling of the font is automatic as long as there is fluid in a above the level of the tube b.

40
Close-up of burner and font
Argand lamp, New Brunswick Museum

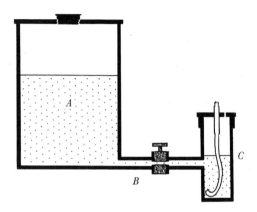

A somewhat more sophisticated version of the Argand lamp is preserved in the New Brunswick Museum as part of the Odell collection (figures 39 and 40). From the design of the burner it may be concluded that this lamp dates from between 1820 and 1840. The general form suggests the so-called student lamp, an Argand kerosene lamp popular in the 1870s and later, but the reservoir is mounted on the support as in the original Argand.

This support is a ⅜-inch brass rod with a ring at the top and an ornamented conoid base. The rod goes through a hole up the centre of the reservoir and the height may be set by means of a sleeve with a set screw. The 2-piece reservoir consists of a cylindrical canister into which fits a removable can. On the bottom of the can, off centre, is an opening which is closed by a disc when the can is upright, but which opens when the can is inverted for filling. A pin projects from the disc valve. When the can is placed in position in the lamp, this pin presses against the canister bottom, thus opening the valve and allowing the fuel to flow down a sloping tube to the font and burner. The flow is regulated on the bird-bath principle. The burner is almost identical with that of the mantel lamp, described next. Notice the shelf for the cylindrical chimney, and the four rods that extend from this shelf to the top of the burner. Rotation of the shelf and its various attached parts caused the wick to move up or down. The peculiar shade shows that this was a reading lamp, and not intended for decorative or general illumination.

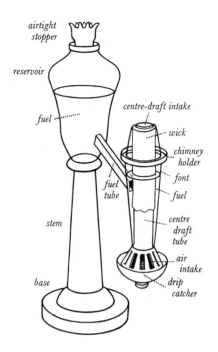

THE MANTEL LAMP

The basic Argand principle of a tubular wick with a centre draft reappeared at least four times during the nineteenth century in slightly different forms. Examples that will be considered later are the astral, the solar, the student, and the Rochester lamp. They differed in appearance from the original Argand mainly because of a rearrangement of parts. A further form which grew directly from the Argand, and differed mainly in its added ornamentation, was the mantel lamp. It was, in fact, simply called the Argand lamp at the time of its popularity, and "mantel" may have been the American name for it. These lamps usually came in sets of three, consisting of a central lamp with a symmetrical pair of burners, and two side lamps, each with single burner, all three being normally displayed in balanced arrangement on the mantel of the living room. O'Dea states (p. 52) that double Argands were used as wall lamps to illuminate the mansion of the Duke of Devonshire. There is a double mantel lamp in the Oil Museum of Canada at Oil Springs, Ont., which was presented by the present Duke of Devonshire, and presumably is one of the lamps referred to by O'Dea.

Late models of the mantel lamp incorporated several improvements on the simple Argand. Such is the case with the lamp shown in figures 41 and 42 (LSR 254). It was purchased from Mr. Pat Cutini of Buffalo, N.Y., who obtained it from a local trading store in northern Maine, so it presumably was used in that area. Similar lamps may have reached New Brunswick or Nova Scotia. The present example was used at one time as a double candle holder, and a quantity of green paraffin had to be boiled out of the burners before they could be taken apart. These burners will be described in detail because they illustrate the construction of the improved Argand burner found in several different lamps of the early nineteenth century.

The lamp is of brass, with a fine golden bronze finish. The reservoir is urn-shaped, and is supported on a cylindrical pillar decorated with 6 vertical rows of acanthus leaves. The base is a square of brass about one inch deep. The 2 burners are supported about 6½ inches on each side of the reservoir by horizontal brass tubes, which extend laterally and then curve forward. The burners are cylindrical and each bears a rectangular plate with the following in raised letters: "MESSENGER & SONS / LONDON & BIRMINGHAM / MANUFACTURED FOR / JONES, LOWS & BALL / BOSTON." According to Mrs. Hebard's book (p. 67), Jones, Lows & Ball was the company name in 1839 of the present firm of Shreve Crump & Low, Inc.

In figure 41 one sees the narrow, tubular fonts projecting below the shade holders. Inside the font, and projecting below it, is the centre-draft tube. The lower end of the tube is threaded externally and on it is screwed a heavy brass bowl with perforated top. Air enters the tube through the perforations, while the bowl catches any dripping oil.

Inside the font the centre-draft tube has on its outer surface a spiral groove running clockwise from top to bottom. The wick tube seen in the middle of figure 42 fits snugly but freely inside the font. There is a space between the wick tube and the centre-draft tube for the wick holder (at the left), a short tube with a thickened lower part, from which a small stud projects. There is a similar stud inside on the opposite side, not quite

visible in the photograph. The lower end of the tubular wick was slipped over the upper part of the wick holder, where it was held by small sharp teeth. The wick holder fits inside the wick tube, the external stud engaging the vertical slit in the tube.

To assemble the burner, the wick tube with the wick holder inside is fitted into the font, around the centre-draft tube. This pushes the wick holder to the top, but by turning the wick tube clockwise its internal stud can be made to engage the spiral groove on the outer surface of the centre-draft tube; further rotation will then draw down the wick holder. The external stud, fitting into the slit in the wick tube, ensures that the rotary motion of the tube is transmitted to the wick holder, which at the same time is free to move up and down. The wick tube is supported by 2 studs near its top, which ride on the rim of the font.

The shade-holder assembly is seen on the right in figure 42. Its upper ring fits over the top of the font and has 2 notches on its lower rim to engage the 2 projecting studs on the wick tube. Thus the wick can be adjusted by turning the shade holder. The actual shade support is the

41
LEFT: Mantel lamp purchased in Buffalo, N.Y. said to be from northern Maine
LSR 254. ROM *photo*

42
Parts of the mantel-lamp burner
LSR 254: LEFT, *the wick holder*
MIDDLE, *the wick tube*
RIGHT, *the shade-holder assembly*

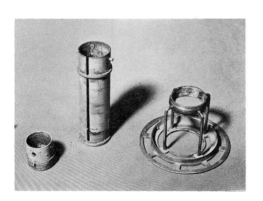

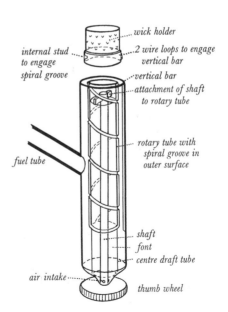

slotted ring suspended by 4 rods from the upper ring. On it the etched-and cut-glass combination chimney and shade rests. It looks like a precarious perch, but although the shade can be displaced, it is kept from falling off by the upper part of the font. Even with the shade in position one can turn the shade holder and so adjust the height of the wick raiser.

This ingenious device for regulating the wick was patented by Nicolas Conne of London in 1819.[33] Conne's patent drawings show the burner on an astral lamp, but the only important difference from the burner described above is that the rotation is accomplished by means of a knurled knob at the bottom of the burner, which can be reached through a slotted area on the lamp stem.

One other part of this mantel lamp should be described, that is, the arrangement to permit control of the flow of oil. The graceful reservoir tapers below to a narrow stem, which screws into the top of the main stem just above the junction of the fuel tubes. Here there is a small chamber into which the fuel tubes open. The stem of the reservoir continues downward inside the chamber as a tube, closed at its lower end by a threaded stopper. The side of the tube is perforated by a $\frac{1}{2}$-inch hole; around the tube at this point is a steel collar which is also perforated by a $\frac{1}{2}$-inch hole. From the collar a soldered-on handle, now lost, projected out through a slot in the threaded part of the reservoir stem. The right end of this slot is marked "OPEN" and the left end "SHUT." Moving the handle to the right brought the hole in the collar over the hole in the reservoir stem, so that oil could flow from the reservoir into the chamber and so into the fuel tubes and burners. Moving the handle to the left closed the opening and shut off the fuel.

It is not clear how the reservoir was filled. It would seem that some upper part of the reservoir should unscrew, but no screw joint can be detected, and it may be that filling had to be done through the narrow opening in the bottom of the reservoir stem.

The handsome brass diadem that fits the shoulder of the reservoir has 2 little eagles opposite each other. Seventeen glass pendants, each of a short and a long prism, hang from this ring. Although the ornament fits snugly on the reservoir, I suspect it to be a later addition, perhaps by the Boston distributor, as the style of ornamentation is so very different from that of the lamp.

ASTRAL LAMPS

The Argand and mantel lamps had two defects. The reservoir, no matter how much offset, still cast a shadow, and the deep form of the reservoir caused a change in the rate of fuel flow as the level went down. The solution to both shortcomings was to make the reservoir in the shape of a large, shallow ring, so spaced from the burner that much light could come down through the space inside the reservoir ring. Lamps with this arrangement are called astral lamps. The credit for their invention is given to the Frenchman J.-A. Bordier-Marcet.[34] Examination of the original *brevet*[35] confirms this but shows that his device was intended to apply only to hanging lamps, especially for public places; hence the evocative name "lampe astrale" or star lamp. Its adaptation to domestic lighting in the form of a table lamp was the work of J.-F. Chopin,[36] but apparently he did not take out a patent, and the "lampe à coronne de Chopin" also became known as the astral lamp, although the name was no longer as appropriate.

The ring-shaped reservoir is supported by two sloping tubes which conduct the fuel to the font. The wide glass shade rests on the reservoir. An improvement on the original design was produced in 1820 by Samuel Parker;[37] in cross-section its reservoir is wedge-shaped, and so oriented relative to the flame that at a short distance from the lamp the reservoir shadow is obliterated. This idea was further modified by

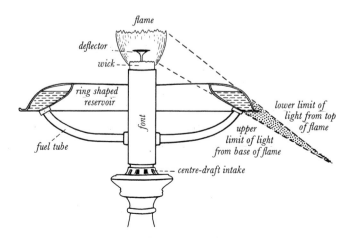

A HERITAGE OF LIGHT 84

George Phillips of London,[38] who changed the wedge to a flattened oval, which was even more effective in getting rid of shadow. Lamps of the Phillips type became known as *sinumbra* or shadowless. Phillips apparently did not take out a British patent, but he obtained a French *brevet d'importation* in 1820 for his "lampe sinombre."[39]

The early astral lamps had simple Argand burners, but in 1820 the spiral wick raiser was incorporated. The sinumbra lamp enjoyed its greatest popularity in the 1840s. By this time the burners had been provided with some device to deflect air onto the flame. The simplest and commonest deflector was the so-called Liverpool button, characteristic of the "Liverpool" lamp.[40] This device was patented by Edwin E. Cassell in 1838;[41] his specifications include simple discs, inverted cones, and cup-shaped deflectors that could be used for priming. The typical button deflector consists of a disc or low inverted cone, supported by a vertical rod up the centre of the draft tube. The deflector is set so that its under surface is slightly above the level of the wick. Air drawn up the centre-draft tube was deflected horizontally against the flame, thus concentrating and intensifying the draft where it could do the most good. It also spread the flame radially, so that this type of burner required a bulbous chimney.

The draft could also be reinforced by directing the external air current inward. This was done by suspending a flat ring above the flame, the opening in the ring being of about the same diameter as the tubular wick. The air coming up the outside of the burner and impinging on this ring would be partly deflected inward toward the flame. This produced a flame that was high and narrow, suitable for a cylindrical chimney. If the inside diameter of the chimney were about the same as the outside diameter of the deflector ring, deflection would be complete. This was the beginning of the "solar" burner, which is described in chapter 6. It is said to have been introduced in 1840 by Benkler of Wiesbaden, Hessen,[42] but an Englishman, George

Roberts, made numerous modifications,[43] involving two or more rings at different levels and with various diameters of opening.

The sinumbra lamp in figure 43 (LSR 253) is typical of the later versions of this graceful lamp, although unfortunately lacking the burner. A good height was desirable to make the most of the sinumbra principle, and this lamp stands 2 feet, 1 inch high to top of reservoir. It is of brass, with a golden bronze finish. The base is a square block about 1 inch deep. The stem is cylindrical with annular decoration in its lower third; the upper part resembles 4 conjoined pillars, with base, shaft, and capital. Above this is a short, constricted annular portion, which supports a slotted drip bowl similar to that on the mantel lamp. From the bowl rises the low cylindrical font, but draft tube and wick raiser are missing. The 2 fuel tubes enter the font from opposite sides near the top; they curve outward and upward to the underside of the reservoir. The latter is ring-shaped, with an outside diameter of 10½ inches. In cross-section it is narrowly and obliquely ovoid, the upper surface being gently convex, the under surface nearly straight. The filler opening is on top, above one of the fuel tubes; it has a screw lid, and a semicircular rim just below to catch spillage. The glass shade rests on the outer rim of the reservoir; it is depressed globose below, narrowing greatly above to form a chimney which is shaped like an inverted bell. The surface is etched, with incised clear pattern of leaves, flowers, and berries. From the sophisticated shape of the reservoir I deduce that this is a rather late model of the sinumbra, probably about 1840. The missing burner presumably had the spiral wick raiser and the button deflector. This lamp was purchased from Mr. Pat Cutini of Buffalo, N.Y., and is said to have come from a home in that city, where it had been converted into an electric table lamp.

A sinumbra lamp that was probably used in Canada West is displayed in the "Pastor's House" at Upper Canada Village, Morrisburg, Ont.[44] It is not as tall as the previous example – 16½ inches exclusive of shade – but in other respects there is a close resemblance. It has the same square base, tall stem, ring-shaped reservoir flattened ovoid in cross-section, and combination shade and chimney. The burner is present and is interesting in having the 2-ring deflector patented by Roberts. This dates the burner, at least, as later than 1843. The lamp was purchased from the Chelsea Shop in Toronto.

43
*Sinumbra lamp
said to have been in a home
in Buffalo,* N.Y.
LSR 253. ROM *photo*

Another sinumbra lamp presumably used in Canada is in the collection of Mrs. Janet E. Ehnes of South Monahan, Ont. It is similar to the one in Upper Canada Village but a little smaller. The original burner had been replaced by an electric light fixture before Mrs. Ehnes acquired the lamp from the estate of the Burnham family of Port Hope. The conversion to electricity appears to have been of 20th-century date, so it is probable that the lamp was brought to Canada and used in its original form.

That astral lamps actually were used in Canada is proven by a drawing made by Anne Langton which shows her with her mother, brother, and aunt in their Sturgeon Lake home in 1840. The lamp by the light of which they are working has the tall stem and characteristic shade of the astral. It is impossible to tell from the drawing whether it is a sinumbra or the earlier form of astral, but at that date it was probably the former. Such a lamp would have been a great luxury in a backwoods home in 1840, but the Langtons were well educated and cultured people, and a good light for reading or social intercourse would have been important to them. This one was probably sent out by William Langton in England, because his brother John, in a letter dated November 30, 1840,[45] implies that the "lamp-glass" arrived broken.

THE MODERATOR LAMP

Colza oil and the cheaper grades of whale oil were too viscid to flow readily up the wick of the usual whale-oil lamp. Additional pressure from a mechanical source was first provided in the Carcel lamp, already mentioned, which had a series of pumps built into it. A somewhat simpler device for providing the extra pressure appeared about 1850, under the name of moderator lamp. According to the *Glasgow Practical Mechanic's Journal*,[46] the inventor's name was Hadrot, and

LEFT: *Moderator lamp, Copetown, Ont.*
LSR 325. ROM *photo*

45
Close-up of burner and regulator moderator lamp. LSR 325

the manufacturer or distributor, Cronin & Co. of Glasgow. For a time these lamps were very popular, and I have seen rows of them collecting dust on an antique dealer's shelves in Philadelphia. Part of the attraction may have been that in many instances the cylindrical reservoir was enclosed in a ceramic shell which was ornamentally coloured or decorated.

Moderator lamps could have come to Canada direct from England or by way of the United States but so far I have found no reference to them in Canadian newspapers or books of the time. That some were used here is proven by an example (LSR 325) purchased from Mr. Harold Luscombe of Hamilton, Ont., and obtained from an old home in Copetown, a village about twenty miles to the west.

This lamp (figure 44) is 21½ inches high, which is unusually tall, even for a moderator. It is entirely of metal, mostly brass, with a bronze finish decorated with painted flowers and a bird that suggests the Lazula bunting. The base is a square of brass, actually an inverted tray, 5⅜ by ⅞ inches. The cylindrical reservoir rises through it, with a brass flange at the juncture. The reservoir has an annular cover at its top, into which is screwed a tall and slightly tapering tube, at the top of which is the burner assembly.

The burner proper (figure 45) is a simple Argand type, with 2 brass tubes, one within the other, with space between for the wick. This space, closed below, is also the true font, and from the bottom a flattened tube extends down for a total length of 6 inches. This tube is part of the fuel line and also houses a slender, toothed rack which is raised and lowered by a pinion and an external key (now lost). The burner assembly is supported on the flange of a short brass tube, which acts as a cap for the external tube. Opposite it the other support is a brass casting through which extends a horizontal shaft with a pinion on the inside, and another larger key on the outside. The pinion engages a stout rack which extends up from the reservoir and of which more later. In the centre of the short, supporting tube is a narrow, stout tube, extending up ½ inch and down into the lamp body 9½ inches. Within this tube is a long steel rod or spindle, projecting out at both ends. The lower end of the rod is pointed, the upper end splayed. Just below the level of the supporting flange the centre tube is connected to the wick-raiser tube by a short, horizontal junction tube. Evidently the centre tube with its rod is also part of the fuel feed.

The burner assembly is normally enclosed in a thin, perforated cylinder, through the ornamental openings of which air could enter to reach the centre-draft tube of the burner. At the top is a flange that might have supported a shade. The chimney holder is another tube that fits inside, with a coronet-like upper rim. Inside this holder 4 radial partitions extend to another, smaller tube, which embraces the outer tube of the burner. In this way the chimney is centred on the burner opening. The chimney evidently was a narrow glass tube, perhaps a little constricted above the flame.

Until this lamp is completely disassembled the description of the remaining mechanism has to be based on the account referred to above and other sources. The rack that extends down into the lamp body is attached below to the support of a dome-shaped leather diaphragm, which can be moved up and down in the reservoir by turning the key one way or the other. However, between the top of the reservoir and the top of the diaphragm is a helical spring, wound conically so as to be able to fold within itself. So if the diaphragm is raised by the rack and key, the spring promptly pushes it down again. The central tube with the pointed rod extends through an opening in the centre of the diaphragm support.

Its operation was something like this. The wick-raising rod was racked up out of the burner and the short cylindrical wick attached. This was then racked down into place. The oil was poured slowly into the cup-shaped upper end of the lamp body, where it ran through the open part of the burner support and accumulated on top of the leather diaphragm. Now if the diaphragm were raised, the turned-down edges of the leather would allow some oil to be squeezed past into the lower part of the reservoir. By alternately adding oil and raising the diaphragm, the reservoir could be almost completely filled.

The static pressure of the spring on the diaphragm would force some of the oil up the centre tube around the loosely fitting rod, then through the short junction tube to the wick-raiser tube and up into the font. With moderate pressure the rod would remain suspended in its tube by the splayed upper end. As pressure increased, the rod would be lifted, but its weight, and the narrowness of the space around it, would retard the flow to a moderate rate, hence the name of the lamp. Excess oil that did not pass into the wick-raiser tube would spill out the top of the centre tube and fall back onto the diaphragm.

All of this sounds complicated and a little impractical, but the popularity of the moderator lamp just before the introduction of kerosene shows that it was an adequate, reliable, and probably economical source of light.

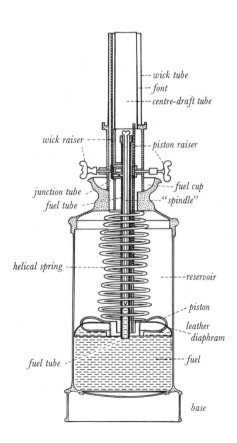

46
*Burning-fluid lamp
burning mixture of
alcohol and rectified turpentine
West Milton, Pa.* LSR 28. ROM *photo*

CHAPTER V

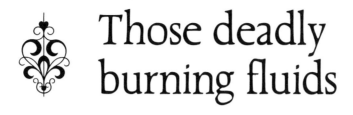

Those deadly burning fluids

AS THE PRICE of whale oil rose in the mid-nineteenth century, a new kind of fuel gained popularity throughout North America. "Burning fluid" was a mixture of high-proof alcohol and redistilled turpentine. It was cheap and very fluid. The lamps that burned it were simple to make and operate. It produced a white, smokeless flame. But it was also one of the most dangerous lighting fuels ever to gain wide use. Hundreds of people were injured or killed in accidents involving it.

A lamp burning the modern equivalent of burning fluid, a ten to one mixture of 95 per cent alcohol and rectified spirits of turpentine, is shown in figure 46. The wicks are of twisted absorbent cotton. Although slightly smaller than average, this lamp from Pennsylvania (LSR 28) is typical of the many that were used in Canada and the United States during the 1840s and 1850s.

Today these distinctive lamps designed for burning fluid are rather common in antique collections, and as many of them are attractive, they figure prominently in the trade. They are commonly referred to as camphene lamps, but there was a difference between camphene and burning fluid. An article in the *Scientific American* in 1860 clearly states that camphene is simply spirits of turpentine redistilled, whereas burning fluid was a mixture of alcohol and camphene in the proportions of about four to one respectively.[1] A fuller description appears in an account of the manufacturies of Philadelphia in 1857.[2] Alcohol, *it is generally known, is distilled from whiskey—nine gallons of the latter making about five of the former. Alcohol, for burning-fluid, is 95 per cent, while Druggists' Alcohol is but 84 per cent, being reduced to that standard after distillation.* Pine Oil, *or* Camphene, *is distilled from Spirits of Turpentine, the well-known produce of the pine forests of North Carolina. This loses in distillation about one gallon in a barrel, or two and a half per cent.* Burning Fluid *is made by the admixture of one gallon of Pine Oil to four gallons of Alcohol.*

Some of the confusion may arise from the fact that in Britain the name camphine was applied to what was called burning fluid in North America, but the slight difference in spelling helps to distinguish the two usages. Furthermore, there actually were lamps designed to burn camphene.

Burning fluid was first patented in 1830 and in the next decade its use spread quickly. Its very low viscosity allowed it to be burned in simple lamps, and even its tendency to vaporize was exploited in crude vapour lamps (described in chapter 11). As the price of whale oil climbed, the price of burning fluid fell because of increased production. By 1857 over a million gallons were manufactured in Philadelphia alone, and sold for about 60 cents a gallon.[3]

THE JENNINGS PATENT

A mixture of camphene and alcohol was tried as an illuminant as early as 1820. Professor Robert Hare, M.D., wrote a letter to the *American Journal of Science & Arts,* describing his experiments.

I have lately found that the addition of about $\frac{1}{17}$ of the same substance [oil of turpentine] to alcohol will give this fluid the property of *burning with a highly luminous flame, and that there is a certain point in the proportions at which the mixture burns without smoke like a gas light.*

This observation may be of some use where spirits are cheap, as in our western states, and even in the northern parts of the Union where it is made from potatoes.

It might be serviceable to morals if the value of the article could be enhanced by a new *mode of consumption.*[4]

In spite of this clear statement of preparation and use, ten years passed before a patent was issued for burning fluid, and then it was in the name of Isaiah Jennings of New York City,[5] who had already obtained the previous year a patent for an improved Argand lamp. In his claim, Jennings explained how the liquids were combined: "To produce light from alcohol and spirits of turpentine, mix equal or unequal parts of each, agitate them that they mix together; let them stand awhile, and the alcohol will be combined with a small quantity of turpentine, and the remainder will be separated; draw off the alcohol, and the small portion of turpentine combined, which is about one-eighth part, and it will be ready for use."

One year later Jennings' invention appeared in a Canadian patent issued to John Ratcliff of Odelltown, Que.[6] The directions for preparing it are almost identical with those of Jennings. In those days only a British subject could be granted a patent in the Canadas, and it would be charitable to think that Ratcliff's action was with the permission and approval of Jennings. However, American inventors complained for many years, and with some justification, about the pirating of their ideas by Canadians.

Jennings' new lamp fuel had a very favourable reception at first. Among those impressed was the editor of the *Journal of the Franklin Institute of Philadelphia*, who wrote:
We have seen the above mixture in combustion in an Argand lamp.

The flame was clear, dense, and brilliant. The light may be made greatly to exceed that from oil, without the escape of any smoke, and there is not the slightest odour of the turpentine. The patentee says the mixture is as cheap as spermaceti oil, and that he is making arrangements that will enable him to afford it at a cost considerably below that material. The wick is scarcely blacked by the combustion; there is no dripping from the lamp and no grease.

The writer ends his appraisal with his version of Professor Hare's little joke. "The friends of temperance will not object to the burning of alcohol."[7]

No sooner was Jennings' invention seen to be a financial success than various people began "improving" it. Samuel Casey of Lebanon, Me., got a patent for "Carbinated Alcohol,"[8] which was just Jennings' mixture with the addition of camphor. Henry Porter, of Bangor, Me., added camphor, rosin, and tincture of curcuma. His patent for a "Portable Burning Fluid" appears to be the first use of the term.[9] Potassium nitrate appears in other formulae. Probably the ultimate was reached by Horace H. Davidson of Montreal, who patented a "portable Lamp-Fluid" which was a mixture of alcohol, nitre, olive oil, camphor, turpentine, and camphene.[10] It would seem that about the only thing left for Mr. Davidson to add was the kitchen sink.

Jennings himself came up with a modification in 1839.[11] He found that the addition of "oil of whiskey" to the alcohol enabled it to dissolve a much larger amount of camphene. What he meant by oil of whiskey evidently was the mixture of higher alcohols that was in those days a waste product from the distillation of alcohol from whiskey. The proportions recommended by Jennings were: two parts of spirits of turpentine, one of alcohol of 93° above proof, and one of oil of whiskey. Jennings also tried mixing these three ingredients with spermaceti oil. He did not claim greater safety for these mixtures, but it would seem that any reduction in the proportion of alcohol present would correspondingly reduce the risk of explosion. None of these other mixtures, however, displaced the original burning fluid.

BURNING-FLUID LAMPS

As noted above, one of the first demonstrations of Jennings' burning fluid was in an Argand lamp. Probably the majority of other early users tried it in ordinary whale-oil lamps. They were the common lamps of the time but about the worst that could be chosen. The short upper part of the wick tube on the whale-oil burner would bring the flame too close to the font, and the relatively wide diameter of the tube would produce a large flame and considerable vapour. With a drop burner, rather than the screw-on type, an accident would be almost inevitable. It was not long before these dangers were realized and a special type of burner developed, which, if used with precautions, could handle the new fuel with relative safety.

The most distinctive feature is the shape of the wick tubes. They extend about an inch and a half above the base plate and not at all below it, so as to keep the flame away from the font. The tubes are narrower than those of whale-oil burners, and have a distinct taper from bottom to top. This gives a tight fit, with less chance for vapour to escape and ignite. If there are two or more tubes, they diverge from base to top; separate flames create less heat. Each tube has a deep metal cap, usually attached to the base plate by a fine chain. This served as an extinguisher, and prevented evaporation of the volatile fluid when the lamp was not in use. Two-wick burners are the commonest, but burners with single, triple, quadruple, and quintuple tubes are known. The burner base plate screws into a threaded collar on the font, and there is no vapour vent.

The fonts of burning-fluid lamps are characteristically much higher than wide, and taper from top to bottom. There is less area adjacent to the flame than in a spheroid font; and whether intentional or not, the tapering shape results in less surface area of fuel to vaporize as the space above becomes larger and able to accumulate more vapour. This shape of font is sometimes found in whale-oil lamps, but then the glass is usually free-blown and thin. Glass fonts for burning fluid are moulded and have thick walls to reduce the danger of breakage. The extra thickness made decorative patterns possible.

Newspaper accounts and advertisements of the 1840s and 1850s show that burning fluid was used in many parts of what is now Canada. Burning-fluid lamps are not common today in collections, but there is a representation from Nova Scotia to Ontario. Originally most, if not all, must have been imported from the United States.

The pewter lamp shown in figure 47 is in the Nova Scotia Museum at Citadel Hill, Halifax. It has a disc-like base gracefully curving to a conoid stem. The font is shaped like an inverted cone with a dome-shaped top. The 2-tube burner is of brass; the extinguisher caps have been lost. Height of the lamp including burner is 9 inches. There are no data with this lamp but it must have been obtained somewhere in Nova Scotia.

Tin burning-fluid lamps have not yet been found in Canada, but from just across the St. Lawrence River, in Ogdensburg, N.Y., I obtained the example (LSR 151) shown in figure 48 from Mrs. Maple Adams, who assured me that it came from a local home. The font is like part of an inverted cone with a low dome top. A curved metal strip soldered to the side forms the handle. The base is a saucer-shaped tray, like that of some candle holders. The burner is of pewter with brass wick tubes, and screws into the collar of the font. The 2 extinguisher caps are attached by a Y-shaped chain. The lamp is finished in a dark, purplish brown enamel, with a little decoration in yellow lines. Over-all height with caps in place is 6 inches, and the diameter of the tray is $5\frac{3}{16}$ inches. A similar lamp in the National Museum of Canada (NMC H-41) was obtained in West Winfield, N.Y.

47
Pewter burning-fluid lamp
Nova Scotia Museum, Halifax, N.S.

48
BELOW: *Tin burning-fluid hand lamp*
Ogdensburg, N.Y. LSR 151

49
RIGHT: *Glass burning-fluid lamp*
Belliveau's Cove, Digby County, N.S.
LSR 308. ROM *photo*

The handsome glass lamp (LSR 308) shown in figure 49 was purchased from Mr. Malcolm Horton of Yarmouth, N.S., and was obtained by him at Belliveau's Cove, Digby County. The font is 6-sided, with a dome-shaped, free-blown top. Each panel on the sides bears the image of a 4-string harp. The stem is 6-sided and conoid, and rests on a 6-sided flat base, the combined stem and base being hollow. There are 2 mould seams on the stem/base, in contrast to 3 on the font. The collar of the font and the burner are of brass. One of the extinguisher caps has been lost. Over-all height of the lamp is 11⅛ inches. Mrs. Lee has described the harp pattern in various glass objects including a large whale-oil lamp on a glass standard.[12] Perhaps her example was actually a burning-fluid lamp similar to the one described above. She ascribed the pattern to M'Kee Brothers of Pittsburgh but said that earlier examples may have been made at Sandwich, Mass.

From the Province of Quebec comes the lamp (NMC A-1314) shown in figure 50. It has a base and stem almost the same as that of the lamp from Yarmouth, but the font has a pressed pattern of large, sharply pro-truding diamond shapes. The metal collar has been removed from the font opening. Height as preserved is 11 inches. This lamp was purchased at an antique show in Montreal.

The slender lamp (LSR 291) shown in figure 51 was purchased from Mrs. Sally Earle of Napanee, Ont. The font is elongate pear-shaped, very narrow below, and has 4 panels, slightly hollowed, and rounded above. It obviously was mould-blown in one piece. The stem is 8-sided, and shaped like an inverted cup below. The inside is sharply ribbed. The con-fluent base is a square plate. There are only 2 mould seams. The collar and burner base plate are of pewter and the wick tubes of brass. Both caps are present, as is a wick, which is in one piece, with its ends both in the wick tubes. This wick is probably original, as it is a peculiar braided cord, about 5/16 inch in diameter but capable of being squeezed much narrower. Over-all height of the lamp is 11⅛ inches.

The glass lamp shown in figure 52 (NMC D-705) has a very elaborate form. The font has a hemispherical free-blown top, resting on a 6-sided shoulder rim. Below this rim the sides of the font are concave, with petal-like panels, terminating in another 6-sided rim below. The stem has 6-sided annular decorations, and flares below to the 6-sided base. The

50
LEFT: *Glass burning-fluid lamp
purchased in Montreal, Que.* NMC A-1314

51
RIGHT: *Glass burning-fluid lamp
purchased in Napanee, Ont.*
LSR 291. ROM *photo*

height without burner is 11 inches. This lamp was purchased from Mr. T. G. Wrightmeyer of Belleville, Ont., and was probably used locally. Lamps almost identical with this one are illustrated by Hayward and by Mrs. Lee.[13] All probably date from the late 1840s.

In the 1850s the all-glass lamp was replaced in part by the composite lamp. The glass font was retained, with little or no change, but it was set into a tubular brass stem, which was bolted to a square marble base. A good example is shown in figure 53 (NMC D-950). The glass font is cylindrical, with a free-blown hemispherical top, and the sides are ornamented in circular areas with a diamond pattern. The brass stem has a spiral ornamentation, and its juncture with the marble base is concealed by a brass flange. Height of the lamp without burner is 10½ inches. It was purchased from Mr. R. L. Donaldson of Sheffield, Ont., and is said to have been used in the Galt district. A similar composite lamp with the same provenience, but with a different shape of font, is in the author's collection (LSR 73). Exactly the same kind of font attached to a glass stem and base is shown by 2 lamps illustrated by Hayward.[14] This is a good demonstration of the fact that fonts formerly made for all-glass burning-fluid lamps were duplicated for the later composite lamps.

Miniature burning-fluid lamps were common and today are usually called sparking lamps, the tradition being that when the small font was empty, it was time for the young man to go home. Actually such lamps were used in hotels, and were intended to provide the guest with light while he went to his room and retired, but not enough to permit him to sit up reading.

An example of these burning-fluid night lamps was obtained from Mr. Jacques Rivard of Hudson Heights, Que. (LSR 48). It is made of plain, thick glass, with a disc-like base and a spheroid font. The collar and burner are of brass. There is a single wick tube with no taper, and slipped over it is another, snugly fitting tube, which can be drawn up telescope-fashion to increase the height to 2 inches. A cap was originally present, as shown by the small hole for the chain on the rim of the burner

base plate. Height of the lamp, with wick tube not extended, is 3⅞ inches. This lamp may have been of Canadian manufacture, but similar lamps are present in American collections, including that of the U.S. National Museum.

ACCIDENTS AND DISASTERS

The potential dangers of such a volatile lamp fuel were recognized early in its history, yet burning fluid continued to be used widely until the introduction of kerosene. As Thwing (p. 60) points out, reasonable precautions could make its use safe enough, but for people accustomed to the almost fool-proof whale oil, such caution was hard to keep in mind. Many conflagrations, injuries, and deaths were blamed on burning fluid. Some were caused by leakage or spillage from a burning lamp. In other accidents the generated vapour within the lamp exploded. Sometimes, almost incredibly, people tried to refill the lamps while they were still burning.

Watkins (pp. 399–400) has recorded a number of such unfortunate events, mostly based on reports in the *Scientific American* and beginning in 1847. In 1853 this journal reported thirty-three fatal explosions due to burning fluid and related lamp fuels in the preceding year. Explosions were most frequently reported, and there are even two reliable reports of "camphene" lamps that exploded while unlit, one with fatal effects.[15]

Search of Canadian newspapers for the 1840s and 1850s has not revealed very many records of fires blamed on burning fluid. This probably means that the fuel was less widely used in the British provinces than in the United States. Canadians certainly were no more careful, as the following three examples illustrate.

Early in March 1845, a fire broke out in a dry-goods store on St. John Street in Quebec City. The flames spread to an adjacent jewellery and watch-repair shop, and while people were trying to rescue its valuable stock, a "camphine" lamp exploded. Several of the salvage party were severely injured. One man lost his life in this fire, although not as a result of the explosion.[16]

An example of an accident that resulted from failure to appreciate the dangerous nature of burning fluid occurred in Lambton, Canada West, on or about August 13, 1856.[17] A young woman had lit a burning-fluid lamp, and then attempted to "prime" it with more fuel, probably because she was accustomed to do this with lard lamps.

The burning fluid promptly exploded, showering flaming liquid over clothes and furniture. Fortunately help was close at hand. The foolish girl escaped with painful but not dangerous burns, and the fire in the house was extinguished promptly.

The most disastrous fire in Canada attributable to burning fluid appears to have been the destruction of the St. Louis Theatre in Quebec City on June 12, 1846.[18] The following account is based mainly on the report of an eyewitness, Sir J. E. Alexander of the 14th Regiment.[19]

The St. Louis Theatre was a stone building in the Upper Town, close to a surviving wing of the old colonial government palace, the Château St. Louis, which was on the site of the modern Château Frontenac Hotel. A former riding-house, the building had been converted into a theatre for the garrison. As part of the stage lighting a number of "camphene" lamps were used under the supervision of an experienced operator. Regular performances under military auspices were carefully regulated, but on the fatal night the theatre had been engaged by a Mr. M. R. Harrison for the showing of his "illuminated dioramas." To supplement his two hundred oil lamps he rented four "camphene" lamps but did not employ the regular operator. The audience of about three hundred was "very respectable," including a number of families that would not have attended a regular dramatic production.

About 10 P.M., when the audience was starting to leave at the close of the performance, one of the burning-fluid lamps behind the lowered curtain was knocked over by a boy, presumably a member of the stage crew. In a few moments the scenery was ablaze, and yellowish smoke began to fill the theatre. Some of the audience still inside escaped by forcing open the side door, but the main exit, at the foot of a staircase, became blocked; one or two people fell and the subsequent panic jammed those behind into a mass from which few could escape. Firemen and soldiers rushed to fight the flames. There was much confusion but little water. In a few minutes the flames had enveloped the helpless victims. Fire-fighting resources were finally organized in time to save the adjacent wing of the Château St. Louis, but the theatre was completely destroyed.

The following morning forty-five charred bodies were brought out of the burned-out shell – soldiers, civilians, women, and children. This fire, although not as destructive of life as many of the tragic theatre fires of the nineteenth century, had all the standard ingredients: inadequate exits, careless stage hands, panic in the audience. To these was added the rapidity with which a fire fed by burning fluid could take hold and defy immediate efforts to extinguish it.

PARTIAL REMEDIES

Besides the standard burning-fluid burner, a number of ingenious ideas were put forward to reduce the dangers that accompanied this fuel. Jennings was one of the first to explore the possibilities, long before the risks were fully appreciated. In his patent,[20] he describes a burner with a brass wick tube about two inches high, closed at the upper end except for several minute holes. The internal wick does not project through any of these openings, but brings the fuel by capillary action to the top of the tube, where its vapour escapes through the holes and can be ignited.

Again in 1836 Jennings[21] attempted to decrease the danger of burning-fluid lamps by surrounding the wick inside the font with a tube having only small perforations. If such a lamp were upset, only the small amount of fuel inside the perforated tube would be spilled, but one imagines that no amount of burning fluid was too small to be dangerous.

No important changes were suggested for burning-fluid lamps during the 1840s, but in the following decade a series of "improvements" were described in patent specifications and some were actually made. A few of these were marketed in Canada. It is ironic that all this effort to make the burning-fluid lamp safe took place at a time when kerosene was about to make it permanently obsolete.

R. V. De Guinon of Williamsburgh, N.Y., added an overflow chamber to the bottom of a metal font.[22] When the fluid expanded with heat from the burner, it would pass into this chamber though a tube, rather than emerge via the wicks. The De Guinon lamp was of the Argand type; use of such lamps with burning fluid must have been very unusual. The inventor wrote of "those fearful accidents and great losses of life which so repeatedly occurred," the like of which his invention was intended to prevent.

John Newell of Boston, Mass., patented an idea admittedly borrowed from the Davy safety lamp.[23] The typical Newell lamp has two cylinders of wire gauze, one inside the other, extending from the collar to near the bottom of the font. The cylinders are closed with gauze discs at their bottoms; their wire, of copper or brass, is silver-plated to prevent corrosion. The base plate of the burner is minutely perforated to prevent pressure build-up. Newell lamps were certainly made and used. Hayward described in detail a well-preserved example in the collection of the Worcester Historical Society.[24] Thwing mentioned (p. 61) a number of others in which the gauze had been corroded, showing that the lamp had actually been used. But wire gauze could have done very little to reduce the dangers of burning fluid. In the Davy lamp it confines the flame of burning gas. In the Newell lamp it is liquid that lies on either side of the mesh. A modification that may have been more effective was produced by Seth E. Winslow of Philadelphia in 1857,[25] in which there was only one gauze barrier, and that was short and conical, above the level of the fluid.

A simple, and presumably effective, device was patented by D. H. Chamberlain of Roxbury, Mass.[26] Basically it consisted of a conventional wick or vapour lamp in which the font was filled with granulated pumice. This left little space in which vapour could accumulate, yet the mass was porous enough to contain a working quantity of fuel. Even breaking such a font would be less dangerous, for the liquid contents would not escape immediately. The same idea was patented in England six days later by G. T. Bousfield.[27] Whether or not there was collaboration between these two patentees is not known, but the closeness of the dates is a curious coincidence.

Another burning-fluid lamp that came into use was patented by William Bennett.[28] It held the fuel in a rubber bag within the font. Thus the vapour could expand without breaking the font, and if the font were accidently broken, there would be no leakage. A fine example of this lamp, complete with rubber bag, is displayed in the Henry Ford Museum at Dearborn, Mich. The Bennett lamp was advertised for sale in Toronto in 1856.[29] The notice included a comparison with the Newell lamp, and this suggests that the latter was also available in Toronto at that time.

RELATED LAMP FUELS

In 1839 A. V. H. Webb of New York City patented a process for distilling turpentine with water and potash to produce a purified form he proposed to call camphene or camphene oil.[30] This apparently was the first use of the term. At the same time he obtained a patent for a lamp especially designed to burn his new fuel.[31] The burner consisted of two incomplete cones, one inside the other, with the wick between. The fuel was fed from a separate reservoir, and the base of the cylindrical chimney could be raised or lowered to control the draft.

Closely related to burning fluid was a lamp fuel patented by Ephram Howe of Brooklyn, N.Y.[32] He found that powdered rosin could be dissolved in an equal weight of the "essential oils" that remain after the distillation of whiskey. These are the same higher alcohols that Jennings added to his burning fluid. The fluid devised by Howe was used either in a vapour lamp or in a conventional burning-fluid lamp.

During the 1850s a number of patents were obtained for lamps designed to burn "rosin oil." There has been some uncertainty among historians of lighting as to what this substance was. According to some, it was alcohol in which some rosin had been dissolved—evidently a reference to Howe's mixture. But the *American Encyclopedia* for 1883[33] has the following statement under *Rosin*: "When the distillation is performed on a larger scale, the gases evolved are air, carbonic acid and carbides of hydrogen; at a higher temperature the oxygen disappears. The first portion of the liquid distillate is yellow and mobile; later a viscid, fluorescent oil passes over, called rosin oil." According to this source, rosin oil is a medium-viscosity product of the distillation of rosin, analogous to the "coal oil" produced by the distillation of coal.

A slightly different interpretation appears in Freedley's account (p. 370) of the manufactures of Philadelphia. He lists the products of the distillation of rosin as "Rosin Oil, Acid, Naphtha, Pitch, and Tar." Presumably the "Naphtha" came over first, and corresponded to the yellow, mobile liquid of the *Encyclopedia*. But this, according to Freedley, was the lamp fuel, and the rosin oil, a heavier fluid, was used in industry. I understand that some rosin oil is still manufactured for use as an ingredient in paints and other products.

Whether "Rosin-oil" lamps burned true rosin oil, as their name would suggest, or "Naphtha," as Freedley states, they certainly used a distillate of rosin. The first of them was patented by Francis Blake of Boston, Mass.[34] It is a centre-draft lamp, with a burner similar to that of the more advanced astral and sinumbra lamps. The patented features are circuitous intakes on both the internal and external drafts, and a method of raising and lowering the deflector button by turning a portion of the lamp stem. Apparently the successful use of rosin oil as a lamp fuel depended on a precise adjustment of the drafts and the absence of extraneous air movements.

A fine example of the Blake lamp is displayed in the "Doctor's House" at Upper Canada Village (figure 54). At first glance it appears to be a solar lamp (see chapter 6), but on the movable portion of the stem is an oval plate bearing the inscription "F. BLAKE / BOSTON / PATENTED / July 17, 1855." What appears to be the lower part of the font is actually a cup-shaped draft regulator which, by turning, can be raised or lowered, thus closing or opening the air intake under the shoulder-like periphery of the font. Air entering here emerges through slots on top of the font, within the rim supporting the chimney. This lamp was purchased at Thornhill, Ont., and may be presumed to have been used in that part of Canada West.

Other patents for rosin-oil lamps were obtained by Prentice Sargent of Newburyport, Conn.,[35] and Isaac Van Bunschoten of New York, N.Y.[36] Like the Blake lamp, theirs have Argand-type burners with deflector buttons and the patented parts are those that permit precise regulation of the drafts. I have no evidence that either of these lamps was manufactured commercially.

54
Blake rosin-oil lamp, in the "Doctor's House," Upper Canada Village Morrisburg, Ont.; said to have been purchased in Thornhill, Ont.

CHAPTER VI

Lard becomes respectable

"Lard," wrote Mrs. Traill in 1862, "is now used as a substitute for oil in parlour lamps."[1] The "now" extended over the period from about 1840 to the early 1860s. This is much the same period as that during which burning fluid was popular, but the two fuels represent extreme opposites. One is very fluid, the other viscid to solid. Burning fluid is dangerous, lard is safe. Both fuels were cheap, but burning fluid had to be bought at a shop, whereas lard was produced on the farm, and this was probably the main reason for its popularity.

The lamp shown in figure 55 is actually burning lard. It proved to be a practical fuel, easy to use. To prepare the lamp I made wicks of folded flannelette and fitted them in place as described on page 122. With the priming pan at the top of the lamp removed, I filled the font with melted lard obtained from the supermarket. The wicks got well impregnated during this process. After the lard solidified, I spooned a little out and put it in the priming pan, and replaced the pan on the lamp. It required a little persistence to light the wicks the first time, but once they were going they melted the priming lard and soon had communicated enough heat to the fuel in the font to liquify some of it. The peculiar pointed flame gave a good light, and seemingly could have gone on burning for an hour.

55
Flat-wick centre-draft lard lamp
burning lard; purchased in Windsor, N.Y.
LSR 159. ROM *photo*

Most of us have a general idea of what lard is, but the following nineteenth-century definition contains information that would not be readily available today.[2]

Lard is the fat of swine, the quality of which depends not only on its purity but also on the part of the animal from which it is taken. The best lard (leaf lard) consists of the fat that surrounds the kidneys, the caul fat, and the fat that underlies the skin, which is firmer and less easily melted than the fat obtained from the abdominal viscera. Bladder lard should be of the best quality, melting at about 40° C. (105° F.), while the unselected fat, sometimes termed keg lard, melts at about 32° C. (90° F.). Neutral lard, made from the leaf fat of newly slaughtered animals, contains scarcely any free fatty acid, and is chiefly used in the manufacture of butter substitutes.

Most lard lamps worked well enough with natural lard, but some were designed for a more fluid derivative, lard oil.[3]

Lard oil is the limpid and nearly colourless oil obtained by subjecting lard to pressure, the more solid portions which are left behind constituting what is known as "lard stearin"; the proportion which the oil expressed bears to the stearin depends to a great extent on the temperature at which the pressure takes place. Lard oil consists of olein with variable proportions of palmitin and stearin. Its sp. gr. is about 0.915 at 15.5° C. (60° F.). It is chiefly used in this country as a lubricant, but it is employed in America for lighthouse lamps.

The main difficulty with lard as a lamp fuel was its viscosity. Too soft to be used normally for candles, it is nevertheless a solid at room temperatures and cannot flow up a wick. Even lard oil is a viscous fluid, and congeals readily. Lamps that burn lard successfully needed some special means of making it flow. The problem of bringing the fuel to the flame stimulated much ingenious invention, and provided a fascinating period in the history of lighting.[4] Two methods were used, separately or together; the fuel was forced into the burner by mechanical or gravitational pressure, or the heat was conducted from flame to fuel to melt the latter and keep it fluid.

Many patents were granted between 1840 and 1860 for lamps designed to burn lard. Some are not represented by any extant example, and others appear only in patent-office models in the collection of the U.S. National Museum. The following discussion is limited almost entirely to lamps that are known from specimens which obviously have been used and must have been available to the public in their day.

LARD LAMPS ACTUATED BY PRESSURE

A popular form of lard lamp was patented in 1842 by B. K. Maltby of Rootstown and J. Neal of Middlebury, O.[5] The wick tubes were mounted in a cylinder which acted as a plunger into the font. As the lard was consumed, the plunger was pushed down, forcing more lard up and around the wick tubes. There some heat from the flame would warm the fat enough for it to flow up the wicks.

This lamp is well represented in American collections and at least 3 examples are known with Canadian backgrounds. One of these (figures 56 a–c) was obtained some years ago from the estate of a resident of Markham Township, Ont. It is constructed of tin, with soldered seams and joints. The font rises from the centre of the circular, saucer-shaped base. It has a gently convex top with a large central opening, the rim of which is turned up as a ¼-inch vertical collar. Into this opening fits a plunger-like tube, which can be drawn up or pushed down about 3 inches. At its top is a lens-shaped chamber ("bulb"), capped by a small shallow bowl. The 2 vertical wick tubes project through the bottom of this bowl about ⅜ of an inch. They are about 3/16 inch in diameter and have a slot on one side for wick adjustment.

The top of the font is a detachable lid, which can be lifted off with the plunger tube and burner assembly. The lower end of the plunger (figure 56c) bears a piston, called a follower in the patent. It consists of 2 slightly convex discs fitted around the lower end of the plunger tube about ⅛ inch apart. Between these discs is a leather washer, now shrunk, which when new evidently projected slightly beyond the discs to give a seal. The lower, concave face of the piston bears 2 low vanes which are tangential to the rim of the plunger tube opening. They are not mentioned in the patent, but if the plunger were depressed with a clockwise rotation, they would tend to direct the lard into the opening.

The wick tubes reach within ⅝ inch of the bottom of the plunger. Their lower ends are chisel-shaped, and are attached together by a metal sheath not shown in the patent. If the ends were open, the wick might be forced out of the tube by the upward pressure of the lard as the piston was depressed. Instead, the melted lard reached the wick through vertical slots at intervals along the wick tube. According to the patent, the wick was pushed the full depth of the tube by means of a little wire with a slightly forked end. This is missing from all specimens I have seen.

The handle is a curved metal strip, like the handle of some candle holders; it is soldered to the font at the top and about ⅓ down the side. Principal dimensions of this lamp are: over-all height with piston elevated, 8¼ in.; with piston depressed, 5⁷⁄₁₆ in.; diameter of base, 5⅜ in.

A nineteenth-century housewife using this lamp would first put the wicks in place, and then, with the lid removed, fill the font almost to the top with lard. She would replace the lid and push down the plunger as far as it would go without undue pressure. Next she would have to put a little lard in the bowl around the tops of the wick tubes, and light the wicks. The burning primer would heat the wick tubes, causing the lard around them in the plunger to melt and seep through the slots, saturating the wicks. Once the melted lard worked up to the top, a good flame would result. When it showed signs of decreasing, the housewife would push the plunger down by hand, forcing more lard up the tube. One can imagine that the plunger might be a little hot for grasping after the lamp had been in use for some time.

Two other examples of this lamp are in the Paul collection of the Hastings County Museum, Belleville, Ont. One of these (no. 227) is similar to that from Markham, the other (no. 228) is considerably larger. According to Dr. Paul's records, they both came from Port Hope, Ont. The Maltby and Neal lamps in the U.S. National Museum and in the Morton collection are like the Markham specimen, at least externally. Seven more are on display in the Ford Museum at Dearborn, Mich., but two of these have a single flat wick tube instead of two cylindrical tubes. A small discrepancy exists between actual lamps and the model represented in the patent drawings; the latter appears to have a cast ring-shaped handle riveted to the under side of the rim of the base. There is also a curious disagreement in the spelling of the name of one of the inventors. On the printed patent specifications it appears as "Mateby," on the drawing, "Maltby." To try to clear up this question, I examined the original claim in the U.S. National Archives, but the result was inconclusive. The peculiar signature could be interpreted either way. However, comparison with the same handwriting in other parts of the claim supports interpretation of the name as "Maltby."

The Maltby and Neal lamp has been described in detail because it was used in Canada, and because it was the first of the pressure-operated lard lamps. Several other patented lard lamps using pressure are represented in American collections, and may well have been brought to Canada.

One such lamp, patented by Ira Smith and John Stonesifer of Boonsboro, Md,[6] has a separate cylindrical fuel reservoir centred on a circular saucer-like base. From near the bottom of the reservoir the font rises as an offset tube, expanding gradually from the joint to the burner at the top. The unique feature is the screw-operated piston within the reservoir, by means of which the unmelted lard could be forced up the font as required. The patent specifications describe a burner with a flat wick and an adjustable extinguisher. This type is illustrated by Thwing (pl. 51). The specimen in the U.S. National Museum, shown on the right in figure 57, has 2 cylindrical wick tubes. There is a good example of the Smith and Stonesifer lamp, lacking only the handle for the piston shaft, in the Paul collection (no. 232) of the Hastings County Museum, Belleville; however, it was purchased in New England.

It is a curious fact that a lard lamp almost identical with that of Smith and Stonesifer, except that it was smaller, and its piston was pushed rather than screwed down, was patented 12 years earlier by John Grannis of Oberlin, o.[7] It is represented by a Patent Office model in the U.S. National Museum, shown on the left in figure 57, and also illustrated by Watkins (pl. 8). Apparently the Grannis lamp did not go into production, whereas the Smith and Stonesifer lamp is represented today by at least 12 examples in collections, showing that it enjoyed a moderate popularity.[8]

Gravity supplied the pressure in the lard lamp patented by Dexter Chamberlain of Boston, Mass.[9] The font is a cylinder, pivoted horizontally on the ends of a Y-shaped support. One of the 2 pivot pins can be tightened to set the font in any desired position. The 2 wick tubes, which are flat, project tangentially. There is a circular filler hole, which in the normal operating position is at the top of the lamp. As the fuel was consumed, the font could be rotated manually so as to tip the melted lard

57
Lard lamps in U.S. National Museum
LEFT: *Grannis lamp, no.* 251789
RIGHT: *Smith and Stonesifer lamp no.* 337408

against the wicks. When the flames were extinguished, the font would be in such a position that the lard would congeal around the wicks and so permit easy relighting. Although evidently produced commercially, this is one of the rarer lard lamps. The one illustrated (figure 58) is in the Paul collection (no. 296) of the Hastings County Museum, Belleville, and is unusual in being mounted as a sconce lamp. There is one example in the U.S. National Museum and two in the Ford Museum. I have seen one other in an antique shop in Connecticut.

A lard lamp invented by James D. Hayes of Mount Norris, Ill.,[10] superficially resembles the Chamberlain lamp in having a cylindrical font, but the font does not rotate. Instead, there is an internal axial shaft to which is attached a vane. The shaft could be rotated by means of an external handle, so as to push fresh lard towards the wick tubes. There is an example in the Ford Museum.

LAMPS ACTUATED BY HEAT ALONE

The earliest lard lamp that depended on heat alone to keep the fuel in contact with the wick was patented by F. H. Southworth of Washington, D.C.[11] This might turn up in Canada, so an example in the U.S. National Museum is illustrated (figure 59). It has two simple wick tubes, actually folded copper strips. Another double copper strip held between them helped to conduct heat from flame to fuel. The problem with such a lamp is to get it started. People used wicks already impregnated with lard, and placed a little priming lard in the cup-shaped base of the burner. Once a good flame was established, the high heat conductivity of the copper wick tubes and reflex strip would ensure that much of the lard in the font became fluid. The patent specifications describe a lamp with a glass font, like those of some whale-oil lamps, but the numerous examples in modern collections all seem to be of metal. The Ford Museum has six or more.

58
Chamberlain lard lamp
Paul Collection no. 296
Hastings County Museum, Belleville, Ont.

The popular lard lamp invented by Delamar Kinnear of Circleville, o.,[12] looked very different but employed the same principle of conductivity. From the large number that have survived, it must have been used in considerable numbers in the 1850s. The Kinnear lamp font is very broad in one horizontal direction and very narrow in the other, and in cross-section resembles an axe-head. From the flat upper surface the wick tubes project. The main one is flat and unusually broad, with slots for wick adjustment. Beside it is another wick tube, small and cylindrical, from which a strip or wire of copper extends inside the lamp down to the bottom of the font. The small wick tube provided a night light, and its heat, conducted by the copper, would keep the lard in the font partly melted so that the large wick could be lit easily if required. In the original Kinnear lamp the font was filled by sliding a part of the top towards one end, exposing an opening, but later models had a circular filler hole with a cap. Early Kinnear lamps had a simple rectangular tray for a base, and a curved metal strip for a handle. Later the right to manufacture Kinnear lamps was obtained by S. N. and H. C. Ufford of Boston, and most of their models were produced with conical cast-iron bases, variously ornamented with raised designs and openings. They placed a rectangular brass plate on one side of the font, with the makers' and inventor's names, and the date of patent.

There are several Kinnear lamps in Canadian collections. In the National Museum of Canada there is one of the late models produced by the Uffords (NMC H-12; figure 60). It was purchased from Mrs. Eva Boire of Mooers, N.Y., but was obtained by her from near Lacolle, Que. The brass plate on the side reads "S.N. & H. C. UFFORD. / 117 COURT ST. / BOSTON / KINNEAR'S PATENT / FEB. 4. 1851." It is interesting that the ornamental design of the conical cast-iron base of this lamp is not the same as that of the otherwise identical lamp in the U.S. National Museum. Evidently more than one mould was used by the Uffords in casting these bases. The Paul collection in the Hastings County Museum,

59
Southworth lard lamp
USNM 377198

Belleville, Ont., includes an example (no. 229) with the rectangular tray and the sliding filler cover; unfortunately the provenience is not recorded. There is a Kinear lamp in the New Brunswick Museum at Saint John, but it lacks the base. The U.S. National Museum collection includes examples of the earlier as well as the later models. The Ford Museum has a series, and there are examples in the Morton and O'Connell collections. The Museum of the New Haven Colony Historical Society, Conn., has a curious one with angulate, rather than curved, sides. An example (LSR 317) with the usual shape of font and the Ufford plate, but on a saucer base, was obtained at Searsport, Me.

The Argand principle is used in another lard lamp, patented by Samuel Davis of New Holland, Pa.[13] It superficially resembles the Southworth lamp, but the burner is tubular. The inner tube is for the centre draft; it is connected to the stem, in which there is an opening to admit air. The outer tube is cone-shaped, open at the bottom, and has slots for adjusting the wick. The two wicks were flat strips of doubled flannelette; two guide flanges within the cone formed each

60
TOP: *Kinnear lard lamp, Ufford model Lacolle, Que.* NMC H-12

61
LEFT: *Davis-type lard lamp purchased in North Hatley, Que.* LSR 285

wick into a semicircle, so that between them they produced a tube. The lower part of the flannelette hung down into the lard of the font.

The air hole in the stem could be closed conveniently with a thumb or finger, and this was supposed to be a way of extinguishing the flame. Some lamps had means of regulating the centre draft. A lamp in the Ford Museum has a snugly fitting collar around the stem at the level of the opening; this collar is perforated, and, by turning it, the air intake can be opened or closed as the two openings are made to coincide or separate.

There are at least 9 Davis lamps in the Ford Museum and 2 in the O'Connell collection. Some of these are marked "SAM.ᶫ DAVIS / PATENTED / MAY 6TH 1856." Nothing exactly like them has been found in Canada so far, but a tin lamp (LSR 285) obviously based on the Davis design was obtained from Mrs. Anne Beaulieu of North Hatley, Que. (figure 61). Like the original Davis lamp it has a saucer base, a tubular stem, and a loop of metal strip for a handle. The cylindroid font tapers from top to bottom, rather than from bottom to top. The opening for the burner has a ¼-inch collar, and there is a centre-draft tube of copper, ½ inch in diameter, projecting through the opening. The burner consists of a concave base plate through which extends the short wick tube, about ¾ inch in diameter, with 2 vertical slots for wick adjustment. On the underside, between the wick tube and the rim of the base plate, there is a vertical collar which fits inside the collar of the font. The main difference between this lamp and the typical Davis version is that the air intake to the stem and centre draft is through 4 small holes just below the font, and that there is no division of the wick space to provide for 2 flat wicks. The height of this lamp is 6⅝ inches.

A centre draft could also be used with 2 flat wicks. Such an arrangement is found in a lamp (figure 62) from Markham, Ont. This differs from the Southworth lamp, which also had 2 flat wicks, but no centre draft. The Markham lamp has a cast-iron base, which is conical rather than saucer-shaped. Like the lamp from North Hatley, the air intake is through small holes in the stem. The saucer-like priming pan, part of

62
Flat-wick centre-draft lard lamp private collection, Markham, Ont.
ROM *photo*

the burner in the North Hatley lamp, is here a separate part, which rests on the font opening and has a rectangular hole for the wick tube. A similar lamp is in the Black Creek Pioneer Village near Toronto, but I have not seen one in any other collection, and it may be that this particular lard lamp was of Canadian manufacture.

A lard lamp with a similar burner but a different general shape was obtained from Mr. Miner Cooper of Windsor, N.Y., but is said to have come to him from New Jersey. This is the one shown burning lard in figure 55 (LSR 159). The base, stem, and handle are the same as in the Davis lamp, including the single large hole for the centre-draft intake. The font is cylindrical and the priming pan is a separate part. The modern wicks were made by following the directions supplied with the Davis lamp.[14] Closing the air intake with the thumb has very little effect on the flame.

A flat-wick lard lamp with centre draft was patented by Charles von Bonhorst of Hancock, Md.[15] but the font is shaped more like that of the Kinnear lamp. It is probable that the flat-wick lard lamps with centre draft, such as the one from Markham, were derived from the Davis lamp, and not from the later von Bonhorst lamp.

The weirdest of all lard lamps was patented by Zuriel Swope of Lancaster, Pa.[16] It has the usual saucer base and tubular stem with handle. The font is of a peculiar shape – flat on top and sides, with a semicircular bottom – but the really unusual feature is the device for conducting heat from flame to fuel. This starts with a conical hood or funnel, which is suspended over the burner by a swan-neck tube arising from the font. Swope figured that hot air from the flame would be collected by the hood and forced to pass down into the font and around through a curved tube emerging at the other end. An extension tube on this vent was apparently intended to increase the draft by inverted siphon action. Both the tube and the hot-air collector could be removed, and in some examples have been lost. There are two examples in the Ford Museum, one of them incomplete, as is the specimen in the U.S. National Museum.

THE SOLAR LAMP

In many mechanical details the solar lamp resembles the astral lamp, and it could burn whale oil or olive oil. But it is best known as the lamp that made lard as a fuel both convenient and fashionable.

Its distinctive features are in the burner. The general design is that of the typical Argand burner with spiral wick raiser, but there is added a low, dome-shaped deflector with a circular opening just a little wider than the diameter of the wick. This directed the external draft inward against the flame. Together with the centre draft it produced a high, narrow flame which was described as very bright. Additional force to the draft was given by the high, almost tubular chimney.

The beginnings of the solar type of deflector are to be seen in lamps invented in the early 1840s by Englishmen such as Thomas Young and George Roberts.[17] A deflector even more like that of the solar lamp was introduced by Benkler of Wiesbaden, Hessen,[18] but Redwood refers to the Birmingham "Solar" lamp, evidently implying that it was an English invention.[19] In America the solar lamp is especially associated with the firms of Cornelius & Company, and Archer, Warner, Miskey & Co. of Philadelphia.

Solar lamps were offered for sale in Toronto, apparently for the first time, on October 5, 1847, by Sanford and Fuller of 48 King Street.[20] Numerous other advertisements for them appeared in 1848. So far, however, no example with the original solar burner has been found in Canada. There are three or four in the Ford Museum. The specimen in the writer's collection (LSR 255) is complete except for the original chimney (figure 63). It was purchased in St. Joseph, Mo., and was said to have come from a home in Kansas City. It may be considered as essentially the same as the lamps that were being sold in Canada in the late 1840s, although perhaps a little more ornate than the standard model.

63
*Solar lamp, with original burner
and shade; the chimney has been added;
purchased in St. Joseph, Mo., said to
have come from a home in Kansas City*
LSR 255. ROM *photo*

The base consists of 2 square marble slabs, the smaller one resting on the larger, with a bronze moulding of leaves fitted into the angle of the step. From the upper slab the stem rises; the bottom is circular and above is a slightly conical portion with 8 heavy flutings. Then comes a constricted portion and 2 bulbous portions. The upper bulb has a ring of 13 holes through which air for the central draft could enter. The lower part of the font is like an inverted cone, ornamented in lotus-flower fashion. The upper part is a depressed sphere, with a projecting rim at the periphery. On this rim rests a ring from which are suspended 12 glass pendants, each consisting of a short and a long prism, with sunbursts cut into the flat side. All metal parts so far described are finished in a handsome golden bronze. The font is widely open on top, revealing the burner projecting up from the interior.

A solar lamp with dissected burner is illustrated by Thwing (pl. 58). A complicated brass piece fits over the top of the font, largely covering the opening. The central part of this piece is the deflector, a flattened dome with an opening a little larger in diameter than the burner. Around the deflector is a channel and rim, to receive the lower end of the chimney. From this rim 6 convex spokes radiate to an outer, wider channel and perforated rim, which rests on the flange of the font and supports the glass shade. All this piece, which might be called the deflector assembly, is stamped from ordinary brass.

On the rim of the chimney support are 2 square slots, which fit over 2 upright bars projected from a brass ring inside the opening of the font. From this ring 4 spokes slope inward and downward to a brass collar which encircles a steel tube a little below its top. In the tube are 2 circular openings about $\frac{1}{2}$ inch in diameter which allowed fuel to reach the wick.

The wick holder is a brass tube about one inch in height, and of such diameter as to slip loosely within the steel tube. There is a projection from the lower rim that slides up and down in a vertical slot which extends from the top of the steel tube almost to its bottom. Opposite, and on the inside, is a much smaller projection. The upper two-thirds of the wick holder is smaller in diameter than the lower third, and has small barbs to engage the inside of the tubular wick.

The centre-draft tube rises from the bottom of the font and is sealed from it, but opens into the stem where there are air-intake holes. The tube has a square-cut spiral channel on its outer surface. When the wick holder, inside the steel tube, is dropped into the draft tube, and the assembly is turned slightly, the small projection on the inside of the wick holder is engaged in the spiral groove. By turning the steel tube clockwise the wick holder can be made to descend. Usually the steel tube was rotated by turning the whole deflector assembly, which meshed with the 2 vertical projections on the wheel-like ring.

In operation the lower end of the tubular wick was fitted over the wick holder. With this in place, as described above, the wick could be lowered into the steel tube and so into the font, and the height of the upper edge adjusted by turning the deflector assembly.

The shade on this lamp is probably an original. The lower two-thirds is almost globular; the part above is constricted but still wide. The upper rim is flaring and has 12 scallops. The outer surface is etched, with clear decoration of circles and fronds.

The chimney shown in figure 63 is of much later manufacture, the original chimney being missing. Typical solar chimneys may be seen in the Ford Museum. They are high and narrow, like the flame, without any expanded or constricted portion, but taper slightly from the middle to the top in a rather ungraceful curve.

Solar lamps worked well with olive or whale oil, but in North America they were used mainly with lard. Their success with this fuel presumably resulted from the all-metal construction of the font, deflector assembly, and burner. The steel tube must have been especially effective in conducting heat to the fuel. Robert Cornelius rather gilded the lily in an invention[21] which involved a deflector separated from the chimney and shade holder, but connected to a tube extending down into the font. This deflector tube and the slotted steel tube were suspended so that there was little heat transfer to the body of the lamp but much to the fuel. I have not seen an actual example, but a number of solar lamps that have been converted to burn kerosene still bear the Cornelius patent plate. An example is shown in figure 64 (LSR 44). The plate is of brass and oval in shape, and is attached to

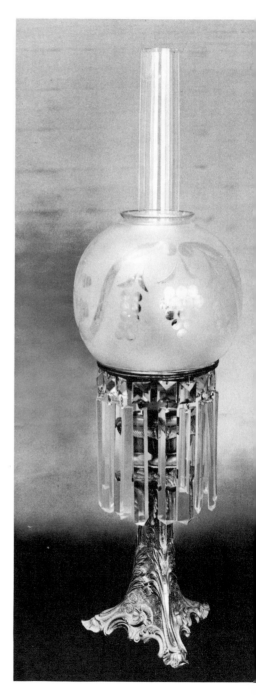

the side of the font. It bears the following inscription: "CORNELIUS & CO. / PHILAD. / JULY 24TH. 1842 / PATENT / APRIL 1ST. 1843."

As noted previously, the solar lamp is closely connected with the firm of Cornelius of Philadelphia. The history of this family would make an interesting study. The earliest record seen by the writer is in *The Philadelphia Directory and Stranger's Guide* for 1825, which lists Christian Cornelius as "Silver plater & patent lamp manuf." The following changes in name and direction of the company are from subsequent issues of Philadelphia directories, and may be useful in dating lamps or other lighting devices:

1839: Cornelius Co. Lamps (C. Cornelius and R. Cornelius).

1845: Cornelius, C., lamp and chandelier manuf.
Cornelius & Co., Lamps (R. Cornelius).

1853: Cornelius, Baker & Co., Lamps and Chandeliers. (R. Cornelius and Isaac F. Baker).
Cornelius, C., lamp and chandelier manufactr.

1856: Cornelius & Baker, Lamps and Chandeliers (Robert Corneluis, I. F. Baker, Robert Cornelius, Jr.).

1857: Cornelius & Baker, Lamps & Chandeliers (Robert Cornelius, Isaac F. Baker, Robert C. Cornelius).

1860: Cornelius & Baker, Manufrs of lamps, gas fix., &c (Robert and Robert C. Cornelius, Isaac F. and William C. Baker).

1861: Cornelius & Baker [the name of John C. Cornelius added to those of 1860].

1863: Cornelius & Baker [same names as for 1861; Charles E. Cornelius also appears listed separately but at the same address].

1868–9: Cornelius & Baker [same names as for 1861 with Charles E. Cornelius added].

1870: Cornelius & Sons (Robert, Robert C., John C. and Charles E. Cornelius) [no mention of the Bakers in the Directory].

1887: Cornelius & Hetherington.

64
Solar lamp, purchased in Ridgeway, Ont. said to have come from a home in Westfield, N.Y. It bears the Cornelius patent dates of 1843 and 1849 but was converted to burn kerosene, and subsequently altered to serve as an electric light. LSR 44

1888: Cornelius & Rowland [George L.].

1891: Cornelius & Rowland.

The Cornelius firms were noted for the manufacture not only of fine lamps, chandeliers, and gas fittings, but also of ornaments and statuettes cast in brass and finished in a characteristic golden bronze. The Cornelius products won almost every possible award and citation in the exhibitions held by the Franklin Institute of Philadelphia between 1824 and 1874. Freedley (p. 355), after giving an excellent account of the Cornelius & Baker processes, states that the products are often sent to "Cuba, South America, the Canadas, and sometimes China and India."

Another Philadelphia firm that achieved some success in the manufacture of solar lamps was that of Archer, Warner, Miskey & Company.[22] A handsome catalogue of what was evidently the same firm, but with Warner, Miskey & Merrill on the cover, shows coloured lithographs of whale-oil lamps, vapour lamps, and a large series of solar lamps.[23] The date must be about 1850. A curious point of nomenclature appears in this catalogue, not seen elsewhere. The term 'Solar Lamp" is restricted to those in which the speroidal shade rests on the outer edge of the font, as in the lamp described above. Those lamps in which the shade rests on a rim immediately around the burner, leaving most of the font exposed, are labelled "Supper Lamp." There does not seem to be enough difference to justify making this distinction today, but the two styles should be recognized.

The majority of solar lamps now seen in collections and antique shops have at some time been converted to burn kerosene. This usually was done by removing the burner and closing the opening into the font with a brass cover, in which was set a collar for a kerosene burner. Although this burner may have been one of the tubular-wick kinds that appeared after 1869, there was no attempt in the conversion to preserve the Argand principle of operation. Mr. Carleton Brown of the Ford Museum has expressed the opinion to me that most of these conversions were done by the manufacturers themselves, and the sophisticated manner in which it was done and the matching materials used strongly support this conclusion.

Lithograph plate from a catalogue of "Patterns" by Warner, Miskey and Merrill New York, ca. 1850

From left to right and top to bottom peg lamp (burning fluid?), four whale-oil lamps, solar wall lamp solar hand lamp, Argand lamp "supper" lamp, solar hand lamp two "supper" lamps, solar lamp two "supper" lamps (By permission of the Metropolitan Museum of Art Whittelsey Fund, 1958)

Dr. Abraham Gesner

CHAPTER VII

The coming of kerosene

1854 to 1860

In 1846 Dr. Abraham Gesner, a Nova Scotia physician and geologist, gave a public demonstration of a new process he had discovered. By heating coal in a retort he distilled from it a fairly clear, thin fluid which – as he showed his audience – made an excellent lamp fuel, burning with a bright yellow flame. By coincidence Gesner's talk that evening took place in Charlottetown, P.E.I., where eighteen years later other talks would be the first move towards Canadian Confederation; Gesner's demonstration was the beginning of a technological and social revolution as great in its way as the forthcoming political changes. By 1864 "coal oil," the popular name for the liquid he named kerosene, was the almost universal lamp fuel in North America. It proved efficient, relatively safe, and cheap enough to be used by both city merchant and backwoods farmer. It transformed home lighting, and in its development gave rise to the giant international oil industry many years before the invention of the motor car.

Abraham Gesner was born in 1797 in Annapolis Township, near Kentville, N.S.[1] His father and uncle had fought on the British side during the American War of Independence and had come to the Annapolis Valley in 1784. After youthful adventures at sea, Abraham went to London, where he studied medicine and took lectures in geology and chemistry. He began medical practice in Parrsboro, N.S., but his real interest was geology, and in 1836 he published a book on the minerals of Nova Scotia, especially those of the Minas Basin region. This led to his appointment in 1838 as Provincial Geologist of New Brunswick. When this ended four years later, he tried to start a public museum in Saint John, but failing to get the needed support he returned to the family farm near Kentville which he had purchased from his father in 1841. There he practised medicine and carried out experiments on elctromagnetism and on the distillation of coal. He was engaged in a geological survey of Prince Edward Island in 1846 when he gave the public demonstration in Charlottetown.

In 1848 Gesner sold back the farm to his father and moved to Sackville, N.S., and later to Halifax. About this time he published books on the natural resources of New Brunswick and Nova Scotia. In Halifax Lord Dundonald, the admiral commanding the British naval forces in the western Atlantic, encouraged him to continue his experiments on illuminants. He gave public demonstrations of his new lamp fuel, for which he coined the name "Kerosene" – a contraction of the Greek "keroselaion," meaning wax-oil – but he could not get financial support. In 1854 he moved to New York City, where he interested a group of business men. They formed the North American Kerosene Gas Light Company, to which he assigned his patents.

Across the Atlantic, meanwhile, another inventor was proceeding along independent but parallel lines. Gesner was, after all, building on earlier discoveries. People had been roasting coal for nearly two generations to produce illuminating gas, and one of the by-products of this process is coal tar, the raw material of a host of chemical compounds. Michael Faraday is credited with discovering some of these compounds in 1825, including the light oil called benzol.[2] This was patented as a lamp fuel in 1847 by C. B. Mansfield of England, but the smoky flame proved unsatisfactory. A clear flame could be produced by burning benzol vapour in a current of air and this was done in the "atmospheric" lamp, but it was a complicated piece of apparatus that had little if any use in North America.[3]

In the late 1840s both Gesner and a British chemist, James Young, hit independently on the idea of distilling coal at temperatures well

James Young

below those required to produce illuminating gas (800° F. as compared with 1,000° F.). The principle product was an oil similar to benzol, but which, with suitable purification, could be made to burn with a clean, bright flame.

James Young (1811–1883) was born in Drygate, Scotland. After a modest education he became assistant to Thomas Graham, professor of chemistry at Anderson University and later at University College, London. Subsequently he worked for various chemical manufacturers. In 1844 he went to Manchester as the manager of Messrs. Tennant, and there in 1848 he experimented with oil seeping in a coal mine as a source of lubricating and illuminating fluids. When the source became exhausted he tried the dry distillation of coal, especially the very resinous "boghead" coal, from which he was able to produce a number of useful liquids. One of these he called paraffine oil, because at low temperatures it congealed to a substance resembling paraffin.[4] Young took out a patent on his process and its products in 1850,[5] and two years later obtained an American patent[6] for the same invention. These patents were upheld in both England and the United States in a series of lawsuits. As a result of the success of "paraffine oil" as a lamp fuel, and the royalties that other producers had to pay him, Young became wealthy. He retired to Scotland, but continued to make chemical inventions and devised experiments to determine the velocity of light. He was the principal patron of the missionary-explorer David Livingstone, a friend of Glasgow days.[7]

In spite of clear priority of discovery, Gesner did not obtain his first kerosene patent[8] until 1854, two years after Young's American patent. But Gesner's method of purifying the product of the initial distillation seems to have been superior, resulting in a cleaner and less malodorous fuel. Manufacture of kerosene under the Gesner patents began in New York in 1854, and later in Boston. The raw materials were bituminous coal and oil shale.

Saint John and Fredericton Business Directory, 1862 (*The Ganong Library, New Brunswick Museum*)

The Canadian Directory for 1857–58
(Oil Museum of Canada, Oil Springs,
Ont.)

With the bad luck that had followed him all along, Gesner lost the chance to exploit the richest source of kerosene he knew. In northeastern New Brunswick there was a thick vein of natural asphaltum, subsequently named Albertite after Albert County. Gesner tried to acquire the mining rights but in an almost incredible court decision a "jury of farmers" ruled that the asphaltum was a kind of coal and therefore part of a mineral grant already issued to other parties. These people reaped the profits that should have been Gesner's, selling lamp fuels distilled from Albertite as "Albertine"[9] and "Portland Kerosene."[10]

During the late 1850s Gesner's kerosene enjoyed a slow but steady increase in popularity, thanks to the efforts of J. H. and G. W. Austen, the Kerosene Company's sales managers. In 1857 it was available in both Montreal and Toronto.[11] By 1860 it had reached St. John's, Nfld.,[12] although in the Maritimes it did meet some competition from Young's paraffine oil[13] and the products of Albertite. Much was made of the safety as well as the brilliancy of the kerosene light. Explosions did occur and were publicized by the manufacturers of other fuels, but these accidents were found to have been caused by improperly distilled fluid, in which the votatile fractions (what we would call naphtha and gasoline) were included.[14] By 1859 kerosene, commonly sold as coal oil or carbon oil, was available in most of the settled parts of British North America. It was still, however, too expensive for general use. The revolution in lighting was yet to come.

In addition to serving as chemist for the Kerosene Company, Gesner found the time to write the first text-book on the distillation of hydrocarbons.[15] In 1863 he returned to Halifax and began preparation of a second edition. At this time he obtained a Nova Scotia patent on kerosene.[16] He was appointed Professor of Natural History at Dalhousie University but before he could assume his academic duties or complete his book he died on April 29, 1864. His son,

George W. Gesner, completed and edited the second edition,[17] but it was nearly seventy years later that his grave in Camp Hill Cemetery was marked; the credit for this goes to Imperial Oil Limited.

The introduction of kerosene brought to an end the age of confusion in lamp fuels, which was also the age of ingenious invention in lamps. Kerosene is a member of the large family of hydrocarbons. These are relatively simple compounds of carbon and hydrogen, the basic form being the gas methane, with a molecule consisting of one atom of carbon and four atoms of hydrogen (CH_4). From this one can trace an apparently endless series of compounds in which the number of carbon and hydrogen atoms are multiplied in regular fashion. With increase in size of molecule the hydrocarbon becomes more dense, and so progresses from a very light gas to a volatile liquid to a heavy oil to a solid. Hydrocarbons occur in nature in all these stages and in various mixtures. Natural gas is methane and other gaseous hydrocarbons. Petroleum is the liquid form usually found in nature; it is widely disseminated in some sedimentary rocks but when concentrated it may seep as oil springs or flow from wells. Solid hydrocarbons occur nearly pure as asphaltum, bitumen, or pitch, disseminated in "tar sands" or mixed with other organic or mineral matter in the various grades of coal.

KEROSENE FROM PETROLEUM

Dr. Gesner was well aware that kerosene could be distilled from liquid hydrocarbons, and in his patents he mentioned petroleum as one of the sources of the new fuel. For many years petroleum had been a scientific curiosity but little more. An oil seepage in what is now southwestern New York was examined by Jesuit missionaries and was skimmed and used as an ointment by Indians and white settlers. The

site was visited in 1833 by the famous professor of natural history, Benjamin Silliman, who collected samples and distilled them back in his laboratory at Yale University. He obtained a clear and very inflammable "naptha," but apparently did not try to use it as a lamp fuel.[18] Probably this was the first scientific distillation of petroleum. The site of this seepage can be visited today northeast of Olean, N.Y.

Similar oil seepages, hardened into "gum beds," were encountered by the early settlers in Enniskillen Township, Canada West. In 1850 the Canadian geologist T. Sterry Hunt reported on their occurrence. Charles N. Tripp organized the International Petroleum and Mining Company, chartered on December 18, 1854,[19] to exploit them, but within a year he sold out to J. M. Williams of Hamilton,[20] a prominent manufacturer of wagons and railway cars. Williams began shipping the crude oil to Hamilton in 1858 and by 1860 had a refinery operating there in which he made a form of kerosene and sold lamps in which to burn it.[21] At first Williams obtained his oil from shallow, hand-dug wells, which penetrated only the superficial clay over the bed rock.[22] This was the beginning of the Canadian oil industry.

In the United States the petroleum age began in northwestern Pennsylvania. The occurrence of oil in springs and salt wells of Alleghany County was mentioned in 1833 by the geologist S. P. Hildreth.[23] He stated that it was gathered and used locally as a lubricant and an ointment; after being filtered through charcoal it also served as a lamp fuel. The first organized exploitation of it took place in 1853. Dr. F. B. Brewer of Titusville was part owner of the local lumber mill, and he got the idea of collecting the oil seepage from the surface of the spring pools by floating blankets on the water. The wool absorbed the oil in preference to the water and could subsequently be wrung out. Dr. Brewer used the oil as fuel for his lumber-mill furnace. It also proved to be a good lubricant for the machinery and even served as fuel for the flares. Some of this or other Alleghany County petroleum was bought by S. M. Kier of Pittsburgh, who refined and marketed it as a cure for all manner of diseases including "Scrofula or the King's Evil."

The demand for petroleum led Dr. Brewer and his associates in 1854 to organize the Pennsylvania Rock Oil Company, with capital mostly obtained from New Haven, Conn., but incorporated in the State of New York. This is famed as the world's first oil company, but Tripp's company in Canada West anticipated it by about a month.[24] Because of difficulty in raising funds for a New York company, the New Haven directors subsequently organized a branch under the laws of Connecticut. It was this organization that sent "Colonel" Edwin L. Drake to Titusville in 1857 to see what could be done about increasing the supply of oil. Drake had no experience that would qualify him for such a mission, but as it turned out, a more fortunate choice could hardly have been made. After a leisurely investigation

Reconstructed derrick and spring-pole drill on site of first oil well dug in Enniskillen Township Ont., by J. M. Williams in 1858 (Oil Museum of Canada, Oil Springs, Ont.)

The Daily Spectator and Journal of Commerce, *Hamilton, Ont. July 4, 1860*

he conceived the idea of drilling a well similar to the numerous salt wells in the region but expressly for petroleum. He encountered many difficulties but through his own perseverance and ingenuity and the skill of his driller, "Uncle Billy" Smith, he brought in a producing well on Oil Creek on August 27, 1859, at a depth of 69.5 feet. Whether or not Drake's well was completed before or after those of Williams at Oil Springs in Canada West depends upon the definition of an oil well. Drake's was the first well drilled, rather than dug, for oil, and the ancestor of all the oil wells since.[25]

Drake's success brought on the first oil boom in history. Soon the valley of Oil Creek was dotted with derricks. The kerosene factories in New York were quickly converted to use petroleum instead of coal as the raw material, and new refineries were set up near the oil fields. The excitement spread to Canada and by April 1860 another oil boom was in full swing in Enniskillen Township. Before the end of 1859 Williams had successfully drilled for oil, and in 1862 H. N. Shaw brought in a spectacular gusher. New refineries sprang up, like that of J. W. Esmonde at Oakville, 1865.[26] Nevertheless, much Canadian crude oil was sold to the United States. So great was the demand for kerosene that by 1861 the same refineries that bought this oil were selling part of their kerosene back to Canada,[27] a south-north flow of raw material and finished product that was to be repeated in many forms in later years.

By 1861 kerosene made from petroleum was displacing other kinds of lamp fuel in the United States and Canada. Formerly it had been available only to the well-to-do; now it was in reach even of the poor. An advertisement of 1861[28] offered "refined coal oil," presumably made from petroleum, at 30 cents a gallon, and "Albertine Coal Oil" at $1.00 a gallon. The farmer going about his pre-dawn chores, the student cramming for his examinations, the workman on the night shift, the actor behind the footlights, each had a brighter, cheaper, and safer source of light. Man's working day had been increased to twenty-four hours.

This was really a social revolution but it made surprisingly little stir in the records of the time. A few advertisements for "coal oil" and lamps are about all the evidence to be found in the newspapers of 1860. On the individual level the impact must have been more memorable. Imagine the excitement and anticipation in a Canadian home as the family gathered round to watch father light their first kerosene lamp. Sometimes the event was a little too exciting. A lamp in the Oil Museum of Canada at Oil Springs, Ont. (figure 65), is said to be the first in Moore Township, near Lambton. Its label recounts that "Mr. John W. Callum who was born in 1848 was one of the neighbors visiting the home that evening when the lamp was first lit; it flickered and everyone thought that it was going to explode so all ran out of the house."

A somewhat different reaction greeted the appearance of the first kerosene lamp in the Red River Settlement (now Winnipeg). William Drever, a prominent fur trader and business man of the colony, brought it back from St. Paul, Minn., in 1858, and lit it one evening with appropriate ceremony. Seeing the glow, his neighbours rushed over thinking the house was on fire.[29]

What were they like, those first kerosene lamps that fortunate people had been using for over five years, and which in 1860 became available to almost everyone?

KEROSENE LAMPS OF THE 1850s

VIENNA BURNER   The original experiments with kerosene as an illuminant were carried out on simple whale-oil or burning-fluid lamps, which must have produced considerable smoke as well as light. The

65
"First oil lamp in Moore twp."
Oil Museum of Canada, Oil Springs, Ont.

RIGHT: The Daily News, *Kingston, Canada West*
May 14, 1861, and June 9, 1862

various lamps that used the Argand burner with a chimney, such as the astral and the solar, probably gave moderately good results. Nevertheless, John H. Austen, one of the sales managers for the North American Kerosene Gas Light Company, searched the United States and Europe for a device that would give maximum light from the new fuel with minimum smoke. He found what he was looking for in Austria and brought it back to sell in the United States as the "Vienna burner." This was the prototype of all kerosene burners subsequently developed, according to Gesner, writing in 1863.[30] But beyond Gesner's account, there are few references to the Vienna burner. A U.S. Supreme Court patent ruling of 1872[31] mentions a Vienna burner that was exhibited in evidence, and notes that its deflector rests directly on the base plate.

No student of lighting in Canada or the United States I consulted had any additional knowledge of the Vienna burner, so I wrote to Dr. Josef Nagler, Director of the Technisches Museum für Industrie und Gewerbe in Vienna. With his courteous reply Dr. Nagler sent photographs of illustrations from a 1917 catalogue of the firm of R. Ditmars, Gebrüder Brünner of Vienna. There in a page of burner illustrations, in place of honour in the upper left corner, was the picture of a simple burner labelled in three languages, "Wiener Flachbrenner/Bec plat viennois/Vienna Flatburner."

Shortly after having learned in this way what a Vienna burner looked like, I began finding examples. Mr. Godfrey Moore of St. Catharines, Ont., supplied two, one on a handsome peg lamp. A third was obtained from Mrs. Catharine Van Camp of Toronto. A fourth was seen on the lamp of a child's lantern-slide projector. As Dr. Nagler warned, the Ditmars Company went on making the typical Vienna burners for many years, so that no individual burner can automatically be presumed to be one of the earlier imports. The first example described below came on a peg lamp that cannot be older than the

1870s. But because there was little change made in this burner over the years, and because these examples fit the few clues in the records, we may assume that they are the same as those Austen introduced into North America about 1856.

The first burner (figure 66; LSR 264) is of brass and is small by later standards, being 1⅞ inches high and 1½ inches in diameter. The base plate is deeply cup-shaped, with a large number of vertical slits to admit air. In the bottom of the plate is a small chamber, the lower part threaded to screw into the collar of the font. Through this chamber the wick tube, flattened oval, ⁹⁄₁₆ inch in diameter, passes, and with it are 2 wick wheels to engage the flat wick. The wick-wheel shaft is long and ends in a thumb wheel which is marked "DITTMARS/MADE IN AUSTRIA." The upper rim of the base plate is extended as a simple vertical collar ⅜-inch high, with 4 vertical slits to give springiness. This is the chimney holder. The deflector is a high dome with oval blaze hole. It is firmly attached to the base plate below the chimney holder by 2 small lugs that fit into slots on the rim of the base plate. Mr. Moore, who supplied the peg lamp which included this burner, states that it came from a home between St. Catharines and Niagara Falls.

The second example (LSR 265) is somewhat larger, the diameter being 2¾ inches, but the basal screw is the same size ¾-inch diameter). The collar for the chimney is relatively higher. The thumb wheel is marked "WIENER FLACHBRENNER." The provenience is uncertain, but it is presumed from somewhere in the Niagara area. The third Vienna burner (LSR 289) is of the same size as the first but has a higher chimney holder (⁷⁄₁₆ inch). There is no inscription on the thumb wheel.

The distinctive features of the Vienna burner are the simple, collar-like chimney holder and the deflector that is secured to the base plate. With these characteristics to watch for, it is likely that more examples will be found, and indeed some have already been identified in prominent collections. There was nothing particularly new in the wick assembly; flat wicks were used in several earlier lamps, going back to that of Rumford, and the Samuel Rust lamp had a rotary device to

66
*Vienna "flatburner"
made by Ditmars of Austria and
introduced to North America about 1856
for use with the new fuel kerosene;
this example is said to be from a home
near St. Catharines, Ont.* LSR 264

67
*Jones burner
1858, the first American burner
designed for kerosene
purchased in East Aurora*, N.Y. LSR 208

adjust the height of the wick. But the Vienna burner's high, dome-shaped deflector was copied in most of the flat-wick kerosene burners that followed it.

JONES BURNER   The first practical kerosene burner designed in North America was that patented by Edward F. Jones of Boston in 1858.[32] The patent claim specifically applied to a spring-loaded lever which secured the chimney within the serrated rim of the base plate (coronet chimney holder) and held the dome-shaped deflector which was otherwise loose on the plate. The wording of the patent suggests that the lever is the only important difference from the Vienna burner but of course the coronet instead of the plain collar chimney holder and the loose deflector are other obvious differences.

Of the various burners in my collection that were derived from the Jones patent only one example (LSR 208) accords closely with the specifications (figure 67). It was purchased from Mr. and Mrs. Paul Shelley of East Aurora, N.Y. It is much larger than the Vienna burner, with a diameter of 2¼ inches. The base plate is cup-shaped, concave on the outside, and is perforated with numerous small round holes. There are 3 wick wheels in the flat chamber at the bottom. The coronet has 20 pointed serrations. The chimney lever is continued internally as a spring-metal strip braced against the lower part of the wick tube. The deflector is hat-shaped, with a row of perforations near the base of the dome. The rim is slightly turned down at the edge and has a shallow notch which fits over the metal strip and keeps the deflector from turning. It and the spring-loaded lever are the only things holding the deflector in place. The thumb wheel is inscribed "E. F. JONES PAT. MAY 4. 1858."

68
*Modified Jones burner
from Bond Head, Ont.* LSR 96

Four other burners in the writer's collection seem to be intermediate between the Jones burner and the Neilson burner described next. Three of them look like miniature Jones burners, having a diameter of 1¾ inches, but the chamber at the bottom of the base plate is conoid and contains only 2 wick wheels. Of these three burners one (LSR 96; figure 68) has the chimney lever loaded by a loop of wire which goes almost completely around the inside of the base plate. The deflector is like that of the typical Jones burner except for 4 little bumps on the rim. The thumb wheel is not inscribed. This burner came with a tin sconce lamp, and was purchased from the Misses Wilson of Bond Head, Ont. The other two have the lever braced against the chamber of the base plate. One of these (LSR 74), bought from Mr. R. H. Perry of Lambeth, Ont., lacks the deflector but the other (LSR 113), bought from Mr. and Mrs. Gordon McNair of Ilderton, Ont., has the deflector rim corrugated, as in the Neilson burner. Both have the same inscription on the thumb wheel: "HOLMES BOOTH & HAYDEN'S / PAT JAN 1860 / E. F. JONES / PAT JAN 11TH 1859." The Jones date is that of the patent reissue; the other date is of the Neilson patent. The fourth burner (LSR 209) has the same inscription but is much larger, with a diameter of 2¼ inches. It also differs in that the spring on the lever consists of a U-shaped piece of wire looped over the end of the lever and coiled at each tip, which is fastened to the top of the base-plate chamber. The rim of the deflector is coarsely corrugated. This burner was purchased from Mr. and Mrs. Paul Shelley of East Aurora, N.Y.

NEILSON BURNER George Neilson of Boston patented a burner that resembles the Jones burner in some respects and assigned the patent[33] to Holmes, Booth & Haydens of Waterbury, Conn.

An example (LSR 210; figure 69) was obtained from the Shelleys of East Aurora, N.Y. It has no lever to retain the chimney. The rim of the loose deflector is corrugated in such a way as to admit air under the lower rim of the chimney. This is the basic part of the patent. There is a small peg and notch to prevent rotation. The wick tube is vertically corrugated, not smooth as in the patent. The chamber of the base plate is dome-shaped on top. The thumb wheel is marked "HOLMES BOOTH & HAYDENS / PATENT / JAN 24 / 1860."

OTHER EARLY BURNERS Several other burners expressly designed for kerosene were patented before 1861 but no actual specimen of any of them has been seen by the writer. It is not certain that they

69
Neilson burner, 1860
made by Holmes, Booth & Haydens
purchased in East Aurora, N.Y. LSR 210

were ever available for public purchase. However, they will be mentioned briefly in case examples should come to light.

Christian Reichmann of Philadelphia[34] patented a burner in which the deflector was supported well above the base plate by a sleeve fitting over the upper end of the wick tube. The chimney was held in place by 8 vertical prongs rising from the scalloped rim of the deflector. That such a burner was manufactured commercially is suggested by the fact that the holder of the Reichmann patent brought suit against the makers of the "Comet" burner for infringement of patent, the case being decided for the defendants by the U.S. Supreme Court.[35]

William F. Shaw of Boston patented a burner in which the deflector was finely perforated or made of wire gauze.[36] He claimed this provided a better distribution of the draft, rather than concentration of it all at the blaze hole.

Michael A. Dietz of Brooklyn, N.Y., a famous manufacturer of lanterns, obtained two patents for burner modifications in 1859. The first[37] provided for a large chamber in the bottom of the base plate; air entered the chamber and was distributed to the wick. The second patent[38] described a method of attaching the deflector to the chimney holder by means of an annular groove into which the rim of the deflector fitted. The drawings of both patents show burners with chimney holders in the form of a slotted collar, like that of the Vienna burner but higher. As Dietz had the resources of a lamp factory at his disposal, it is probable that his burners were in commercial production for a time. Dietz[39] also claimed to have invented the first flat-wick burner for kerosene in 1857, but I have not found a Dietz patent for that year, and of course the Vienna burner was even earlier.

John L. Drake of Cincinnati, O., took out two patents[40] which combined to characterize the Drake burner. One patent applied to the use of 2 separate wick tubes and wicks; one was the burning wick and was adjustable, the other was of open-weave designed to bring oil to the burning wick. The second patent was for a disc-shaped flange around the combined wick tubes, about half-way up the interior of the deflector; it was supposed to direct the draft to the outside of the chamber and keep the deflector cool. The Drake lamp was described approvingly by the

Scientific American[41] soon after the patents were granted, and shortly afterwards was the subject of another note[42] which explained that it was intended to burn "coal oil, being adapted to both the heavy and light varieties." In view of the obvious omission of this statement in either of the Drake patents or the first *Scientific American* article, there is a suspicion that the mention of "coal oil" was a belated attempt to get on the kerosene band-wagon in view of the Alleghany County oil boom just getting under way.

Rufus S. Merrill of Lynn, Mass., devised a special deflector which he called a director. It was a tent-shaped piece of sheet metal fitting the vertical edges of the wick tube and sloping away on the sides, so that some of the draft from below was concentrated on the base of the flame. Around it was placed the conventional dome-shaped deflector.[43]

LAMP BODIES Kerosene burners from the start were made with screws that fitted the collars of burning-fluid lamps. As a result a distinctive body form for kerosene lamps was slow in emerging. During the transitional period of the late 1850s and the first half of the 1860s three style trends can be recognized. The most common was the composite lamp, evidently derived from the handsome solar lamp but having some predecessors among burning-fluid lamps. Its glass font was cemented or bolted to a cylindrical brass stem, which in turn was fastened to a square marble base. No doubt the earliest models were simply burning-fluid lamps like that shown in figure 53, but were soon displaced by ones with more globular, turnip-shaped fonts. A good example is shown in figure 70 (LSR 30).

The spheroid font is obviously mould-blown, but shows no seam marks. The top is smooth but from the shoulder down it is ornamented in a pattern of fine and coarse fluting. The stem is a brass tube with spiral ornamentation. It has circular flanges above and below and rests on a brass disc like an inverted saucer, which spreads the weight over the base. The latter is a plain square plaque of pale grey, slightly mottled marble. Font, stem, and base are held together by an iron bolt, secured at the base by a nut. When this nut is unscrewed the lamp comes apart, revealing

70
*Composite kerosene lamp body, late 1850s purchased in Ridgeway, Ont.
said to be from Buffalo,* N.Y.
LSR 30. ROM *photo*

that the upper flange of the stem is part of a brass cup into which the glass of the font is cemented; at the bottom of this cup is a nut, into which the upper end of the bolt is screwed. Height to top of collar is 8⅛ inches; sides of the base are 4 inches. This lamp was purchased from Mr. C. F. McDougal of Ridgeway, Ont., who obtained it from a home in Buffalo, N.Y. The date is presumed to be about 1858.

Composite lamps in the late 1850s might have pressed patterns as above or elegant cut-glass designs often employing the cased or overlay form of decoration. In this the glass is in two layers of different colour, and the designs are cut through the outer "case" to expose the inner layer. Usual colour combinations were red overlay on clear glass and milk-white overlay on red. A few examples have been found in Canada and one is described in the following chapter. It is probable that such elegant lamps were seldom used in Canada until after 1860, when kerosene became inexpensive. The most ornate of them were very tall, with slender glass stems joined to the conventional glass font and marble base by short brass couplings and long bolts. In these the art of overlay cutting reached its peak.[44] A dealer in Burlington, Ont., told me that she found one example locally and sold it to a collector from the United States. Beautiful examples may be seen in the Ford Museum at Dearborn, Mich.

The second major type of early kerosene lamp was the all-glass table lamp. The division into font, stem, and base was still preserved. This type was derived from the all-glass burning-fluid lamp and early examples may have been used for either fuel.

An example is shown in figure 71 (LSR 33). It was purchased from Mrs. Allie Howe of Dunnville, Ont., and is said to have been used in the district. The glass is thick, with bubbles and swirl marks, and there are 2 faint mould seams. Evidently it was mould-blown. The stem and base are without seams and a spiral flaw indicates that they were spun by hand. The stem is a narrow column, tapering slightly upwards, and surmounted

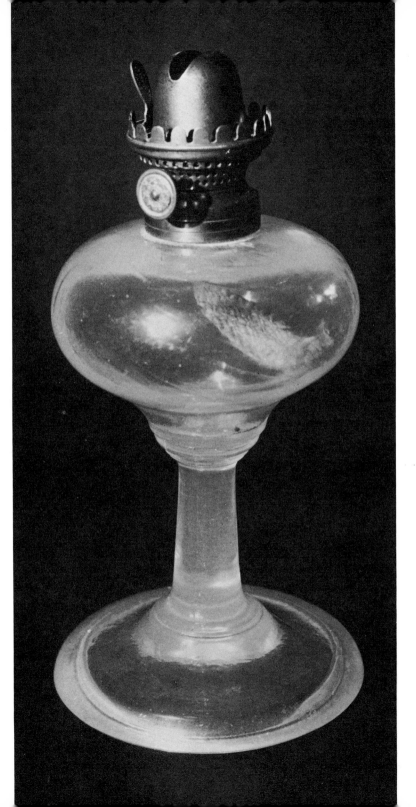

71
*All-glass kerosene table lamp
late 1850s; Dunnville, Ont.* LSR 33

by a capital of 3 rings. At the bottom the juncture with base is flaring, with an annular groove. The base is shaped like an inverted saucer. All the glass is faintly milky. Height of the body including collar is 6⅝ inches and the diameter of the base is 4 inches. An almost identical form of body is shown in the drawing for the Jones patent of 1858; if the present example is not that old it is at least identical with lamps of that time. One very similar is shown by Hayward[45] with a burning-fluid burner. The mate to it is a lamp body (LSR 123) from an old home in Toronto; it is of clear glass, with very faint mould seams, and an annular ornamentation of the font.

The third type of lamp used in this period was the all-glass hand lamp. It had no stem or base, the bottom of the font resting on the table top. The first of these were whale-oil lamps, like the one shown in figure 31, with kerosene burners substituted. Later models were made specifically for kerosene, with lower, wider fonts. They can be distinguished from later hand lamps because they are narrower at the top than at the bottom, and the handle is free-formed and applied.

72
Glass hand lamp
type used in the late 1850s
purchased near Lindsay, Ont.
LSR 350. ROM *photo*

This shape persisted into the 1870s before being replaced. A good example (LSR 350; figure 72) was purchased from Mr. and Mrs. A. Burridge of Pleasant Point, Ont. There is another in the collection of Mr. Peter Eisenbach of Grand Bend, Ont.

CHIMNEYS The chimneys brought over with the Vienna burner must have been the same as those sold with it later, with a cylindrical lower part to fit the vertical collar of the burner (figure 73; LSR 289). With the advent of the Jones burner and others having the coronet-type chimney holder, a new form of chimney appeared. This is illustrated in figure 74 (LSR 395). It is tall, and relatively less expanded in the middle than the Austrian chimney. The characteristic feature is in the lower part; the middle curvature is continued almost to the bottom but the rim is turned out to form a small flange which would provide a better grip for the coronet and any associated clip or screw. This feature appears in chimneys down to the twentieth century, for burners with coronets continued to be made, but other differences developed. The example shown is almost identical with chimneys represented in patent drawings of the late 1850s. Notice how the expanded lower half is distinct from the upper, nearly cylindrical portion. In later chimneys of this sort the outline is a more continuous curve and still later the turned-out lower rim becomes exaggerated. The specimen illustrated was obtained from Mr. and Mrs. Paul Shelley of East Aurora, N.Y.

73
Lamp chimney, made in Austria
type used with Vienna burner
purchased in Toronto
LSR 289. ROM *photo*

SHADES   No special type of shades appears to have been developed for the early kerosene lamps and in fact most illustrations show them without shades. Two types were carried over from the solar-lamp period, however, both made of blown glass. The first was the familiar globe, usually of etched glass with cut ornamentation. The second was vase-shaped, with a flaring, scalloped upper rim. A variant that appeared about 1860 had no globular expansion of the "vase"; instead, the sides flared out gradually but continuously from bottom to top. All these shades were supported on metal rims that projected between collar and burner, as in the "supper lamp" version of the solar lamp.

74
Lamp chimney, characteristic of late 1850s and early 1860s; used with Jones and similar burners; purchased in East Aurora, N.Y. LSR 395. ROM photo

75
Composite kerosene lamp, early 1860s
fitted with Jones burner
and burning kerosene; Toronto area
LSR 140. ROM *photo*

CHAPTER VIII

Those new-fangled lamps

1861 to 1869

AFTER THE REVOLUTIONARY kerosene inventions of the 1850s and the frenzy of the petroleum discoveries of 1859 and 1860, the 1860s may seem anticlimactic. It was a decade of consolidation. The oil fields of Pennsylvania and Ontario expanded, and with better techniques the wells went deeper and recovered more oil. Refineries grew not only more numerous, but better designed for economy of operation and quality of product.

In the home the kerosene lamp gradually replaced other forms of lighting. First to go was burning fluid, although it was still being sold in 1866. Lard, readily available in rural areas where the "coal-oil" dispensers were slow to arrive, held on for a few years longer. But the only serious rival of the kerosene lamp at this time was the paraffin candle, never to be completely displaced.

The 1860s saw little change in the styles of lamps. The composite table lamp remained the predominant type, though new manufacturing processes made it possible to substitute glass for marble in the base, and intricate patterns of moulded glass for the elegant overlays of earlier models. But in the field of burner design the decade was a time of experimentation. Yankee ingenuity, formerly expressed in curious lard lamps, now appeared in complex burners. To the basic design, brought from Vienna, inventors introduced new deflectors, base plates, and chimney holders. Some of these innovations had brief popularity and examples have survived. Though they originated in the United States, many if not all were used in Canada. By 1873 a design of flat-wick burner had been developed (the Atwood burner) which was to remain unmodified in fundamentals to the present day.

A curious feature of this spurt of burner development was the lack of interest in the Argand type, the cylindrical burner with tubular wick and centre draft. The Kleeman student lamp, which used this type of burner, was patented in 1863, but did not achieve its deserved popularity until the 1870s. Burners in which a tubular wick was produced by bending one or two flat wicks were being devised by the end of the 1860s but their story also belongs to the next decade.

In summary, the 1860s saw kerosene progressively become the universal illuminant. While this was being achieved, and the basic burner type standardized, the kerosene lamp itself was subject to little innovation.

BURNERS

NEWMAN BURNER   The first significant burner invention of the new decade was made by Carlton Newman of Pittsburgh, Pa.[1] I have found no evidence that the Newman burner was ever made commercially, but it was described and illustrated in the *Scientific American*,[2] and was the subject of patent reissues in 1876. It seems likely therefore that it was actually manufactured and used.

Its significant feature was the arrangement of deflector and chimney-holding rim as a single unit, hinged at one point to the periphery of the base plate. This permitted deflector, chimney holder, and chimney to be swung back, exposing the wick for trimming. A similar arrangement was incorporated later in the popular Marcy burner and other, lesser known designs, but Newman was the first to use it. He also built in a filler tube next to the wick tube, which made it possible to add fuel to the font without removing the burner. This device seems to have had no general acceptance.

DYOTT BURNER   An ingenious modification of the Jones burner was patented by M. B. Dyott of Philadelphia[3] (figure 76). As in the Jones burner, the dome-shaped deflector with its perforated basal flange rests loosely on the coronet-shaped ring which receives the lower rim of the chimney. But this assembly is separate from the basal part of the burner, a deep, perforated cylinder which screws into the font collar, and contains the flat wick tube with its three-wheel wick raiser. The unique feature is a set of three slotted metal strips, which extend spirally downwards and clockwise from beneath the chimney holder. These strips are engaged by inward projections near the upper rim of the perforated cylinder. As a result, an 80° rotation of the chimney ring counter-clockwise causes it to rise about ⅜ inch, on the principle of the Archimedes screw. This elevation is just enough to permit insertion of a knife blade or small scissors to trim the wick.

76
*Dyott burner, open
purchased in East Aurora, N.Y. LSR 211*

There are 2 Dyott burners in the writer's collection. One (LSR 211; figure 76) is almost identical with that depicted in the patent drawings. The thumb wheel is marked "DYOTT'S PAT. JAN. 6. 1863." Height of the burner, not extended, is 2⅛ inches. The other (LSR 212) is similar, except that a double-channel, open-work, stamped shade ring has been fitted snugly around the chimney holder. Both were purchased from Mr. and Mrs. Paul Shelley of East Aurora, N.Y.

The name of Dyott is well known in the history of Philadelphia. He is said to have been a self-qualified medical doctor who established a successful glass manufactory in a community that he named Dyott-ville. To encourage thrift, he established a bank, but overextended his own investments and went bankrupt. Convicted of incompetency if not of fraud, he served a short prison term, and when released, established with his sons a prosperous patent medicine business.

An examination of Philadelphia city directories from 1825 shows that two individuals are confused in this account. There is a "Dyott, T. W., M.D. & druggist" and a "Dyott, M. B., Glass manuf. Dyottville." I shall have to leave it to the historians of Philadelphia to untangle the Dyott clan, but a plausible interpretation is that it was Michael B. Dyott, the inventor of the Dyott burner, who operated the glass factory in the 1830s and after whom Dyottville was named, that he went bankrupt, and that after clearing his financial position, he set up as a manufacturer of lighting devices. "Dr." T. W. Dyott was another individual, who was the banker, and who went to jail.

MARCY BURNER   The burner most characteristic of the 1860s and used well into the next decade was introduced in the patent of John J. Marcy of Meriden, Conn.[4] Its most conspicuous feature was a hinged deflector and chimney holder, but this, as we have seen, appeared earlier in the Newman burner, and Marcy claimed no originality for it. His innovation was to add to the hinge a curved rod with an expanded end. This rod served as a stop to prevent the hinge from opening more than about 60° (figure 77).

The popularity of the Marcy burner over other hinged burners of the time may be due to the fact that he assigned his patent to Edward Miller of Meriden. The Miller firm was one of two or three great makers of lamp burners, and through it the Marcy burner obtained wide distribution. Pages of the Miller catalogues have been reproduced by Freeman (pp. 55–57); these are not dated but evidently were printed in the 1870s.

There are several Marcy burners in the collection of the National Museum of Canada and eleven in the author's collection. Most have

77
Marcy burner, 1863
purchased in East Aurora, N.Y. LSR 192

the Baldwin vapour vent and are not older than 1867. The inscriptions on the thumb wheels vary greatly, even between burners that look otherwise identical. Some simply refer to "E. MILLER & CO. MERIDEN CT." Others give the patent dates of the Marcy burner, the Baldwin vapour vent, and the Ambrose vent (see below). Two burners of Marcy type (LSR 40 and LSR 116) were used in incubator lamps and have chimney holders almost 3½ inches in diameter; the chimney was a sheet-metal cone, with a circular mica window. One of these burners has a simple loop on the wick-wheel shaft instead of a thumb wheel. Another Marcy burner (LSR 111) is a double-wick or duplex burner.

Marcy burners must have had a wide use in Canada during the late 1860s and the 1870s. Examples have been obtained at Ilderton, Jordan, Preston, and Ottawa, Ont., Huntingdon, Que., and in the United States as far south as Pilot Mound, N.C.

78
Marcy burner, 1868 *or later purchased in East Aurora,* N.Y.
BELOW: *deflector closed*
RIGHT: *deflector open to show vapour vent*
LSR 217

BALDWIN VAPOUR VENT   Although it means departing somewhat from strict chronology, this safety invention ought to be mentioned here because it was almost universally incorporated in later Marcy burners. George E. Baldwin, of West Meriden, Conn., obtained a patent[5] for placing a small flattened tube, like a miniature wick tube, alongside the actual wick tube (figure 78). Through it gases formed by vaporization of the fuel could escape easily and be burned without pressure build-up. As a further safety precaution, the lower part of the burner base, starting at the screw, was sealed off as a separate chamber through which the wick tube and the vapour tube passed.

Baldwin assigned his patent to E. Miller and Co., as had Marcy, and the vapour vent became an integral part of the Marcy burner. It also appears in the "Sun Hinge" version of that burner put out by Plume & Atwood, and in the Plume & Atwood burner of the 1870s (see chapter 9). Actually the auxiliary vapour vent first appeared in a patent by J. E. Ambrose in 1860,[6] as was acknowledged by inclusion of the Ambrose patent date with others on the thumb wheel of many Marcy burners.

TAPLIN BURNERS   Albert Taplin, of Providence, R.I., took out several patents for improvements in lamp burners during the early 1860s. The most significant[7] was for a hinged burner similar to those of Newman and Marcy. The difference was in the hinge. Taplin's had two cylindrical "eyes" on the lower part and one "eye" on the upper, held together by a pin. This is a conventional three-segment hinge, except that the middle part of the lower half was not cut away. It was retained instead as a flat "fender" or stop to prevent the chimney holder from swinging back too far, and in this sense was a substitute for the little curved rod in the Marcy burner. In this Taplin patent the hinge was made from extensions of the metal of the chimney ring and base plate. In a later patent[8] in 1864 Taplin stated that the hinge parts "may be made separately, and fastened on in any of the usual ways." In the latter patent there are two hinges. One connects the chimney holder and base plate, the other connects the base plate and the screw that fits the collar of the lamp body, permitting easy filling of the font. This new hinge is different from that of the earlier patent: it consists of a projecting strip on the upper half which fits loosely into the turned-over edges of the lower half, the two being held together by a separate strip of metal which passes through slots in both upper and lower halves. This seemingly improbable design for a hinge apparently worked very well.

Another patent for a hinged burner was taken out four years later by Alvin Taplin of Somerville, Mass.[9] This does not seem to differ in any important way from the Albert Taplin burner of 1864. It must be more than a coincidence that two men named Taplin obtained patents on the same idea, that of a hinge between base plate and chimney holder.

The circumstances become even more curious when we examine some burners that bear the name Taplin.

79
Taplin burner
1868; *purchased in East Aurora, N.Y.*
LSR 221

The one shown in figure 79 (LSR 221) was purchased from Mr. and Mrs. Paul Shelley of East Aurora, N.Y. It superficially resembles a Marcy burner, but has the thumb wheel marked "TAPLINS PAT. / MAR. 4. 1864 / AND FEB. 25. 1868." Apart from the three-day error in the first date, these correspond to the Albert Taplin patent of 1864 and the Alvin Taplin patent of 1868. The curious feature is that the essential part of both patents, the hinge between base plate and screw, is not present. The hinge between chimney holder and base plate is like that of the 1864 patent, except that the strip of metal that holds the two parts together is an extension of the lower half of the hinge, and acts as a stop as in the Taplin patent of 1862. There is also a suggestion of another Taplin patent of 1862,[10] in which the base plate is deeply channelled between the outer perforated part and the inner disc that supports the wick tube. This was supposed to augment the draft. Thus it appears that this burner, made in 1868 or later, was based mostly on the Taplin patents of 1862.

Two burners of a different sort are also marked "Taplin." They have the sloping sides of the base perforated, not with numerous small holes, but with a row of large rectangular openings. This, and the presence of a Baldwin vapour vent, suggest that they are not as old as the burner described above. The hinge is a variant of that of the Taplin patent of 1864, but the strip holding the two parts together is a projection from the upper half of the hinge. One (LSR 64) was obtained from Mr. Stan Ashbury of Preston, Ont. The thumb wheel is marked "TAPLINS / HINGE / PAT. MAR. 4. 1864," a repetition of the three-day error in date. The other burner (LSR 222) is from the Shelleys of East Aurora, and is simply marked "TAPLINS / HINGE."

Other manufacturers produced hinged burners in the latter part of the nineteenth century. The "Sun Hinge" was probably the commonest, but another version was made by the Manhattan Brass Company of New York City.

The discrepancies between patent specifications and actual burners make it hard to say what should be called a Taplin burner. Until examples with the double hinge are found, the name might reasonably be used for all burners in which the hinge between chimney holder and base plate is provided with a projecting strip of metal as a stop, in contrast to the Marcy burner in which the stop is a curved metal rod.

WEBB BURNER Numerous attempts to devise a kerosene burner that would give a smokeless flame without a chimney were made during the 1860s and later. Most of them employed specially shaped deflectors or wick tubes to provide an increased draft to the flame. The most successful were those used in lanterns, for the lantern case itself functioned to some extent as a chimney. A detailed discussion of lantern burners does not belong in a history of domestic lighting, but one example will be described because it was developed early and was sometimes used in lamps.

William Webb of Waterbury, Conn., obtained the patent.[11] His burner's most conspicuous feature is an elaborately slotted deflector, designed to dissipate heat from the flame and thus reduce vaporization of the fuel in the font. The ends of the blaze hole are expanded to admit more air to the base of the flame, and there is a horizontal shield inside the deflector to reduce the draft caused by suddenly lowering the lamp. I have not seen a burner that exactly fits the specifications of the Webb patent but one sold under the name of Callender burner is very similar.

80
Webb burner, 1864, on a lantern font purchased at Aberfoyle, Ont. LSR 118. ROM *photo*

An example (LSR 118; figure 80) is set on a rectangular brass font, and was evidently part of a lantern or headlight. It was said to come from Palermo, Ont. The deflector is relatively higher than that shown in the Webb patent drawings, but is slotted in exactly the same alternating pattern. The internal draft shield is level with the ends of the blaze hole, and these ends are not specially expanded. The thumb wheel is marked "E. MILLER & CO. MERIDEN / CONN." An apparently identical burner is illustrated in the Plume & Atwood catalogue of 1907, under the name of "Callender." That these are really Webb burners is confirmed by an example in the U.S. National Museum (no. 75364, Cultural History Division). It is part of a lamp with a sheet-metal font supported in a swivel just above a saucer-shaped base. In the burner the sides of the deflector are completely cut away except for two uprights at the ends of the blaze hole. The draft shield is in the same position as in LSR 118, but the ends of the blaze hole are expanded. Although this USNM specimen differs as much as does LSR 118 from the Webb specifications, its thumb wheel bears the inscription "PATENTED APRIL 5TH / 1864."

NEVILLE BURNER   Anthony Neville of Ernestown, Ont. (the township in which the present village of Odessa is located), obtained two patents[12] in the middle 1860s for other types of burners designed to produce a smokeless flame without a chimney. He used a tall, flat-wick tube with a variety of tips. The second patent includes a description of a special wick, made up of an outer envelope with a core of two or three string-wicks, like those of candles.

The writer's collection includes 3 bronze lamps with the name Neville, purchased from Mr. C. L. Graham of Napanee, Ont. The largest of these (LSR 2; figure 81) has a conoid font with rounded shoulder and a ring-shaped handle riveted to the side. The collar is part of the font. The lower part of the burner is a chamber, with the under side threaded to fit the collar and the upper side a low dome. Inside this chamber are the 2 wick wheels. The wick tube, which extends through it and projects about 1¼ inches above it, is a flat tube, ½ inch wide; the tip is flared, with 5 small holes in a row in the flaring on each side. The thumb wheel bears the inscription "NEVILLE'S PAT. MAY 14. 66." Over-all height of the lamp is 4³⁄₁₆ inches; base diameter is 3¹³⁄₁₆ inches. A second example of this lamp (LSR 51) is slightly smaller but otherwise almost identical. The third lamp (LSR 3) is much smaller, the base diameter being 2⅛ inches, and the wick tube is narrower, with only one perforation on each side of the tip. The thumb wheel is marked "NEVILLE'S PAT. NOV. 23 65," but the differences between this lamp and the other two are so slight as to suggest that they were all made at the same time.

I have been unable to obtain the correct size of wick to test these lamps. One can speculate that the tall wick tube allowed a maximum of oxygen to reach the flame, and that there would be little if any smoke as long as the amount of exposed wick were carefully controlled. A very similar lamp but with a cord-shaped wick was made in the United States much later under the name of Planter's lamp. It is described in a later chapter.

COLLINS BURNER   A short-lived but popular group of burners were invented by Michael Henry Collins of Chelsea, Mass. The

81
LEFT: *Neville hand lamp*
1866; Napanee, Ont. LSR 2
82
BELOW: *Collins burner*
1865; Preston, Ont. LSR 168
83
BOTTOM: *Collins burner*
1868; purchased in Mooers, N.Y.
National Museum of Canada

first, which appeared in 1865,[13] combined the deflector with a device to hold the chimney from the inside.

The deflector, instead of being a graceful dome, is shaped like an inverted saucer, from the rim of which radiates a ring of petal-like flanges. These are springs, which press against the inside of the chimney well above the basal rim. The bottom of the chimney rests in the rim of the base plate, which is well below the deflector. The base plate is shaped like a low dome, and is well perforated. An example of the early Collins burner (LSR 168), purchased from Mr. Stan Ashbury of Preston, Ont., is said to be from the Paris, Ont., area. This example (figure 82) differs from the Collins patent drawings of 1865 in that the deflector is supported by 4 instead of 2 uprights, and has 16 spring flanges instead of 28. The thumb wheel bears the date of the early patent "SEP 19 1865" but is marked "HOLMES, BOOTH & HAYDENS," the firm to whom Collins appears to have assigned all his patents.

Collins obtained another patent [14] in 1868 for a modification of his original burner. The new one was larger, but had the same arrangement for holding the chimney. The special improvement is that the combined deflector/chimney holder is slipped over the wick tube, so that both it and the chimney can be lifted off to permit trimming the wick.

There are 3 examples of later Collins burners in Canadian collections. One (figure 83) is in the National Museum of Canada, purchased from Mrs. Eva Boire of Mooers, N.Y., but said to come from Hemmingford, Que.; the other two are in the author's collection, LSR 117 coming from Mr. Gordon McNair of Ilderton, Ont., the other, LSR 148, from Mr. Richard Bourcier of Malone, N.Y. There is a curious discrepancy between these actual specimens and the patent specifications of 1868. The burners have the deflector/chimney holder firmly attached to the base by 4 uprights, so that the assembly cannot be lifted off. Nevertheless the National Museum burner and LSR 148 have the later as well as the earlier Collins patent date on the thumb wheel. The example from

Ilderton has a confusing inscription: "PAT SEPT 21 / 58 REISSUED 3082 PAT SEPT 19TH 1868." The first date is that of the Reichmann patent mentioned in chapter VII, and the second date seems to be an erroneous combination of the two Collins patent dates. The Collins burner appears again in slightly different form in the early 1870s.

COMET BURNER   The name of Lewis J. Atwood of Waterbury, Conn., appears many times in the history of the kerosene burner. During the 1860s he was foreman in charge of lamp manufacture with Holmes, Booth & Haydens Manufacturing Company, and took out a number of patents which he assigned to himself and that firm. Later he helped to established the Plume & Atwood Manufacturing Company, of which more later, and devised other burners, one of which became a standard type that is still being made.

The burner patented by Atwood in 1868,[15] fifteen days ahead of the second Collins patent, was known in its day as the Comet burner. It was obviously intended to compete with the Collins burner, and evidently had some success. The main difference from the Collins burner is that the pressure to the inside of the chimney is applied by a spiral spring which forms the rim of the deflector.

An almost perfect example (LSR 79), obtained from Mr. John Player of Mallorytown, Ont., was said to have come from the Kingston district (figure 84). The deflector with its spring and the perforated base plate with its vertical serrations form an assembly which can be readily lifted off the wick tube and the top of the screw. The thumb wheel is marked "HOLMES, BOOTH & HAYDENS PATENT JAN 21 1868," and around the perimeter of the deflector is the inscription "COMET ATWOODS PATENT OCT. 13, 1863." The latter date is of an earlier Atwood patent,[16] which seems to have little in common with this burner except that the deflector obstructs the interior of the chimney.

ARNOLD AND BLACKMAN BURNER   The same year saw the beginning of a long series of burners in which the chimney is held

84
"Comet" burner, 1868
Kingston district, Ont. LSR 79

by four vertical spring strips projecting up from the rim of the base plate. The patent was obtained by Alonzo C. Arnold and Ebenezer Blackman of Norwalk, Conn.[17] Two examples are available to me. One in the National Museum of Canada is from the estate of Dr. Robert Bell of Ottawa. The other (LSR 82; figure 85) was purchased in Mooers, N.Y., from Mrs. Eva Boire, but may have come from the Hemmingford district of Quebec. The deflector is firmly attached to the base plate. The lower part of the deflector is cylindrical, but the upper part is the typical dome. The characteristic feature is the set of four spring-brass strips which project upward from the rim of the base plate. The upper part of these strips is bent in, then out, to form an angulation which fits into an annular groove on the special chimney. This holds the chimney solidly, but must have made it awkward to clean the wick.

85
Arnold and Blackman burner
1968; purchased in Mooers, N.Y. LSR 82

86
Toof burner
1868; purchased in Morristown, N.Y.
LSR 153. ROM *photo*

TOOF BURNER Edwin J. Toof of Madison, Ia, obtained a patent[18] for a burner (figure 86) which was descended from the Reichmann burner but had some unique features. The deflector is placed well above the base plate and consists of a low dome in the centre of a flat plate. From this plate four U-shaped spring-brass strips, bent down and back up, provide four slots into which the bottom of the chimney fits. Two of these springs are free, but a third is attached to the base plate of the burner and the spring opposite it serves as a catch. The result is that the deflector, with its chimney-holding springs and chimney, can be hinged back about 80°.

The base plate is well perforated, with a rim of vertical serrations. In the middle is a low dome, from which the flat wick tube projects about half an inch. On one side of the dome is a rectangular opening, the upper end of a vapour vent. From the patent drawings and specifications it appears that there is a valve in the lower part of the vent tube, which allows gas to escape upwards but prevents flame from being drawn down.

The flat part of the deflector is ornamented with a pattern of rays and a rope-like rim. Adjacent to the rim is an inscription, some letters of which are covered by rivets and in the following transcription are enclosed in brackets: "TO[O]FS P[A]TENT AUG. [1]1 18[6]8." There is no inscription on the thumb wheel. This example (LSR 153) was purchased from Mrs. Evelyn Holloman, Morristown, N.Y.

BURNER MANUFACTURERS The best-known maker of lamp burners in North America during the 1860s was the firm of Holmes, Booth & Haydens of Waterbury, Conn.[19] It was established in 1853 by Israel Holmes, John Camp Booth, Henry Hubbard Hayden, and Hiram Washington Hayden. The two Haydens were only distantly related, but their presence on the original board of directors produced the puzzling plural form of the third name in the firm's title. The principal products at first were copper and brass sheets, tubes, and wires, but later they made various objects in brass or copper. In 1856, Holmes, Booth & Haydens were advertising in the Toronto *Globe*[20] as manufacturers of various objects in brass, copper, and German silver, including daguerreotype plates, but there is no mention of lamps. They apparently began making burners in 1859 or 1860, just about the time kerosene derived from petroleum began coming on the market. Lewis J. Atwood was made foreman of the new department, and began his long series of inventions in 1862.[21] Most of his patents of the 1860s were assigned jointly to himself and his employers. H. W. Hayden was also an inventor and took out a number of patents in various fields including lighting. Besides the various Atwood and Hayden inventions, the firm made Collins burners and Marcy-type burners using a modified Taplin hinge.

In 1869, Holmes and Booth left the company to help form what was later known as the Plume & Atwood Manufacturing Company (see chapter 9). The Haydens continued to operate the parent company until the 1890s, but it was no longer a major manufacturer of

Lewis J. Atwood

lamp parts. Other Connecticut companies, such as Scovill of Water-bury and Edward Miller of Meriden, were making lamp burners in the 1860s, but they became more prominent later and are discussed in chapter 9. R. E. Dietz of New York City was also in the burner business, but was more famous for lanterns.

There is some suggestion that kerosene lamps or burners were made in Ontario during the 1860s. It is said that Robert Young of Hamilton began manufacturing "coal oil" burners in 1857.[22] Yet in an advertisement the next year Young and Brother (Robert and William) listed only plumbing fixtures and gas fitting.[23] In an 1862 directory the firm appeared as "Wholesale and Retail Dealers in COAL OIL LAMPS."[24] Two years later they were listed as manufacturers of coal oil lamps.[25] A Toronto company, Parson Brothers, who were selling "coal oil" in 1858, advertised themselves in 1861 as manufacturers and wholesale dealers in improved coal oil lamps.[26]

It seems a bit doubtful that burners and lamp bodies were actually being made in Canada during the 1860s. The big brass and glass companies of New England and Pennsylvania were already in the field and until 1866 enjoyed a duty-free entry into the Canadian market. Most likely these Canadian "manufacturers" were merely assembling lamp parts imported from the United States. I hope that further searching of museums and collections will prove me wrong.

LAMP BODIES

The extraordinary diversity and ingenuity shown in the development of lamp burners during the 1860s were not matched by variety and innovation in the other parts of the lamps. The three main types of bodies established before 1860 persisted with little change, the composite table lamp, the all-glass table lamp, and the glass hand lamp. In the composite lamp some clever inventions permitted moulding in elaborate patterns, and bases of moulded opaque glass replaced the square slabs of marble. Better methods of moulding were also applied to all-glass lamps. But although many of the lamps produced at this time were graceful and attractive, the concept of a lamp as an elegant focus in room decoration was reserved for a later decade.

ATTERBURY LAMPS   The firm of Hale, Atterbury and Company of Pittsburgh, Pa, was established about 1858.[27] The first lamp patent associated with the company was assigned to them in 1861 by Jacob Reighard of Birmingham, Pa.[28] It was for a method of mould-blowing a lamp font with two openings, a central one for the collar and an eccentric one for filling. Reighard used a two-piece mould with a second opening in the upper part along the line of the mould seam, directed upwards at right angles to the inner surface of the mould. This opening was closed with a temporary plug before molten glass was introduced. When the glass was blown in the mould, it formed a closed tube projecting upward in the second opening. Afterwards this tube could be cut open and a brass rim with cap cemented to it.

An example of the Reighard lamp (LSR 9) was purchased from Mr. Don Dunham of Agincourt, Ont. (figure 87). Unlike the font described in the patent, it was made with a 3-piece mould. The font is pear-shaped, with a pattern of angular flutings ("icicle pattern") below the periphery. The filler opening, now broken and without its cap, is situated on one of the mould seams and is surrounded by a circular seam about one inch in diameter. It may be that the original design of the Reighard mould made freeing the filler tube difficult, and that the secondary hole in the mould was therefore much enlarged and partly filled by 2 pieces forming a hollow cylinder; when the main pieces of the mould were removed, these two auxiliary pieces would remain around the filler tube and could be removed with special care. Outside the circular seam there is a

87
*Glass table-lamp body
with Reighard filler opening, 1861
Toronto district.* LSR 9. ROM *photo*

concentric inscription reading "PATENTED JULY 1861." The stem and base are a separately press-moulded, hollow piece, the stem portion being 6-sided and curved-conoid, the base discoid, with the periphery made up of 15 convex flutings. Height of this lamp body is 8 inches; diameter of the font is 3⅞ inches.

In 1862 a group of patents was issued to J. S. Atterbury, T. B. Atterbury,[29] and James Reddick, which had to do with the production of hollow glass ware. In each case a lamp font was used as the example. These patents[30] ingeniously combined the techniques of press-moulding and mould-blowing. The part of the lamp below the shoulder was first press-moulded. Then a lump of molten glass on a blowpipe was held close above it and the mould was closed with two upper pieces. When the top was blown in it fused to the pressed part to complete the font. This method permitted ornamentation of at least that part of the font below the shoulder with elaborate patterns resembling those of cut glass. In one version the pattern was pressed on the inside of the font and subsequently covered by blown glass; thus ornamentation was combined with a smooth inner and outer surface, less likely to accumulate dirt. Another technique involved two colours of glass, creating an effect analogous to the overlay ornamentation of earlier lamps.

I have not seen an example of the composite-moulded Atterbury lamp body as described in the patent, but 2 lamps in my collection bear the appropriate patent dates and are evidently variants. One of these (figure 88) is a small hand lamp (LSR 32) with cast circular handle, the seam of which coincides with that of the font. The upper surface of the font is concave, with annular grooves. There is a distinct shoulder with an annular seam mark, below which the side of the font is concave and narrows towards the base. The side of the font is ornamented with a reversed icicle pattern, and the base with radial fluting. None of this ornamentation can be felt on either the outside or the inside of the font, and is, in fact, between layers of glass. The font, including the handle, up to the shoulder was evidently press-moulded, forming the fluting on the inside. Then the upper part of the mould was placed in position around a lump of molten glass, which was blown not only to complete the font at the top but also to cover the internal pattern with smooth glass. The base of the font bears a faint inscription, "PATENTED / FEB 11 JUNE 4," with "1862" in the centre. The second date must be an error for June 3. Height of the font to top of collar is 2¾ inches; diameter of the base is 3⅛ inches. This lamp was purchased from Mrs. Allie Howe of Dunnville, Ont.

Another, more puzzling, Atterbury lamp is LSR 59 (figure 89). It is an all-glass table lamp in which the font is a plain depressed spheroid, with 2 mould seams, obviously mould-blown. It is attached to a bell-shaped stem and base, with a handle shaped like a question mark, evidently all pressed together in a 2-piece mould. Inside the hollow base is

88
Atterbury hand lamp, 1862
Dunnville, Ont. LSR 32. ROM *photo*

89
Atterbury table lamp
1862; Milton, Ont. LSR 59

an inscription meant to be read through the glass: "PAT^D FEB 11TH JUNE 3RD 1862 REISSUED JULY 20TH 1869." The first two dates are those of the Atterbury patents mentioned above, but the font obviously was not produced by any of the techniques described in those patents. It may be that the combined base and stem was a stock item, frequently attached to fonts of the composite-mould type, but also used for simple lamps of the kind represented here. The over-all height of this lamp to top of collar is 8⅝ inches, and the diameter of the base is 5 inches. It was purchased from Mrs. Catharine Van Camp, formerly of Milton, Ont., and was said to have been obtained in that district.

In 1863 the Atterbury brothers patented[31] a new way of attaching collar to font by setting the metal collar in a separate ring of glass or porcelain which sat on the neck of the font. This was supposed to reduce the passage of heat from burner to fuel. I have not seen an example of this ring, but in all probability it was manufactured.

Several patents for lanterns were taken out by the Atterburys in the middle 1860s, but in 1868 they returned to innovation in lamp-font casting.[32] They designed a mould in four pieces, two lower and two upper, with the horizontal seam going through the upper part of the font-to-be and handle matrix. In use, the lower part of the handle matrix was first partly filled with molten glass. Then the blower put his ball of glass into the body of the mould and closed it on top. When he blew, the glass would not only take the shape of the mould but would unite with and augment the glass in the handle matrix, producing a completed handle attached to the font.

The lamp represented in the patent drawing has no ornamentation, but simple patterns suited to mould-blowing could be used. An example (figure 90) of this is seen in a small hand lamp (LSR 131). The font is a low cylinder with a belt-buckle pattern around the nearly vertical periphery. From the mould-seam marks it is evident that the upper two pieces of the mould merely served to close the top of the font cavity and complete the handle matrix. The handle is ring-shaped and smooth, almost as if free-shaped, but there is a faint bulge indicating the position of the seam. The base, which seems to have had a separate mould piece well inside the periphery, is marked in faint raised letters, "PATD JUNE 30TH 1868." This lamp was purchased from Mrs. Allie Hazelgrove, of Kingston, Ont.

90
Atterbury hand lamp, 1868
Kingston, Ont. LSR 131. ROM *photo*

This method of attaching the handle could have been used for glass mugs as well as lamp fonts. A lamp that is reminiscent of the Toby jug has been illustrated by Revi (p. 40). Another example (LSR 36; figure 91) was purchased from Mrs. Ruth Baird of Chatham, Ont. The design on the outside of the font is of a grotesque female head. Her face is opposite the handle. Her hair covers three-quarters of the remaining surface, straight above, hanging in ringlets below. The vertical mould seam goes through her nose. The horizontal seam encircles the font just above her eyes and meets the upper base of the handle. As in the lamp previously described, the handle is smooth as if free-formed, reflecting the low pressure inside the handle matrix when the glass was blown. The original filling of the handle matrix ran over into the font chamber of the mould

91
Atterbury hand lamp
1868; *London, Ont.* LSR 36. ROM *photo*

and remained distinct, although it is well fused to the font and has taken on part of the pattern. The nearly flat base had a separate mould piece with the inscription, "PAT^D JUNE 30TH 1868."

The last Atterbury patent of the 1860s was for a method of uniting foot and stem in composite lamps.[33] This was usually done by cementing with plaster the plain glass plug of the font into the cup-shaped upper end of the brass stem. The new Atterbury plug was relatively long, and had a screw-like thread cast on its surface. Thus it could be screwed into a threaded socket on the upper end of the stem. Examples have been found in Newfoundland, Nova Scotia, New Brunswick, Quebec, and Ontario.

The New Brunswick example (LSR 321) is illustrated in figure 92: it was purchased from Mr. Dave Graser of Fredericton. It is a large lamp, standing 12 inches to the top of the collar. The hollow base is 8-sided below, rising to a conoid form above. The font is almost spherical, with a peripheral ridge. Above the ridge is a short icicle pattern, while below are 6 large loops. Three well-defined mould seams extend from top to bottom. The stem is a brass tube 1¼ inches long, and the same in diameter. It is threaded in 7 volutions, and receives the threaded plug of the font and upper end of the base.

A much smaller version of the same lamp (LSR 320), 8³⁄₁₆ inches high, was obtained from Mr. Harold Pipe of Amherst, N.S. A lamp of intermediate size is displayed in the Newfoundland Museum at St. John's; it is said to have belonged to Samuel Kirby of Harbour Buffett. Mr. Malcolm Horton of Yarmouth, N.S., obtained one from the "French Shore" which has the base moulded in amber glass to look like a swan. A similar lamp is figured by Revi (p. 40). The Quebec example (LSR 290) bears a date of 1873 and will be discussed later.

RIPLEY LAMPS   All-glass lamp bodies of a peculiar form, combining features of table and hand lamps, were made by Ripley and Company of Pittsburgh in the late 1860s. According to Revi (p. 290),

this firm was established by Daniel C. Ripley, George Duncan, Thomas Coffin, John Strickel, Jacob Strickel, and Nicholas Kunzler in 1866. The process of producing the characteristic lamp body was patented by Ripley.[34] His basic idea was to press-mould the base, stem, and handles, and then mould-blow the font so as to fuse it to these parts. The wide-curving handles were easy to hold and also helped to brace the base and font. The inventor expressly pointed out that his process could be used to produce lamps with either one or two handles, but that he preferred double handles for greater strength, and for convenience in passing the lamp from one person to another.

There are 4 Ripley lamps in the writer's collection, all different but all showing the characteristic features. What I take to be the earliest (LSR 43; figure 93) has a plain, depressed-spheroid font, tapering below to a short and square stem, which in turn connects to a base shaped like an inverted saucer. Joining base and font are 2 handles, each about 45° of a circle. On the under side of the base is a circular band of radial striations, but no inscription. There are 2 mould seams in the vertical plane, extending from collar to stem and down to periphery of base. The seams on the outside and inside of the handles are in the same plane. There is an irregular line of junction between press-moulded stem and mould-blown font. The general shape, the obvious mode of manufacture, and the presence of 2 handles, indicate that this is a Ripley lamp body, but the absence of an inscription suggests that it was made before the patent was issued. Height to top of collar is 5½ inches; maximum diameter of font is 4 inches. It was purchased from Mr. C. F. McDougal, Ridgeway, Ont.

The other 3 examples have the patent dates in the inside of the base. One of these (LSR 1) has a font very similar to that already described, but the stem is a short vertical plate, with the 2 edges reinforced by 6-sided columns. The handles also are 6-sided. The clear centre on the inside of the base bears a mark like a reversed number 2. Around this is a ring of pebbly surface, then a clear ring with the raised inscription (reversed so as to be read through the glass), "RIPLEY & CO. PAT^D JAN. 7. JULY 14. AUG. 11. 1868." This specimen was purchased from Mr. C. L. Graham of Napanee, Ont.

In another (LSR 27) the font is more pointed below, the stem is represented merely by a protruding ring, and the handles curve around under the font to rejoin the stem. It was purchased from Mantz Antiques, Snellingrove, Pa. The final example (LSR 99) is similar except that there is only one handle. The depressed spheroid font has a band of vertical ribs around the periphery, and 3 mould seams, one continuing into the

93
Ripley lamp, 1868
said to be from St. Catharines, Ont.
LSR 43

seam on the handle. Only with the single handle was it possible to use the more convenient 3-piece mould for the font. The specimen was purchased from Mrs. Ruth Baird of Chatham, Ont.

COMPOSITE LAMP BODIES Unless the maker can be identified, it is impossible to be sure whether a certain composite lamp was made in the last two or three years of the 1850s or the first two or three of the 1860s. After that, trends in design become evident and lamps of the late 1860s are not difficult to identify. The two described below are believed to date from the first half of the 1860s mainly because they resemble those in illustrations of that period.

Figure 94 shows the finest example that I have studied of an early composite lamp. The pear-shaped font of pale "cranberry" overlay has an attractive design of lines and ovals cut through to the clear glass. The slightly tapering fluted brass stem is certainly an early style, strongly reminiscent of the Cornelius solar lamps. The base consists of 2 pale-grey marble squares, the smaller one resting on the larger, with an ornamental brass moulding filling in the step. Height to top collar is 12 inches; the base is 4¾ inches square. It was sold to the National Museum of Canada (NMC D-925) by Mr. C. L. Graham of Napanee, Ont., and is said to have been used in that district. The combination of ornate font and fluted stem is part of a style that began about 1859 and started to wane about 1862. A good guess for the date of this particular example would be 1861.

A style in lamp bodies typical of the mid-1860s is illustrated in figure 75. The glass font, brass stem, and marble base are still present. The stem, however, is roughly hour-glass-shaped, and its ornamentation is annular rather than vertical. The font is a low spheroid; it has a ring-like periphery, above and below which are 8 large "thumb-prints," that is, oval depressions, the lower ones deeper than the upper. There are 2 mould seams in the vertical plane, rather faint above the periphery, and a circular seam around the top of the periphery ring. This may be an Atterbury font; at least it is obvious that from the top of the periphery ring down it was formed by press-moulding, and above that line by mould-blowing.

94
Composite table lamp
with red overlay, ca. 1861
purchased in Napanee, Ont.
NMC D-925. NMC *photo*

95
RIGHT: *Composite table lamp*
with opaque blue-glass font
and opal-glass base, Taplin burner
ca. 1865; Huntingdon, Que. NMC A-1168

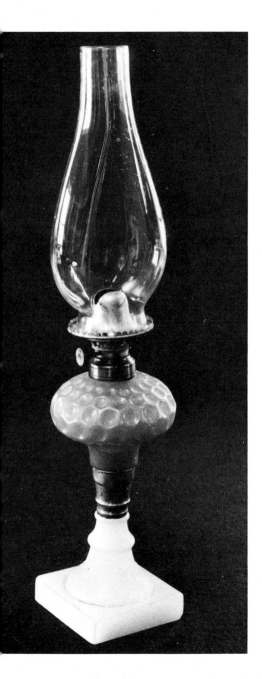

Height to top of collar is 8⅞ inches; diameter of font is 4 inches. This is in the author's collection (LSR 140), and was purchased from The Pennyweight Antique Shop, Toronto. It is said to have come from a home in the Rosedale district of Toronto. It appears to date from some time between 1862 and 1865.

The press-glass lamp base made its appearance about 1865. An early version is shown in figure 95. The simple marble base is imitated in the lower part, and the lower half of the brass stem in the upper. A short section of turned brass represents the upper half of the old brass stem, and joins glass base to glass font.

The font is a depressed spheroid, extended below. It is made of a rather attractive pale blue opaque glass, ornamented with close-set circular impressions. According to Ruth Webb Lee,[35] this pattern is called "Mirror," and was a product of McKee & Brothers of Pittsburgh. Revi (p. 230) calls it "Concave," and lists both it and "Mirror" as *ca.* 1865. The burner came with the body and is a Taplin with Baldwin vapour vent; it is therefore not older than 1867. The lamp body, however, could be as old as 1865, judging by the font pattern and the style of the glass base. This lamp is in the National Museum of Canada (NMC A-1168), and was purchased from Mrs. Eva Boire, of Mooers, N.Y. It is said to have come from the Flynn home, about 5 miles north of Huntingdon, Que. Height of lamp to top of collar is 9½ inches; width of square base is 3³⁄₁₆ inches.

More elaborate designs in press-glass bases were in vogue by 1867. An example (LSR 79) is shown in figure 96. The "stem" portion of the base has vertical fluting on the upper part and around the lower rim. The true base is squarish with scalloped sides. The glass is black opaque rather than white. The font is pear-shaped, with "icicle" fluting on the lower two-thirds. It was blown in a 3-piece mould. The font is similar to, and the base is identical with, a lamp illustrated in 1867,[36] but this style of base is known to have persisted into the 1870s. The lamp body came with the Comet burner, previously described, which dates from 1868. It was purchased from Mr. and Mrs. John Player of Mallorytown, Ont., and is said to have come from a home in the Kingston district. It is a reasonable assumption that a lamp that came unmodified from a home would have a body as old as, if not older than, its burner. If a burner wore out, it would be replaced, but it is unlikely that an old burner would be put on a new lamp body. All this suggests that the body dates from 1867 or 1868. Height of body to top of collar is 8¾ inches; diagonal width of base is 4⁵⁄₁₆ inches.

HAND LAMP BODIES   Hand lamps are more difficult to date than table lamps, especially the earlier ones with little or no ornamentation. In the following paragraphs three glass hand lamps are described, supposedly from oldest to youngest, as typical of the 1860s. All three were used in Canada and probably all three were made in the United States.

A very simple, almost primitive form (LSR 180; figure 97) has a depressed globular font with circular base and almost no ornamentation. It was blown in a mould with 2 side pieces and a base piece. The handle was free-formed by attaching a small lump of melted glass to the side of the font, and then drawing it out and turning it up and back to reattach and form the circle. Height of body to top of collar is 3⁵⁄₁₆ inches; maximum diameter of font is 4½ inches. It was purchased from Mrs. Marge Smith, Thornbury, Ont.

The second specimen (LSR 47) is still simple but somewhat more sophisticated in design. Its font has a convex top, rounded shoulder, concave side, and ring-shaped basal periphery wider than the shoulder. On the underside of the base is a central boss surrounded by radial fluting. The font, like that of the preceding lamp, was blown in a mould with 2 side pieces and a base piece. The handle was free formed in a circle; both ends are fused to the font. Height of font to top of collar is 3¼ inches; diameter at base is 4¼ inches. It was purchased from Mr. Jacques Rivard, Hudson Heights, Que., and was said to have come from a local home.

The third lamp (LSR 186; figure 98) has a font of similar but more exaggerated design, and a pressed handle. The concavity of the side is deeper and the peripheral ring more bulging. The under side of the base is slightly concave but plain. The 2 vertical mould seams are very faint.

96
LEFT: *Composite table lamp*
with black glass base, ca. 1868
with "Comet" burner
Kingston district, Ont. LSR 79

97
BELOW: *Glass hand lamp*
early 1860s; *purchased in Thornbury, Ont.*
LSR 180. ROM *photo*

98
RIGHT: *Glass hand lamp*
late 1860s; *purchased in Ilderton, Ont.*
LSR 186

In contrast the handle has a distinct mould seam and a sharp projection at the top for the thumb. The ends of the handle bulge through the font wall. It appears that the handle was pressed separately, and placed in the mould in its own matrix with the ends projecting into the main cavity; the font was then blown, fusing with the handle. Height of font to top of collar is 3⅞ inches; maximum diameter is 4 inches. This lamp was purchased from Mr. Gordon McNair, Ilderton, Ont.

CHIMNEYS

The chimneys developed for the kerosene lamps of the late 1850s continued in popularity into the late 1860s. The majority were relatively tall, with a less pronounced expansion and a more gradual taper to the top than later chimneys. The basal rim was distinctly turned out to provide a more secure grip for the clamp or set-screw that was used in burners having a coronet-like rim to receive the chimney. Such chimneys were suitable for Jones, Newman, Marcy, Taplin, and Dyott burners. The original Vienna burner, as we have seen, required a chimney with a vertical lower part and no basal rim, to fit the collar-like holder. However, there were few burners produced in the early 1860s for which such a chimney was suitable.

The appearance of the Collins, Comet, and Toof burners later in the 1860s brought about a change. These burners held the chimney in place by pressure from the inside, and required a chimney that was a vertical cylinder at least as far up as the level of the deflector. Chimneys of more modern shape now appeared. For the first 1½ inches or so from the bottom they rose vertically; then came a pronounced expansion which tapered towards the top. The upper rim was still plain.

An illustration of 1869[37] showing a Collins burner with a patent extinguisher depicts a chimney with straight vertical sides but with the

99
Straight chimney, ca. 1865
Preston, Ont. LSR 173. ROM *photo*

upper one-quarter curving in like an incomplete dome to a restricted orifice. Such a chimney was purchased for the author's collection (LSR 173; figure 99) from Mr. Stan Ashbury of Preston, Ont. It is 7½ inches high, and 2½ inches in outside diameter at the base. At the top the curvature is a little irregular, and the opening is slightly less than one inch in diameter. Evidently this chimney was made from simple glass tubing, which was heated and drawn out at intervals. The constricted part was then cut, and the edges rounded in the flame. Each drawing would make 2 chimneys. Such chimneys would be inexpensive to make, but it is not obvious that they had other advantages.

100
Ditheridge oval chimney
1861; *Waterville, Que.*
LSR 299. ROM *photo*

DITHERIDGE CHIMNEYS   The firm of Ditheridge and Company of Pittsburgh and vicinity was an important manufacturer of lamp chimneys in the latter part of the nineteenth century. They held a number of design patents, of which the earliest was obtained in 1861 in the name of Edward Ditheridge, founder of the company, and his son, Edward D. Ditheridge.[38] It was for a chimney of conventional design, such as would fit a Marcy burner, but with the expanded portion distinctly oval instead of circular in cross-section, so as to accommodate better to the linear shape of the flat-wick flame.

An example (LSR 299; figure 100) is shorter and broader than shown in the patent drawing, but has the characteristic oval expansion with circular base and top. It seems to be a combination of the improvement of 1861 with the shorter and wider shape that came into use in the late 1860s. As noted below, a further modification of the oval chimney appears in a Ditheridge model of 1870.

Edward Ditheridge took out a patent in 1869[39] for a chimney with a thickened basal rim. The patent drawing shows a cylindrical chimney, similar to that (LSR 173) described above, except that the basal rim has a distinct "bead." The same basal bead appears on a chimney of more conventional shape (LSR 89) which was purchased with a railway-station wall lamp, probably dating from the 1880s. The purpose of this thickening was to reduce the liability of chipping, and it may well have been adopted by other chimney manufacturers.

EAGLE CHIMNEYS   A variety of chimney shapes appear in a patent issued to Robert N. Eagle of Washington, D.C.[40] They have a circular base and an oval mid-section, as in the Ditheridge chimney, but the oval cross-section extends right to the top. In some there is a constriction above the base, located so as to reinforce the deflector of the burner. I have not seen an example, but the ideas involved are so practical that it seems certain such chimneys were manufactured and used.

MOULDED CHIMNEYS   The majority of glass chimneys used at any time in kerosene lamps were hand-blown or hand-fabricated. However, mould-blown chimneys were produced from time to time, later ones having elaborate patterns to match the bodies.

A moulded chimney (LSR 163; figure 101) made especially for the Arnold and Blackman burner (1868) presumably dates from the late 1860s. It has a cylindrical lower portion with a narrow groove just above the basal rim. About 1¼ inches above the rim is a deep annular constriction of the correct shape and position to receive the distinctive angular bend in that particular burner's chimney prongs. Above this the chimney is oval in cross-section, changing to circular, as in the Ditheridge chimney of 1861. Near the top is an annular bead, above which the rim is distinctly flared outward. There are 2 mould seams, coinciding with the narrow ends of the oval. The chimney was purchased from Mr. Leslie Donaldson of Sheffield, Ont.

101
Moulded oval chimney designed to fit the Arnold and Blackman burner of 1868 and probably based on the Eagle patent of 1869; Galt district, Ont.
LSR 163. ROM *photo*

SHADES

Many illustrations of lamps in the 1860s show them being used without shades. In other cases a shade similar to that of the solar lamps, either spherical or vase-shaped, was carried over. These rested on a rim around the burner. About 1867 a low conical shade appears in pictures, apparently supported by the expanded portion of the chimney. The next year hemispherical shades were in vogue, held by three bent wires radiating from a ring around the burner. Some early shades were made of coloured glass, with or without overlay, but frosted glass was commonest. Later, shades made of white opaque glass became available. Few examples of these shades of the 1860s have survived; we are dependent for our knowledge of them on contemporary drawings and photographs.

102
Lomax table lamp, 1870
purchased at St. Catharines, Ont.
LSR 121. ROM *photo*

CHAPTER IX

Everybody used kerosene

1870 to 1885

THE PERIOD DEALT WITH in this chapter is a transitional one, and the need for continuity makes it necessary to overlap on occasion at either end. The beginning is marked by a gradual decrease in experimentation. The end is approximately the time when the incandescent electric light and the Welsbach gas mantle began to compete effectively with the kerosene lamp.

The 1860s had been a time of great variety in the design of flat-wick burners. During the 1870s, in contrast, burners became limited to three basic forms. The flat-wick burner remained the most popular, but almost entirely restricted to the type here called the Atwood. The other two basic kinds were revivals of the Argand principle, with circular flame and centre draft, but one type had a folded flat wick and the other used a true tubular wick. Among the latter was the burner of the immensely popular student lamp, which differed only superficially from the original Argand lamp of 1784.

While burners became standardized, lamp bodies became diversified. For the almost universal composite lamp was substituted a variety of forms and styles, some functional, others merely unusual. Lamps for special purposes began to be popular: hanging lamps, wall lamps, and desk lamps. This diversity was a forecast of the extravagance of the last fifteen years of the nineteenth century. The ornate shade and the elaborate font were also forerunners of things to come.

During the 1870s, oil production in the United States expanded well beyond the discovery areas of northwestern Pennsylvania. In Canada the Petrolia field surpassed the Oil Springs area in production, but after that there were no new discoveries of major importance. However, production continued at a high level for some years. New centres of refining and distribution, such as Pittsburgh and Cleveland in the United States, and London and Toronto in Canada, became important. Bulk shipments of crude petroleum and later of refined products by railway tank cars were accompanied by the increasing use of long-distance pipelines. But retail distribution was still at a rather primitive level. Kerosene reached the merchant in barrels, from which he filled the customers' simple cans. The tank wagon and the kerosene pump were yet to come.[1]

BURNERS

FLAT-WICK BURNERS   The common kerosene burner of the late nineteenth century – and the one still used on remote farms and in many summer cottages – was the development of one man, Lewis John Atwood of Waterbury, Conn. We have seen him as the foreman of the lamp factory of Holmes, Booth & Haydens, and the inventor of several distinctive burners of the 1860s. In 1869 Israel Holmes and John C. Booth left that company and, with Atwood, established a new firm. The original name was Holmes, Booth and Atwood, but the Haydens succeeded in getting a court order prohibiting any use of the names of the former partners.[2] In 1871 the name was changed to The Plume and Atwood Manufacturing Company, using the name of David Scott Plume, the company treasurer. Israel Holmes, however, was president until his death in 1874. It should be noted that lamp burners bearing the inscription Plume & Atwood or P. & A. cannot be older than 1871. In 1955 the company moved from Waterbury to Thomaston, where it is still in existence as the Dorset Division of the J. B. Williams Company, Inc.

Atwood's last patent under the sponsorship of Holmes, Booth & Haydens was obtained in 1870.[3] Presumably he had worked on it before the partnership broke up. It was for a lamp burner not unlike his "Comet" of 1868, with the chimney supported by coiled wire attached to the periphery of the deflector. However, four springy prongs from the base plate helped to retain the chimney by pressure from the outside. The coil of wire was filled with fabric to provide insulation.

What may have been the first burner produced by the new Plume & Atwood Company is represented by two examples (LSR 295, LSR 328), the larger of which is shown in figure 103.

103
"New Calcium Light" burner, 1870
Bolton Centre, Que. LSR 295

It was purchased from Eldridge Antiques, Bolton Centre, Que., and was said to have been part of the stock of a local store. The smaller burner was purchased at an antique market and reputedly came from a home in Toronto. Both were on low, simple glass fonts, one for a sconce, the other a hand lamp. These burners resemble the Comet and Collins models in having a low, almost disc-like deflector; like the Collins too they have a fringe of "petals" around the rim to press against the inside of the chimney. The petals are shorter and more numerous, however, and are turned down steeply. The underside of the deflector bears a perforated air-distributor plate, through which the wick tube extends. Below this there is an open space of over an inch to the burner base, a small, disc-like chamber containing the wick wheels. From the base of the burner four wires radiate horizontally, then bend abruptly back on themselves for about a quarter of an inch, then turn up to attach to the underside of the deflectors; the bottom rim of the chimney rests on the doubled portion. On the top of the deflector, near the periphery, is inscribed "NEW CALCIUM LIGHT / 1870." The thumb wheel is marked "P. & A. MFG. CO / PAT AUG 16/70."

The patent referred to on the thumb wheel is that of B. F. Adams of Boston, Mass.,[4] the specifications of which fit almost exactly the two burners described above. The only discrepancy is in the "petals." The Adams patent shows them with slit-like perforations for the passage of air. On the smaller of the two burners each "petal" has a small round hole (rather than a slit) near the base, and on the larger burner they have no perforations at all. Perhaps it was decided after the burners were in use that these openings were not essential for the draft.

The origin of the term "New Calcium Light" is obscure. It is not mentioned in the Adams patent. Perhaps it was an attempt to capitalize on the fame of the Drummond or "lime" light, but there is not the slightest resemblance between the two. The Drummond light consists of a blow-torch flame playing on a slab of calcium oxide, making it glow with an intense white light.

A modification of the Adams burner appears in the Atwood patent of 1872.[5] In it the four wires, instead of just providing a rest for the chimney, extend upward with open ends to embrace it. It is thus a combination of the Adams burner and the Atwood burner of 1870. I have not seen an actual example but it is referred to in the inscription on many Atwood burners which do not have the Collins type of deflector, so it may be assumed that the part carried over was the set of four chimney prongs. These, however, go back to the Arnold and Blackman burner of 1868.

What ought to be regarded as the real Atwood burner appeared in the patent of 1873.[6] This is the burner that achieved almost universal popularity during the remainder of the nineteenth century and is still being sold and used. The basic feature is the construction of the deflector in two parts. The lower is conoid, and its bottom rim is not much above the level of the burner's base plate. The upper is more or less hemispherical, and carries the blaze slit. The perforated draft-distributing plate, which in most previous burners was more or less a part of the base plate, is located at the top of the lower, conoid part of the deflector. The dome-shaped part hinges on the lower part, with a simple catch on the side opposite the hinge. The deflector assembly is attached to the base plate by four stout radial strips, from which the chimney prongs project outwards and then curve upwards around the lower rim of the deflector. This leaves four wide spaces between base plate and deflector rim, through which the air can enter. It was claimed that this arrangement greatly improved the intake and distribution of air as well as the dissipation of heat. The chimney prongs appear to be of wire.

In 1872 it became possible for a person other than a resident of Canada to take out a Canadian patent, and a host of names with American addresses now appear in the records of the Canadian Patent Office. In 1875 Atwood took out a Canadian patent[7] for the burner just described. He called it the "Fireside Burner." Good examples have been obtained from Mrs. J. Palmer of Havelock, Ont. (LSR 91), and from Mrs. Allie Hazelgrove of Kingston, Ont., (LSR 132; figure 104). These bear a raised inscription around the rim of the upper deflector: "PLUME & ATWOOD FIRESIDE." The thumb wheel is marked "PAT NOV 26. 72 PAT FEB 11. 73." Absence of the Canadian patent date might mean that they were made prior to 1875, but it is likely that at first the Canadian patent was taken out as a protection against pirating of the design. Later this type of burner was made in Canada.

The basic Atwood burner was made and sold under a variety of names, distinguished by slight differences in proportions and materials. Recently the Dorset Division of Thomaston, Conn., reprinted a Plume & Atwood catalogue of about 1908. It lists and illustrates four models based on the Atwood patent of 1873. The "Eagle" burner, cheapest of the series, is made mostly of thin, pressed sheet iron, and the lower, conoid part of its deflector is very shallow, so that the distributor plate is not much above the level of the base plate. In the "Banner" burner the two parts of the deflector are of

104
Atwood "Fireside" burner 1873; Kingston district, Ont. LSR 132

about equal height. The "Globe" burner has similar proportions but the chimney prongs are perforated brass strips rather than doubled wires. The fourth burner is called "Model"; the upper part of the deflector is shallow and the lower part is deep. It is almost identical with the "Fireside" burner except that the chimney prongs are brass strips instead of wires. The last three models are of all-brass construction. I have not yet been able to learn the dates on which these burners came on the market, but they are all derived with slight modification from the Atwood patent of February 11, 1873. The commonest in Canada seems to have been the "Banner"; examples have been found from Ontario to Newfoundland. Some "Eagle" burners have also been collected.

In 1873 Atwood patented another burner[8] in which the wick tube could be pulled down below the deflector for trimming. Two later patents[9] incorporated a removable deflector and chimney holder. Another in 1883[10] covered a technique for fastening the inner ends of the chimney prongs to the base without soldering or riveting. In 1885 Atwood patented three different designs for burners on the same date.

The first[11] has a deflector and chimney holder that slide up and down on four vertical strips. In this burner, as in the other two to be described, the chimney holder has the coronet rim and set-screw, reminiscent of the Marcy burner. I have not seen an example.

The second patent[12] covers a burner design in which the deflector and chimney holder are raised by a rotary motion, by means of two upright plates, each with a diagonal slot that engages a stud on the inside of the basal shell. The arrangement is reminiscent of the Dyott burner of 1863. No burner exactly like this has been seen, but the same idea is used in the P. & A. "Unique" burner, in which the uprights (strips rather than plates) are attached below to a ring. This ring encircles a cylindrical tube around the wick tube. A diagonal, inward-projecting ridge on the ring engages a diagonal groove on the tube, translating the rotary motion into a spiral and so raising the deflector above the wick. One of these

105
ABOVE: "Unique" burner, Atwood 1885; purchased in East Aurora, N.Y. LSR 232

106
BELOW: Burner, Atwood patent of 1885, chimney holder and deflector in normal position purchased in East Aurora, N.Y. LSR 235

107
RIGHT: Same burner as in fig. 106, with chimney holder and deflector raised

"Unique" burners (LSR 232; figure 105) was obtained from Mr. and Mrs. Paul Shelley of East Aurora, N.Y. That Atwood regarded this as merely a modification of his burner of Patent No. 324,068 is shown by the inscription on the thumb wheel: "P. & A. / PAT. AUG. 11. 1885."

The third patent[13] covers a burner somewhat similar to that of the first of the three patents, in that the wick is exposed by vertical motion. However, in this case it is the perforated basal shell that moves. A low cylindrical chamber surrounds the wick tube and encloses the three wick wheels. From this chamber two horizontal struts connect to the basal shell. Pulling down on the basal shell depresses the chamber, the wick tube and mechanism, and the wick. The burner base, screwed into the font, and the deflector and chimney holder, do not move. In this way the wick can be reached and trimmed under the deflector. An example (LSR 235; figures 106, 107) was obtained from the Shelleys of East Aurora, N.Y. The inscription on the thumb wheel reads "P. & A. MFG CO / PAT. AUG. 11. 85." This type of burner is not represented in the Plume & Atwood catalogue of 1908. It superficially resembles the "Unique" burner, but the outside of the perforated basal shell is concave rather than convex.

Atwood obtained patents for lamp burners after 1885 but these are discussed in the following chapter.

Hiram W. Hayden was the inventor member of the Holmes, Booth & Haydens partnership and took out a number of patents on lamp burner improvements, although none of these is as well represented in collections today as are those of his erstwhile foreman, Atwood.

One Hayden burner that has survived was patented in 1872.[14] It looks much like the Atwood burner of 1870, but the pressure to the inside of the chimney is applied by the petal-like rim of the deflector, as in the Collins burner. Hayden's claim applied to the chimney prongs, which are made by doubling a length of wire, and are fastened to the base plate by spreading the two ends. Also the air distributor plate extends outward to the lower part of the deflector assembly and bears the petal-like rim. Hayden called this part of the deflector the draw plate. The main, dome-shaped deflector is tightly fitted and clipped to it. By removing the deflector the wick can be trimmed and the draft plate cleaned. The Atwood patent of Nov. 26, 1872, is so similar to this Hayden patent that it is difficult to see how the former could have been issued. The question is made even more difficult by the example of the Hayden burner (LSR 54; figure 108) presented by Mrs. R. Brown of Richmond Hill, Ont. In this the draft and distributor plate with its petals is supported by four strips rising from the base plate, as in the Atwood patent, yet the rim of the draft plate is marked "HOLMES BOOTH & HAYDENS / 1872," and the thumb wheel, "PAT. JULY 23. 72 & SEP. 19. 65." The second date refers to the original Collins patent.

OVAL AND RECTANGULAR BURNERS. Various inventors have been struck by the fact that a flat-wick flame is linear in shape, but the deflector and chimney commonly used with it are circular in cross-section. Ditheridge as early as 1861 patented a chimney that was circular below and oval at the flame level. Burners employing oval or rectangular deflectors appeared in the 1870s.

108
Hayden burner, 1872
Richmond Hill, Ont. LSR 54

109
Rectangular-deflector burner, 1878
purchased in East Aurora, N.Y. LSR 245

One of these (LSR 245; figure 109) was purchased from Mr. and Mrs. Paul Shelley of East Aurora, N.Y. It has a circular chimney-holder plate with set-screw, and a Taplin hinge. The deflector is rectangular at its base, and fits into a rectangular opening in the chimney plate. The air distributor below is a rectangular dish, in the middle of which is set the base with its screw for the font collar. The base is closed above to form a little chamber with perforated sides, and from this the wick tube rises, tapering slightly from base to tip. The opening for the wick in the bottom of the base is semicircular, and there are two wick wheels. On the flat under surface of the base is the following inscription "PAT / FEB 19. 61 / MAR 29. 64 / SEP 24. 78 / NOV 26. 78." The third date refers to a patent by James G. Hallas of Waterbury, Conn., assigned to Benedict & Burnham Manufacturing Company,[15] which covers the combination of circular chimney plate and rectangular deflector. The fourth date is that of a patent of Eli J. Blackham of Bridgeport, Connecticut, assigned to Benedict & Burnham Mfg. Co.,[16] for a method of attaching the deflector to the chimney plate by means of a ridge above and a turned-out edge below. The thumb wheel is marked "TRIUMPH / B. & B. MFG. CO." Benedict & Burnham was one of the oldest brass manufacturing firms of Waterbury, and at the time of the above-named patents was under the presidency of Charles Benedict, son of the founder. The company fabricated sheet metal, wire, tubing, and other copper and brass objects, lamp burners being a subsidiary product.[17]

True rectangular burners were manufactured by the Bridgeport Brass Company of Bridgeport, Conn. This firm was established in 1865 and at first produced mainly brass and copper sheet and wire. In the 1880s it was a major producer of elaborate parlour lamps (see chapter 10). The rectangular burner has been found in both Canada and the United States.

110
Rectangular burner
1880; Bowmanville, Ont.
LSR 50. ROM *photo*

A small example (LSR 50; figure 110) was presented by Mrs. Verne Johnson of Bowmanville, Ont. A larger version (LSR 250) was purchased from the Shelleys of East Aurora, N.Y. Except in size, these two burners are almost identical. The rectangular deflector has a horizontal basal flange, with a row of perforations. It fits loosely into the rectangular dish-shaped air distributor, the upper rim of which rises to form the chimney holder. The chimney is held with a retaining screw. The wick tube is straight above, semicircular in section at the bottom. It is surrounded by an outer casing, the basal section of which is a combination of oval and circular. In both burners the bottom of the base plate bears the following inscription between the wick opening and the threaded edge: "PAT'D / JUNE 1. 69 / SEPT. 18. 77 / NOV. 18. 79 APR. 6. 80." The first date apparently refers to a patent of Rufus S. Merrill and William Carleton of Boston,[18] which covers the use of an external sleeve on the wick tube. The second date is that of a patent of Samuel R. Wilmot of Bridgeport, Conn.,[19] which describes in detail a rectangular burner almost identical with these two examples. Essential parts of the Wilmot claim are the rectangular shape of base plate and deflector, the peculiar conoid-oval sleeve around the wick tube, and the semicircular shape of the wick opening in the bottom of the base plate. I have been unable to identify the patents represented by the last two dates of the inscription. The thumb wheel of the larger burner is marked "BRIDGEPORT BRASS CO.," and that of the smaller burner, "BRIDGEPORT / BRASS CO. / LEADER / NQ 1."

111
Double burner, early 1870s; *purchased in East Aurora,* N.Y. LSR 241

MULTIPLE BURNERS   The principle of multiple-wick burners, so characteristic of whale-oil and burning-fluid lamps, was employed in several ways in kerosene burners. In the late nineteenth century, single burners with two wicks were popular. An earlier development, however, had separate deflectors as well as separate wick tubes mounted on a common base plate. Such burners were manufactured in the 1880s by the Rochester Burner Company, and were developed by H. E. Shaffer, the president.[20] They were sold under the name "Perfection."

Two examples were obtained in the Buffalo-Niagara area of New York State. One of these (LSR 241; figure 111) has a deep coronet to hold the chimney, but no set-screw. The two deflectors are side by side on the base plate, and each is outlined by a row of perforations in the plate. The plate is secured by a lug and an opposite clip to the lower part of the base, which consists of a screw, a dish-shaped, open-work shell, and a flat, finely perforated air distributor. At the bottom of the burner base, where the wick tubes open, there is a wire separator for the two wicks in the shape of a low, broad "U." Separate wick-wheel shafts and thumb wheels project on opposite sides of the base. Each wheel is marked "S.P. / BURNER," the initials presumably standing for "Shaffer Perfection." This burner was purchased from Mr. and Mrs. Paul Shelley of East Aurora, N.Y.

A three-wick burner is part of a hanging lamp purchased from Mr. Norman Luff of Hartland, N.Y. (LSR 253; figure 112). It resembles the two-wick version, but the base plate is larger. There are three deflectors, with the blaze slits tangential to the rim of the burner. The hinge is of the Marcy type, with opposite clip. The coronet for the chimney is low, and has a set-screw. The sides of the open-work shell of the base are concave, not convex as in the two-wick version. The three separate thumb wheels are marked "S.P. / BURNER."

112
Triple burner
early 1870s; purchased at Hartland, N.Y.
LSR 253

Shaffer was not the first to design such multiple burners, although he may have developed them independently. A poster-like advertisement in the Barnett Collection of the University of Western Ontario depicts a three-wick burner, with chimney, very similar to that described above. It is called the "Patent Triplex Star Burner," also "Doty Light / Patented 1866." The agents were Prince and Symmons of London.

FOLDED-WICK BURNERS The original Argand lamp used a wick that was woven or sewn into a tube. But in the Davis lard lamp the trick of bending flat wicks into cylindrical form was demonstrated. In the late 1860s and the 1870s a revival of interest in the Argand type of burner led to the invention of a number of devices in which a flat wick was folded so as to assume a circular cross-section at the level of combustion. This method had two advantages over use of a tubular wick. The slit in the lower part of the wick could be used to allow for an air intake to the centre-draft tube, and the burner would work on a conventional font, without an extension of the centre-draft tube through it.

113
"Victor" burner, 1870s;
purchased in Cambridge, Mass. LSR 268

114
Folded-wick burner, 1870s;
purchased in East Aurora, N.Y. LSR 244

The earliest patent covering this idea apparently was issued to Arthur W. Browne of Brooklyn, N.Y.[21] The design is relatively sophisticated. The centre-draft tube is attached to the inside of the wick tube by a hollow oval branch which opens to the outside through a slit of the same shape on the side of the wick tube. The opening in the base through which the wick is introduced is slit-like, and the wick is folded with the open edge on the same side as the air opening through the wick tube. Thus when the wick is raised by means of the four wick wheels, the open edge of the folded wick spreads around the lateral branch of the centre-draft tube, then comes together above to assume a circular shape.

I have not seen a burner exactly like that of the Browne patent, but the burner on a lamp (LSR 145) purchased from Mrs. Eva Boire of Mooers, N.Y., is similar. The centre-draft tube is vertical in its main part but just above the wick wheels it turns at right angles by a miniature elbow joint and emerges as a circular opening in the side of the wick tube. To ensure that the folded wick opens properly to pass around the elbow, there is a blade-like divider extending into the wick tube between wick wheels and elbow. This burner, which came on a converted solar lamp, is marked on the outer part of the thumb wheel: "CHALLENGE / PAT. APLD. FOR.," and in the centre, the letters "W" and "S" in horizontal brackets, with three stars above and below.

Another patent for a folded-wick burner was issued to William D. Ludlow, of New York, N.Y.[22] The centre-draft tube and the wick tube are formed from a single piece of sheet metal, and the centre-draft tube is pinched below to separate the folded wick. The opening for the air intake is a slit where the junction of centre-draft and wick tubes is not completely closed. A modified form of this arrangement is incorporated in the Plume & Atwood "Victor" burner (LSR 268; figure 113), which was still being offered in their 1908 catalogue.

In a third type of folded-wick burner the wick opening in the base is horseshoe-shaped. Two examples (LSR 244, figure 114; LSR 243) were purchased from Mr. and Mrs. Paul Shelley of East Aurora, N.Y. The

wick tube is tall. On one side near the bottom is an opening which leads by a horizontal tube into the centre-draft tube. The latter is closed below the juncture. The wick wheels do not mesh with the wick itself but with a perforated brass strip which grips the wick in a crown-like ring. This arrangement is slightly reminiscent of the wick mechanism in the Rumford lamp. A similar burner but with the wick wheels working directly on the wick was purchased from Monica's Antiques, North Bangor, N.Y. It is of German manufacture, and is marked on the thumb wheel: "BERLIN / SCHMIDT & JAEDICKE."

True tubular-wick burners were well represented in this period by the Kleeman student lamp and its imitators, described later in this chapter.

LAMP BODIES

COMPOSITE LAMPS   The original composite lamp, with glass font, brass stem, and marble base, remained popular into the 1870s, and appears in illustrations as late as 1875. The characteristic table lamp of this period, however, appeared about 1865 and was especially common in the early 1870s. In it the base and lower stem were a single ornate casting of opaque glass, usually white, but sometimes black. As early as 1872, cast-iron bases were introduced instead of glass. They were less fragile, and provided greater stability. But they represented a decline in the graceful form of table lamps so typical up to this time. Some iron bases were shaped to imitate their opaque glass predecessors, others were entirely conoid or polygonal.

The glass font also assumed new forms. The earlier "turnip shape" gave way to one more cylindrical, or more precisely, to an inverted, truncated cone. In keeping with this shape the pressed ornamental pattern became more annular. A firmer attachment of the brass collar was obtained by having it extend as a low conoid flange, cemented to the top of the font.

METAL LAMPS   The manufacture of metal kerosene lamps had long been urged.[23] Glass fonts could break while the lamp was burning and an increasing number of fires was blamed on this cause. An advertisement for an all-metal "Orient Safety Lamp" appeared in 1871.[24] It and similar lamps were made of sheet metal, tinned or nickel-plated, and shaped to approximate the style of the composite lamps of the time.

LOMAX LAMPS   Drip of unburned oil from the lamp burner seems to have bothered people during this period, and a number of font shapes were introduced to catch this. The most popular was patented by George Henry Lomax of Somerville, Mass.[25] It consisted of a raised lip, projecting outward and upward from the shoulder of the font.

The font was formed by press-moulding, with the top wide open so that the plunger could be withdrawn. At this stage the lip was a horizontal shelf. It was relatively easy for a skilled glass worker to bend the upper rim of the globlet-like vessel inward to close the font and slope the lip obliquely upward. Apparently Lomax assigned his patent to the Union Glass Company of Boston and Somerville, a firm established in 1851.[26] One of its catalogues,[27] evidently dating from the 1870s, shows a number of different lamps with the Lomax drip catcher. Revi has reproduced 3 of them.

A handsome example of a Lomax table lamp (LSR 121; figure 102) was purchased from Mr. Godfrey Moore, formerly of St. Catharines, Ont. It has a white, opal-glass base, a short brass stem, and a glass font decorated with the "thumb-print" pattern. The oil-catching lip projects about ½ inch, at an angle of 45°. Height of lamp to top of collar is 10¼ inches. In the Union Glass catalogue this class of lamp is listed as "opal foot," with the thumb-print and several other patterns shown on the

115
"Plain Lomax Kitchen" lamp, early 1870s
Kingston, Ont. LSR 130. ROM *photo*

fonts. A very similar type was represented in the Lomax patent drawings.

Perhaps the commonest Lomax model surviving today is that listed in the Union Glass catalogue as "Plain Lomax Kitchen." I have examples from Mrs. Allie Hazelgrove of Kingston, Ont. (LSR 130; figure 115), and Mrs. Anne Beaulieu of North Hatley, Que. (LSR 283). Both lamps have a depressed globular font, without ornamentation but with the characteristic Lomax lip. The stem is a glass rod with 3 raised rings about mid-height, and the base is low and dome-shaped. The seams indicate that the mould consisted of a basal and 2 lateral pieces, but subsequent manipulation has almost obliterated the seams in the upper part. The under side of the base is inscribed mirror-fashion so as to be read from above through the glass. The larger lamp (LSR 130) reads "PAT^D. SEP. 20. 1870." The smaller lamp is marked "TRADE MARK / * OIL GUARD LAMP * PAT^D SEP. 20 1870."

Union Glass also added the Lomax lip to hand lamps. One of these called the "Globe Lomax hand lamp" (LSR 53; figure 116) was obtained from Ellicott Antiques of Orillia, Ont. It has a low, convex base, a globular font, and a single handle that was moulded with the font. The base is marked "PAT SEP. 20 1870," read from the underside. A similar lamp (LSR 108) was obtained from Mr. and Mrs. Gordon McNair of Ilderton, Ont.

116
Lomax hand lamp, early 1870s; said to be from the Orillia district, Ont.
LSR 53. ROM *photo*

OTHER DRIP CATCHERS An Atterbury patent of 1875 for an all-glass lamp, described below, provided for a drip-catching rim if desired. Simpler devices were used by others. One was a rounded groove between shoulder and brass rim of the collar.

A lamp showing this (LSR 60; figure 117) was obtained from Mrs. Catharine Van Camp, formerly of Milton, Ont. It has the iron base, brass stem, and inverted conoid font described previously. The font pattern consists of a ring of cross-like figures impressed on an etched band. In the drip-catching groove is a raised legend: "PATENTED JULY 2 1872." This should read July 23 and refers to a patent issued to John Bridges of Allentown, Pa,[28] for a mould in which a segmented iron ring fitted to the top two pieces creates an annular depression in the top of the blown font.

Another type of drip catcher produced what collectors call the "cup-and-saucer" lamp. The body of this hand lamp does look almost exactly like a teacup turned upside-down on a saucer. The projecting rim forms the drip-catching channel. An example (LSR 162; figure 118) was purchased from Mr. R. L. Donaldson of Sheffield, Ont. Apparently the font was press-moulded upside-down. The base, attached later, is a hand-spun disc, as indicated by its concentric ripples and pontil mark. There is no indication of age on the lamp body. It came with a 20th-century burner, but it might well date from this period of interest in anti-drip lamps.

ATTERBURY LAMPS The Atterbury brothers of Pittsburgh continued to produce glass lamps until well after the period discussed in this chapter. They and their associates took out a number of patents, most of which are listed by Revi.[29]

An Atterbury composite lamp of this period (LSR 290; figure 119) was obtained from Mrs. Doris Gale of Waterville, Que. It has the opal-glass base and threaded brass tube for the stem, as described for Atterbury lamps in chapter 8. The glass font, however, is very different, being lantern-like in shape, with 8 vertical sides and a low 8-sided pyramid

top and bottom. Each vertical face has an impressed panel, and in one of these is the legend, "PAT. SEP / 16TH 73." After some search it was discovered that this referred, not to a true patent, but to U.S. Design no. 6,882.

During this period the Atterburys also developed a technique for attaching an opal-glass stem and base directly to a clear-glass font, but I have not seen an example of the resulting lamp. A more important advance was marked by the patent granted to Thomas B. Atterbury in 1876[30] for a method of casting lamp bodies and other glass vessels

120
*Atterbury glass table lamp
with drip catcher
Kingston, Ont.* LSR 401. ROM *photo*

in separate sections, to be welded together later. This did away with the necessity of closing the font by mould-blowing or hand-fabricating. Three examples based on this patent incorporate a drip-catching groove, but this possibility was considered a minor element of the patent.

The example shown in figure 120 (LSR 401) has a low dome-shaped font top, evidently cast separately as it is ornamented internally with a kind of grape pattern. The shoulder of the font is reinforced as a heavy rim, and the edge of the font top is inserted below this rim, so that an annular depression is left, forming the drip catcher. Below this shoulder the rest of the lamp resembles a large 10-sided goblet, and was evidently cast in one piece. The conoid base has a reversed inscription on the inside: "PAT·D AUG 29TH 1876." Height of the lamp to top of collar is 8⅛ inches; diameter of font at shoulder is 4⅜ inches. It was purchased from Mrs. E. J. Laschinger of Kingston, Ont. An almost identical lamp (LSR 144), but lacking the internal ornamentation of the font top, was obtained from Mrs. Martin Beattie of Huntingdon, Que., and was said to have come from St. Nazaire. A footed hand lamp (LSR 348) with a font almost identical with that of LSR 401 was obtained from Mrs. Margaret Brandon of Lindsay, Ont.

HOBBS LAMP   A composite lamp of uncertain manufacturer was based on a patent by John H. Hobbs of Wheeling, W. Va.[31] The example shown (LSR 368; figure 121) was purchased from Mr. and Mrs. Paul Shelley of East Aurora, N.Y.

The clear-glass font is a depressed spheroid, with 3 mould seams. There is a narrow peripheral band of vertical fluting, with a pattern of 9 loops on the surface below. The stem/base is of white opal glass, with a squarish scalloped base and 8-sided conoid stem. The distinctive feature of the Hobbs lamp is in the method of connecting font and stem/base. Instead of a threaded brass tube, as in the Atterbury lamp, there is a brass tube with alternating vertical and horizontal grooves. Reference to the patent shows that these coincide with grooves cast in the font plug and the upper end of the glass stem. The brass tube, called the socket by Hobbs, is wider for the plug than for the stem. The vertical grooves were pressed in advance, and when the socket was slipped over plug and stem, prevented rotation. A special tool was used to indent the brass into the horizontal grooves already in the glass. The result was a rigid connection between font and stem that required no cement. On the upper section of the brass tube, between 2 vertical grooves, is the stamped inscription in tiny letters: "PAT. MAY 24, 1870."

According to Revi, John H. Hobbs was the son of John L. Hobbs, one of the founders of the firm of Hobbs, Brockunier & Company of Wheeling, W. Va., a well-known manufacturer of pressed-glass articles from the 1860s to the early 1880s. John H. Hobbs also registered a number of patterns for pressed glass; but one of the best-known patterns of Hobbs, Brockunier & Co., "Blackberry," was registered in 1870 by William Leighton, Jr., another partner in the firm. An example of the Hobbs lamp (LSR 416), purchased from Mr. W. N. Binns of King City, Ont., and said to have come from the Kingston district, has the "Blackberry" pattern on both the clear-glass font and the milk-glass stem/base. From this and other evidence it may be concluded that lamps with the Hobbs patent stem connector were manufactured in Wheeling, W. Va., by Hobbs, Brockunier & Co. between 1870, when the device was patented, and 1881, when the company was dissolved.

RIPLEY LAMPS   Ripley & Company continued to manufacture lamps and chimneys, some of which were based on patents of Daniel C. Ripley, president of the company. One such lamp became known to collectors and dealers as "wedding lamp," "marriage lamp," or "bridal lamp," presumably because it consisted of two fonts and burners on a single support. The fine example shown in figure 122

121
Hobbs composite lamp
1870; *purchased in East Aurora,* N.Y.
LSR 368. ROM *photo*

(LSR 400) was purchased by the Consumers' Gas Company of Toronto in Burlington, Ont., and presented to the writer for use in this account.

The two fonts are identical. Below the distinct shoulder is a short icicle pattern. Above it the dome-shaped top curves to the brass collar. The glass is sky-blue, moderately translucent, and with many fine bubbles and swirl marks. Diameter of fonts at shoulder is $3\frac{11}{16}$ inches.

The central support has a deep cylindrical cup for matches. The patent drawings show a cover for this receptacle, but none has been seen on actual examples. On one side of the cup is the faint, partly undecipherable inscription "PATENTED / SEPT. 20 1—." On either edge of the cup is a reinforced margin, shaped to fit the side of the font to which it is fused. The reinforcements continue below as flanges, converging at the peg. The relatively thin area of glass between them is pebbly. An annular flange rests on the rim of the short brass stem. The remainder of the stem and the base is a single casting of pure white opal glass. The upper part is fluted; below it are annular flanges and grooves, and then another narrow band of fluting. The square upper part of the base is bevelled to the lower part. The 4 sides of the base have the cupid's-bow outline seen in other opal-glass bases of the late 1860s and early 1870s. Over-all height to top of the collars is $12\frac{1}{2}$ inches.

This lamp is based on two patents by Ripley,[32] the first one dealing mainly with the nature and use of the mould, the second with the lamp itself. The first step in making the double lamp was to press-mould the central support. It was then placed in the middle cavity of a special two-piece mould, with cavities on either side for the fonts. The latter were then blown in the moulds by two glass-blowers simultaneously. The fonts, as is usual with mould-blown vessels, have simple ornamentation, whereas the shape of the central support is complex and its pattern sharp.

There is some variation in details of these Ripley "wedding" lamps. Some have the match holder, others do not. Because of the method

122
Ripley "wedding" lamp
1870; *purchased in Burlington, Ont.*
LSR 400. ROM *photo*

of manufacture, glass of three different kinds could be combined. The combination in this example – translucent blue fonts, translucent colourless support, and white opal-glass stem/base – seems to be commonest, but there are examples with blue-glass supports also. In his first patent Ripley described a mould in which a lamp with three fonts could be made. If an example ever turns up, I suggest that it be called, by analogy, "the eternal triangle." Even the two-font type is not common in Canada. My records include five from Ontario, and none from elsewhere in the country. Ripley described his invention as "a glass lamp, having two or more bowls." The more romantic designations came later.

A less spectacular but more widely applicable design for a glass lamp was patented by Ripley in 1881.[33] A hollow stem and base were cast in one piece in such a way that the stem could be painted or otherwise decorated from the inside.

The example illustrated (LSR 52; figure 123) was purchased from Ellicott Antiques, Orillia, Ont. The low font is roughly square in horizontal section, with grooved and rounded corners. Two diagonal seams indicate that it was mould-blown in one operation. A pedestal-like extension below is fused to the top of the stem. Just below it is a square plate with ornamentation on top. Below that comes a short piece of solid stem and an annular "bead," and next the hollow portion, a square pillar with double-grooved corners. At the bottom of the stem is a slight step, and then the base, a low pyramid-like form, with the corners extended as short feet. The under surface of the base has a radial pattern suggesting the shrouds of a sailing ship. The interior of the stem is plain, but the opening is closed with a thin wafer of cork, which bears on its upper surface, within the stem, an artificial flower and twig. The lower side of the cork has a paper cover, now partly damaged, but still showing some of its inscription: "PA———ED / NOV. 15— –881 / JULY 25TH 1882." Height to top of collar is 8⅝ inches.

I have been unable to locate a patent or registration corresponding to

123
Ripley hollow-stem glass lamp, 1881
purchased near Orillia, Ont. LSR 52

the second date on the cork. U.S. patents were issued on July 22 and 29, 1882, but not on the 25th. The earlier patent, noted above, describes a rather simple mould with 2 side pieces, a 2-piece basal plate to form the top of the stem, and a capping ring to finish off the bottom of the base. Casting the stem and base of the lamp described above required a slightly different mould. There must have been 2 lateral pieces, each forming 2 sides of the stem, a single basal piece, providing the upper surface plate on top of the stem, and an upper ring, excavated to form the upper surface of the base. The ornamentation on the underside of the base was impressed by the wide upper part of the plunger. After the glass casting was annealed in the mould, the first piece to be removed would have been the basal plate, revealing the top of the stem. Then the 2 side pieces would come off, and the excavated plate at the top would be slipped down and off the stem.

Hollow-stem glass lamps apparently continued in production well into the twentieth century. In many the stems were circular in cross-section, as in the original Ripley patent. A four-sided stem appears in the table model of a series of lamps with a pyramid-like base, on the under surface of which are four panels with a pattern suggesting a sunrise. Their eight-sided fonts resemble those of other styles known to have been made in the 1890s and the early twentieth century.

WOODEN LAMPS   The search for a safe material for lamp bodies reached one extreme in the wooden lamp. Like metal, wood is relatively unbreakable, and in addition is a good heat insulator. One such lamp was patented by C. D. Moody of St. Louis, Mo.[34] Its essential feature was that the font itself was of wood, coated on the interior with some substance to make it impervious to kerosene. Glue is mentioned in the patent, but other coating substances are hinted at. Various ways of fabricating the wood are suggested, preference being given to turning it on a lathe, and this was the method used on the two examples that I have seen.

One of these is the patent model in the U.S. National Museum (USNM 331321). It is almost exactly like the lamp represented in the patent drawing, with distinct font, stem, and base, and elaborate annular ornamentation. The other example (LSR 178; figure 124) is smaller and less elaborate. It has a carved wooden handle attached by screws to font and base. The brass collar is sunk into the top of the font. The interior of the font feels quite smooth. The outer surface has been given a coat of aluminum paint, but where this has worn off, it appears that the original colour was dark green. This lamp was purchased from Mr. Lee Phillips of Bruce Mines, Ont., and is said to have been owned by a niece of Kellogg, the cereal manufacturer, who had a summer home in the area.

Grenville M. Stevens, of Deering, Me., took out a Canadian patent[35] for a wooden lamp, but his had an inset metallic font. As pointed out by Moody in his patent claim, such construction had no great advantage over the all-metal lamp.

SAMUELS LAMP A lamp which at first glance appears to be a revival of the astral was patented by Marks Samuels of San Francisco.[36] It has the ring-shaped reservoir of the astral, supported by three sloping oil tubes connected to the central font. The patent claim, however, is for a tube which surrounds the font; it is open at the bottom, and attached at the top adjacent to the collar for the burner. In combination with the wide space between font and reservoir, it was supposed to provide good heat dissipation.

There is no provision for the use of a centre-draft burner, although the folded-wick type would have worked. A fine example is in the Dundas Historical Museum, Dundas, Ont. (figure 125). Except for the three-legged cast-iron base and stem, it closely resembles the lamp shown in

124
Moody wooden lamp
1874; *Bruce Mines, Ont.* LSR 178

the patent drawing. The upper surface of the reservoir is inscribed "PAT. MAY 30 1871." The burner is a late version of the Atwood burner ("Queen Mary").

THE STUDENT LAMP

An immensely popular style of table lamp from the 1870s until well into the twentieth century was the so-called student lamp. Actually it was an almost exact revival of the original Argand lamp, adapted to kerosene. The narrow cylindrical font and burner, with tubular wick and centre draft, was connected by a fuel tube to the wider cylindrical reservoir, which provided fuel to font on the bird-bath principle. The two parts were supported at a point on the fuel tube by a sleeve with set-screw, which could be raised or lowered on a vertical rod rising from a heavy metal base. The popularity of this kind of lamp seems to have been due to its adjustable height and its almost shadowless light. Also the separation of font and reservoir prevented dangerous over-heating, even on prolonged use.

KLEEMAN LAMP   The first of the long series of student lamps was patented in 1863 by Carl A. Kleeman of Erfurt, Prussia.[37] Kleeman confined his claims to an arrangement of the reservoir fountain to provide a regular delivery of the oil, use of a spiral groove rather than a slot in the mechanism for raising and lowering the wick holder, and a device for returning unburned excess oil to the font. His lamp seems to have been almost ignored during the 1860s, although it had imitators. Interest developed early in the 1870s, perhaps because American sales were taken over by C. F. A. Hinrichs of New York City. A brochure put out by Hinrichs is in the Barnett Collection of the University of Western Ontario. It shows the usual model of the

ORIGINAL AND ONLY GENUINE
SAINT GERMAIN
— OR —
German Study or Office Lamp.

C. A. KLEEMANN'S PATENT.

Prize Medal of the American Institute Exhibition, Oct. 26, 1867.   Diploma of the "Pennsylvania State Fair," 1868.
First Diploma of the Kings County Fair, 1872.

LIGHT! MORE LIGHT!

Best, Safest, Handsomest, Most Economical.   No Odor. no Smoke.   Pure, Brilliant, Unwavering Light, very agreeable to the Eye.   None Genuine without my name on Chimney-Holder.   This Lamp is all of METAL, Easily Managed.

Trade Mark on Chimney Holders.

"Patented Mar. 10, 1863, Reissued Mar. 29th, 1870, C. A. Kleemann. C. F. A. Hinrichs, New York, Sole Agent.".

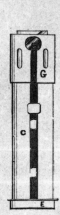
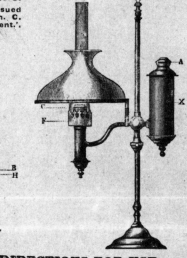

DIRECTIONS FOR USE.

To fill the Lamp, take out the Holder, *A*, invert it and pour in the Oil till it reaches the valve ; then pull up the valve by means of the wire *B*, invert it, holding it above the holder *X* so that any oil which may escape drops into this Holder ; replace it in the Holder *X*. To put on the wick, take off the Chimney holder *F*, take out the Cylinder *C*, take out the smallest Cylinder *D*, tie the wick at the base of Cylinder *D*, then replace the Cylinder *D* in the large one *C*, taking care to push it down as far as the point *E*. Replace everything as before, the large Cylinder *C* having the Brass catches *G* up and the Ring *E* down. To raise the wick turn the Chimney-holder.

This Lamp gives a very superior and steady light, and with ordinary care will emit neither smell nor smoke. One-twelfth, or one eighth of a heavier oil, Sperm, Lard or Olive, mixed with Kerosene, makes the best and safest oil.

Testimonials have been given by highest authority as to its safety against explosions.

Besides the above pattern Lamps, in Brass, as well as in German Silver, I also have Lamps with two burners or Double Lamps ; also, Bracket or Side Lamps, and Double Hanging Lamps or Keroseniers, all with the same St. Germain patent burners.

The wick should be trimmed regularly. If a crust has formed, do not disturb it, but only remove any little point or unevenness that may occur ; do not use the scissors unless the wick, through uneven draft, should have coaled or charred unevenly. By this method you will have an even flame, and the wick will last much longer than when cut frequently. If your Lamp should make a humming noise, which is caused by the shank of the chimney being of the wrong length, raise the chimney slightly, or change it for one with a longer shank.

Use kerosene or spirits in place of water for cleaning chimneys. The brass part of the Lamp may be cleaned with Vienna lime and kerosene, and polished with rouge.

N. B.—Parties returning lamps for repairs will please see that every lamp is properly labelled, with name and address, and also with the complaint.
As there are now being offered to the public, worthless articles, purporting to be chimneys and wicks designed to be used on my ST. GERMAIN LAMP, but really intended to injure its sale, particular attention is called to use a proper sized chimney and wick.
Size of chimney for No. 1 Lamp, full-length, about 10 inches, shank or wide part, 2 inches high, opening in the neck not less than ⅞ inch clear, diameter 1⅜. The chimney for No. 2 Lamp has to be about the same size, except the diameter of shank should only be 1½ inch to fit in the holder. Wicks have to be large enough to fit *close* to the wick holder. A too large wick will be apt to crease or fold and give an uneven circle of light, while burning, besides such a wick will draw the oil quicker than it can be consumed by the flame.

FOR SALE BY
DOUGLAS & McNIECE,
MONTREAL, CANADA.

lamp, together with some of its important parts. There are full directions for filling the reservoir and for adjusting the lamp. A mixture of kerosene with a small amount of sperm, lard, or olive oil is recommended. The invention is said to have won a medal in 1867 and a diploma in 1868. The name of the inventor is spelled "Kleemann," rather than "Kleeman" as on the patent. On the back of the sheet are drawings of sixteen different models of the basic design. They range from the standard form, in brass or German silver, to elaborate two-burner and four-burner chandeliers (p. 219).

The Kleeman lamp used a tubular or "Argand" chimney and an opaque glass shade of conoid form. The manner in which the shade was supported distinguishes this and other early student lamps from the later versions. A square brass rod rises from the fuel tube adjacent to the clamping sleeve that encloses the vertical rod support. This square rod supports a metal ring, which surrounds the burner like a halo, and is recessed to take the rim of the shade. The name of the inventor and that of the distributor are inscribed on this ring or on the burner. A fine example of an original Kleeman student lamp is in the Wolfville Museum, Wolfville, N.S.

OTHER STUDENT LAMPS Even before the belated acceptance of the Kleeman lamp, patents were being taken out on minor modifications of it. Willard H. Smith of New York, N.Y., obtained such a patent,[38] mainly for a diagonal rim around the edge of the wick to catch the overflow of oil and return it to the wick.

Another set of slight modifications appeared in the patent of Bennett B. Schneider of New York, N.Y.[39] The principal innovation was in the reservoir; the outflow of fuel could be regulated by rotating perforated discs in the base, on the same principle as used on pepper cans today. Schneider also made changes in the burner, intended to dissipate heat and prevent the overflow of oil. This patent used the term "student lamp," which does not appear in the Kleeman patent or the Hinrichs literature.

"Improved" student lamps continued to be patented during the 1870s and 1880s. Freeman[40] has reproduced the drawings from a number of such patents. The student lamp most commonly met with in Canada is the "Perfection," manufactured by the Manhattan Brass Company of New York. It may be recognized by the fact that the spiral groove in which the wick raiser works is on the inside of the wick tube, rather than in the centre-draft tube. It is therefore seen externally as a spiral ridge.

MECHANICAL LAMPS

A rather specialized family of lamps in this period employed clockwork mechanism to create an artificial draft, and thus eliminate the need for a chimney. The idea of augmenting the lamp's natural draft had already appeared in the benzine-burning "Atmospheric" lamp, and soon after the introduction of kerosene new designs appeared. They used a spring-driven fan in the base to provide a constant draft.

The earliest patent for such a lamp was granted to Francis B. De Keravenan of New York, N.Y.[41] The font has a double tube up its middle. The inner tube is used for the wick and the space between for the forced draft. Passages through these two tubes led the fuel to the wick. The base contains a paddle-wheel type of fan, driven by a spring motor, which sends air up the stem to the space between the two tubes. A damper in the stem controls the strength of the current.

The difficulty of constructing the central tubes of the De Keravenan lamp led George A. Jones of New York, N.Y., to obtain a patent[42] providing for a simple glass font enclosed in a second vessel of metal, the space between being for the passage of the forced draft. I have not seen examples of either of these lamps, but Jones in his patent claim emphasizes that the De Keravenan lamp was available to the public.

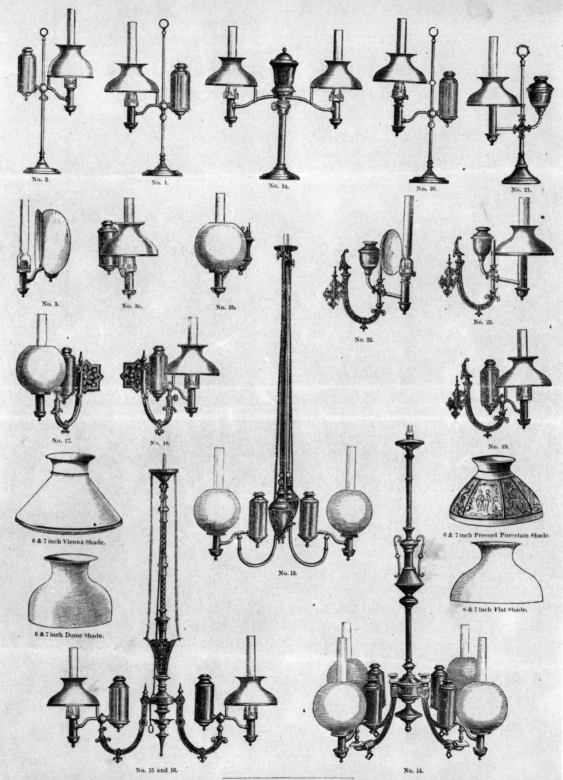

No. 2.

No. 1.

No. 1a.

No. 20.

No. 21.

No. 3.

No. 3c.

No. 3h.

No. 22.

No. 23.

No. 17.

No. 18.

No. 19.

6 & 7 inch Vienna Shade.

6 & 7 inch Pressed Porcelain Shade.

6 & 7 inch Dome Shade.

No. 13.

6 & 7 inch Flat Shade.

No. 15 and 16.

No. 14.

HITCHCOCK LAMPS The most famous mechanically ventilated lamp was patented and manufactured by Robert Hitchcock of Watertown, N.Y. It was designed not only to function without a chimney, but also to use a relatively heavy oil, so reducing the danger of fire. Hitchcock obtained four patents over twenty months in 1872–73, each with progressive improvements in design. In the earliest,[43] both the concentric tubes of the De Keravenan lamp and the space between font and jacket of the Jones patent were incorporated, providing two channels for the air current. For starting the lamp when using heavy oil, a priming reservoir was attached near the top of the burner. This was eliminated in the second patent,[44] which substituted a number of vertical rods in the font to conduct heat from burner to fuel. The wick mechanism is peculiar; the wick is secured to a threaded tube, which receives a long threaded rod. This rod is rotated by a gear mechanism at the top, turned by a long rod extending obliquely through the font to the lower exterior.

In his third patent[45] Hitchcock introduced an oil pump, operated by the same spring motor as the fan, to bring oil from the font to the burner. A third concentric tube within the font provided additional air current. In the fourth patent[46] the spring motor and fan were surrounded by the fuel font, and provision was made to filter the air taken in by the fan.

Hitchcock took out a Canadian patent[47] for his "Forced Blast Heavy Oil Lamp," but this was evidently to protect his Canadian market, which may have been important since he was so close to the border. A handsome example in the National Museum of Canada (NMC D-633; figure 126) was purchased at Tweed from Dr. W. A. Paul of Napanee, Ont. Most of Dr. Paul's collection came from along the north shore of Lake Ontario, and was recently acquired by the Hastings County Museum in Belleville. The fan mechanism is in a cylindrical unit, and the shafts of fan, spring, and winding handle are vertical; hence the fan revolves in

126
Hitchcock lamp, 1872
purchased in Tweed, Ont. NMC D-633

a horizontal plane. The motor is wound by a permanently attached key in the recessed base. Height of lamp to top of deflector is 12¼ inches; diameter of base is 5½ inches. A similar lamp has been illustrated by Thwing (pl. 62).

Two Hitchcock lamps in the U.S. National Museum (USNM 331139 and 251016) differ in having the winding shaft projecting laterally through an opening in the wall of the base; the key in these examples is removable. Five additional Hitchcock or Hitchcock-type lamps in the collection of Carleton Brown are also picture by Thwing (pl. 96). Those with horizontally driven motors have wide conoid bases and those with vertical motors have gracefully cylindrical bases. From the illustrations it is evident that whether the spring shaft is vertical or horizontal the fan shaft is vertical and the fan revolves in a horizontal plane (unlike the De Keravenan lamp). Two of the Carleton Brown lamps illustrated are provided with chimney holders, which seem redundant. The Hitchcock lamps illustrated by Thwing and those in the U.S. National Museum and the National Museum of Canada all have the conventional wick raiser with horizontal shaft and toothed wheels. The screw-driven wick mechanism of the second Hitchcock patent appears to be rare.[48]

Another mechanical lamp, the Wanzer, is described in the following chapter.

HANGING LAMPS

The era of elaborate hanging lamps was yet to come, but by the late 1870s several types of such lamps were in use. The common kind incorporated a heavy rod bent into a triangular or pear-shaped outline. The lamp font with burner rested in a receptacle on the broad lower part of this so-called harp, and the assembly was suspended from the upper, narrow end. Some examples had a conical shade supported part-way up the harp, and at the top there might be a conical or bell-shaped smoke deflector. A hanging lamp of this type with a three-wick

SUPPLEMENT TO THE "LONDON REFLECTOR."

A HIGH-CLASS MAGAZINE FOR THE COLONIES.

Sept. 21st, 1879.   PUBLISHED MONTHLY BY PRINCE & SYMMONS, COMMERCIAL STREET, LONDON.

NEW

LIBRARY LAMP.

Entire Length of Lamp from Top to Bottom,
As shewn, 42 inches.

Pulls down for Lighting, 24 inches longer.

Drawn one-third real size.

Finest American Iron Casting.

Smooth Polish and Gold Bronzed
and Relieved.

Brass Chain.

French Opal Shade.

Height of Shade, 6 in.

Diameter of Shade at
base, 15 in.

No. 1060.

1 inch Burner (American).

PRINCE & SYMMONS, KEROSENE & PETROLEUM LAMP MANUFACTURERS & EXPORTERS.

Complete as Drawn, with Opal Shade, Chimney and Wick, 20/- each.

burner (LSR 253) has already been mentioned. An advertisement for such lamps (preserved in the Barnett Collection of the University of Western Ontario) comes from the supplement to the *London Reflector — A High Class Magazine for the Colonies*, dated September 22, 1879. Another excerpt from the same publication, dated September 21, 1879, shows the "New Library Lamp." Its harp is an ornamental cast-iron ring with a conical open shade attached to the top. Most interesting is the presence of a counterbalanced suspension, a system of four chains with pulleys and a ring-shaped counterweight. This permitted the lamp to be pulled down or pushed up, and to remain stable at whatever height it was left. By the late 1880s this mechanism was widely used on hanging lamps.

Hall lamps were already in use in the 1870s and in fact are a type going back to pre-kerosene days. They differ from other hanging lamps in that the font, burner, and chimney (lamp proper) are inside a glass "globe," open at the top and with draft holes in the metal base. An advertisement in the *Daily Globe*, Toronto, for October 16, 1875, offers "Pelley Hall Lights" for sale. The early hall lamps characteristically had uncoloured etched glass in the "globe," commonly in the form of a six- or eight-sided prism. This type persisted even after highly coloured and gracefully curved globes came into vogue.

COLLARS

The collars of early kerosene lamps were made from short sections of brass tubing, shaped and threaded on a lathe. Later a flat washer shape was stamped into a vertical ring but the threads were still cut on a lathe. These methods required a relatively thick piece of metal, and the cuttings were wasted. The first attempt to produce a threaded collar by stamping sheet metal is described in a patent of Alvin Taplin of Forestville, Conn.[49] Taplin started with a vertical ring stamped from sheet metal but with the upper part left as an inward-projecting horizontal flange. The spiral thread was stamped on this flange. Then the ring was placed in another die and the horizontal flange was stamped into a downward-projecting vertical inner ring. The spiral grooves were thus formed into an inside thread to receive the screw of the burner.

A different method of threading a sheet-metal collar was devised by Frank Rhind of Brooklyn, N.Y.[50] His technique started with a simple vertical ring, stamped or otherwise formed. This was placed between two dies, each composed of several pieces. The inside and outside dies had corresponding threads which were impressed in the metal by a blow applied through a punch.

127
Hand lamp with patent collar, 1876 Niagara Falls, Ont. LSR 326. ROM *photo*

The final step in the production of a practical sheet-metal collar was introduced in the 1876 patent of George W. Brown of Forestville, Conn.[51] He combined the Taplin design of the turned-down upper part with the Rhind method of striking the threads by means of dies. His really original contribution, however, was to impress by die or lathe two deep grooves on the outside of the collar. They gave greater rigidity to the sheet metal, and the ridges produced on the inside provided a stronger grip to the cement that secured the collar to the font.

A small hand lamp in the writer's collection (LSR 326; figure 127) bears the dates of the Taplin and the Brown patents on the outside of the collar. But the presence of two deep annular grooves, as distinct from the slight cuts of earlier models, is enough to date the collar, and therefore the lamp, as 1876 or later. The turned-down threaded portion of the collar is also indicative of the Taplin-Brown innovations. Nearly all lamp collars of later date were made according to the Rhind-Taplin-Brown design.

CHIMNEYS AND SHADES

The introduction of the four-pronged chimney holder, as in the Atwood burner of 1873, brought about a striking change in the shapes of lamp chimneys. The curved lower part with turned-out rim was no longer suitable, and chimneys with this form became displaced by those (figure 141) in which the lower part, for about 1 1/2 inches, was vertical. Above this straight part, beyond the reach of the chimney-holding prongs, the new chimneys swelled out in the usual fashion, except that the bulge was more pronounced than in earlier styles. The relative height was less, but the ornamented upper rim, so characteristic of later chimneys, apparently was not introduced until after 1885, or at least was rare before that year.

Along with this standard form, a number of special shapes appeared during this period. R. N. Eagle of Washington, D.C., obtained additional patents[52] for chimneys that were circular below and oval in cross-section higher up. The cylindrical chimney was the subject of a patent by E. Jones of South Boston, Mass.[53] The oval burner and the rectangular burner required chimneys with lower rims of corresponding shape. Examples of such chimneys (LSR 197, 196; figure 128, 129) were purchased from Mrs. M. Marquart of East Aurora, N.Y. They are mould-blown, with a reinforcing ring at the level where the sides flare out and another at the upper rim. Because they obviously were designed to fit the oval and rectangular burners manufactured after 1878, these chimneys are dated about 1880.

The Ditheridge chimney of 1861, in which the bottom and top are circular and the middle part oval, was mentioned in chapter 8. A modification in 1870 had the oval base formed by flattening opposite sides of a circular base. An example (LSR 34; figure 130) was purchased from Mrs. Allie Howe of Dunnville, Ont. The semicircular areas formed on the sides by the flattening are marked "DITHERIDGE & CO / PITTS" and "PAT / OCT 1861 / AUG 1870." The first date refers to the Ditheridge patent mentioned in chapter 8. With regard to the second date, I have been unable to find a chimney patent for that month and year, and suspect that it refers to a registered design rather than a patent.

The reappearance of the Argand type of burner, in both folded-wick and student-lamp variations, led to the revival of the narrow, cylindrical chimney such as had been used on mantel and astral lamps. These mostly came from Europe and were called Argand or French chimneys. Characteristically they had a deep annular constriction just above the flame level, and were usually narrower above than below – features which increased the velocity of the draft.

It seems a bit incongruous to us who are accustomed to brilliant incandescent and fluorescent lights that people in the nineteenth cen-

128
Oval chimney, late 1870*s or early* 1880*s purchased in East Aurora,* N.Y. LSR 197. ROM *photo*

tury worried about the harmful effects of glare from astral, solar, and kerosene lamps. Not only did they protect their eyes with shades, but they also used coloured glass chimneys.[54] Mr. D. C. MacKenzie of Ottawa obtained a number of Marcy-type chimneys from an old store in Pakenham, Ont. Among them were a few with a beautiful pale blue tint.

Shades were now very popular, but mostly of a simple conical form as in the previous decade. They sometimes sat directly on the upper part of the chimney; however, special frames to support the shade were also available. These were commonly brass rings, channelled to receive the lower edge of the shade. Popular styles of shade were the "Vienna," a simple conoid form with turned-out upper rim, and the "Flat," a low bell shape – both used especially with the student lamp. "Opal Vienna Shades" and "Argand Chimneys" were advertised in Toronto in 1875 for "German Study Lamps."[55] Other shades were

129
BELOW: *Rectangular chimney, late 1870s or early 1880s; purchased in East Aurora*, N.Y. LSR 196. ROM *photo*

130
BELOW RIGHT: *Ditheridge oval chimney 1870; Dunnville, Ont.* LSR 34. ROM *photo*

dome- and globe-shaped. Shades were made of metal, etched glass, or ornamented porcelain, but the commonest material was opal glass.

An arrangement that achieved some long-term popularity was patented by Hiram L. Ives of Troy, N.Y.[56] A bowl-shaped lower part, of clear glass, rested on a reinforced chimney holder on the burner, and was held in place by a set-screw. The upper rim of the bowl was recessed to receive the lower edge of a Vienna or some other model of shade. The lower part of the combination, therefore, functioned as both chimney and shade support. One would suppose that such a wide orifice would not have provided an adequate draft, but the use of this arrangement on a variety of lamps into the 1890s or later shows that it was effective.

MANUFACTURERS AND DEALERS

OIL REFINERIES Canada's pioneer oil refinery, The Canadian Oil Company of Hamilton, had been established by J. M. Williams in 1860. It continued during the next decade, but after that its history grows somewhat uncertain. According to a popular biographical article, Williams left the firm in 1871 and it became the Canadian Carbon Oil Company.[57] But a Canadian Oil Company ("Established 1856") was still advertising in the *City of Hamilton Directory for 1878–79* as "Manufacturers of all kinds of petroleum oils." The proprieter was listed as C. J. Williams, and one might assume that this was the original Williams company continuing under the direction of a relative. The same company advertised in the 1885 and 1887 editions of the *Ontario Gazetteer and Directory* as suppliers of Canadian and American lubricating and illuminating oils.

The Williams company is not among the refineries in Lovell's *Province of Ontario Directory for 1871*, which lists only Prince &

Ontario Gazetteer and Directory 1885

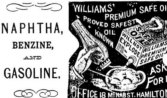

McCulloch of Bothwell and T. & J. Millar & Co. of London. By 1882 the same directory carried the names of twenty-eight refineries, of which twelve were in Petrolia, nine in London (including Imperial Oil Co.), two in Cooksville, and one each in Ingersoll, Sarnia, Stratford, Toronto, and Woodstock. A number of Montreal manufacturers are listed, but no refineries. The Toronto firm was Samuel Rogers & Co. of 33 Adelaide Street East. Their quaint advertisement on page 387 of the directory featured mainly lubricating oils but included "Diamond Burning Oil" and "American Safety Oil." Most of these "refineries" appear to have been importers as well as manufacturers.

BURNER MANUFACTURERS By the 1870s the "brass towns" of Connecticut were well established in the manufacture of lamp burners and other metallic parts. Mention has been made of Holmes, Booth & Haydens and the Plume & Atwood Company. Another important Waterbury firm was the Scovill Manufacturing Company, but their lamp products were more significant later. The oval burners produced by Benedict & Burnham of Waterbury, and the rectangular burners of the Bridgeport Brass Company, Bridgeport, Conn., have been described. Firms in Meriden, Conn., were also getting into the lamp business, notably Edward Miller & Co., but the great days of the Meriden lamps were still to come.

As in the 1860s, a number of Canadian firms of this period advertised themselves as manufacturers of lamps. But as noted for the previous decade, no actual example of a lamp or a lamp part has been seen that can be identified as made in Canada before 1887. In that year Burn & Robinson Manufacturing Co. of Hamilton were making lanterns and burners. This firm became the Ontario Lantern Co. in the 1890s and the Ontario Lantern & Lamp Co. in 1905. Lamp burners were made under both names and it is just possible that

Burn & Robinson lamp burners of the 1880s will be found, but this has not yet happened.

LAMP GLASS   Pittsburgh, Pa, was the centre of glass manufacture in North America during the 1870s and 1880s, and the firms of Atterbury & Co. and Ripley & Co. continued to dominate the lamp business as they did in the 1860s. The Union Glass Co. of Somerville, Mass., was also an important producer of glass lamp bodies. The history of these companies and their products has been discussed by Revi (pp. 25, 290, 304).

The best-known manufacturer of glass lamp bodies in Canada was the Burlington Glass Co. of Hamilton, which was established in 1875.[58] It seems likely that the manufacture of lamps by this company began after 1878, when Murray A. Kerr, who had been a lamp dealer, became associated with the firm. This company has been the object of special study by Mr. Gerald Stevens, and some of his findings as applied to lamps are discussed in the following chapter.

WHOLESALE AND RETAIL DEALERS   By the 1870s all Canadian cities and most towns had outlets for kerosene oil and lamps. It would be pointless to try to list all of them, especially as the names seem to have changed from year to year. Some, however, are worthy of mention, either because they persisted in business for a number of years, or because their advertisements throw light on the products of their times. Among these were H. Piper & Co. of 81 Yonge Street, and Parson Brothers of 51 Front Street, Toronto. Another important firm was Phillips, Thorne & Co., wholesale glass, china, and earthenware merchants of 29 Front Street, Toronto. Its advertisements of 1875[59] list "Kerosene Goods," including chandeliers, pendants, Pelley hall lights, brackets, bronze lamps, German study lamps, opal Vienna shades, and Argand chimneys.

CHAPTER X

Swan song of the kerosene lamp
1886 to 1900

FOR AT LEAST the first twenty years of the present century kerosene illumination remained one of the main forms of domestic lighting, especially in rural areas to which electrical power distribution had not yet extended. But in cities and towns the day of the "coal-oil" lamp was over, except when the power failed, an event that occurred progressively less frequently. The last fifteen years of the nineteenth century saw the transition to this happy state from the days when kerosene was the almost universal illuminant. Competition from electricity and from the newly rejuvenated illuminating gas grew progressively greater. Kerosene lighting met the threat by exploiting the decorative possibilities of its lamps, based on their greater variety and portability, a strategy which fitted with late-Victorian love of lavish decoration.

Elaboration of the kerosene lamp was not accompanied by much real innovation. All the late-Victorian types except for the floor lamp were well established by 1885. What happened afterwards was increased use of coloured glass, of painted glass and china, of elaborate patterns in pressed glass, of prism pendants, of statue-like pedestals, and even of fabric shades and fringes. One is reminded of the elaborate solar lamps that were so popular just before kerosene displaced lard as a lamp fuel.

131
*Vase lamp, 1890s, painted glass
purchased in Huntingdon, Que.*
NMC A-1344. NMC *photo*

Now that kerosene was fashionable as well as universal, the marketing processes became more sophisticated.[1] Patent containers made the fuel easier to handle and less likely to spill in the home. The general store, still the main supplier of domestic needs, installed metal tanks with calibrated dispensing mechanisms, forecasting the gasoline pump of the future. Distribution to retail merchants and bulk users became more efficient; tank wagons made deliveries easier and safer, and enabled merchants to avoid excessive storage. As tank wagons grew larger, there was a revival in the use of the small container, but these were now metal barrels or "drums," much easier to handle and safer to store than their wooden predecessors.

Distribution to retailers, either by barrel or wagon, was centred around the "station," operated by a refining company or subsidiary. Here large metal storage tanks were filled from railway tank cars or from pipelines, and oil drawn as needed to meet retail demand.

Production of petroleum in Canada was limited during this period to the declining fields of southwestern Ontario. Drilling had been attempted in the Gaspé peninsula and in northeastern New Brunswick, with disappointing results. As a consequence, most of the crude oil for Canadian refineries was imported from the United States. This made lake-ports such as Sarnia, Ont., and seaports such as Halifax, logical sites for refineries. The great discoveries in western Canada were still far in the future. Oil seepages in the Waterton Lakes area of southwestern Alberta led to drilling in 1901, and the Dingman discovery well at Turner Valley was drilled in 1913, but western Canada did not become a major producer of petroleum until the development of the Leduc field in 1947.

The last fifteen years of the nineteenth century form the spectacular but rather anticlimactic last act of a drama that began with the lighting of the first Argand lamp in 1783. The next production was already in preparation; the actors were gathering back stage and peering around the wings. The prologue to the new play is the subject of the two following chapters.

ARC LIGHT OIL.

❧The Best Illuminating Oil on the Market.☙

The Maritime Merchant
Halifax, N.S., August 5, 1897

BURNERS

FLAT-WICK BURNERS   The Atwood burner of 1873, by its simplicity of construction and efficiency of operation, quickly became the standard flat-wick burner in North America. The Plume & Atwood Company continued to manufacture it well into the twentieth century, but after the basic patent expired, many companies joined them. Minor variants appeared under numerous trade names, some officially registered, others reserved only by usage. We have noted some of the names used by Plume & Atwood: Eagle, Banner, Globe, Model, and Fireside. Of these, "Eagle" was registered with the

U.S. Patent Office on September 26, 1893, with the notation that it had been in use since January 15, 1879. "Banner" was registered on November 13, 1906. "Fireside" appears in the Atwood Canadian Patent of June 4, 1875. The other names apparently were not registered, either in Canada or in the United States.

Of the Atwood burners made by other companies, one of the more popular was the "Queen Anne" (figure 132), which bears its name in capital letters on the side of the deflector. As usually recorded on the thumb wheel, this burner was made by the Scovill Manufacturing Company of Waterbury, Conn. The name "Queen Anne" was registered in Washington on September 15, 1896, and in Ottawa on November 17, 1914. Queen Anne burners are made of brass, and resemble the Banner burners, but the chimney prongs are ornamentally shaped strips of brass rather than bent wires. A similar burner marked "QUEEN MARY" is common on old lamps. It is made of thin sheet iron with a brass coating, and has chimney prongs of straight, imperforate brass strips. The thumb wheel bears no inscription, and the name Queen Mary does not appear in either the U.S. or Canadian registry of trade names, so it is not yet clear whether this is Scovill's cheaper version of the Queen Anne or the competitive product of another manufacturer.

132
"Queen Anne" burner
1896; *Waterville, Que.* LSR 290

The Bristol Brass and Clock Company, of Forestville, Conn., manufactured and sold two types of Atwood burner, as shown in their catalogue of 1889.[2] The "Parlor" was a conventional Atwood and the "Prize" was similar, with the addition of a Baldwin vapour vent alongside the wick tube.

Another Atwood-type burner commonly encountered is marked on the deflector "WHITE FLAME," with the name of the manufacturer – the White Flame Light Company of Grand Rapids, Mich. I have not found the name in the U.S. Registry, but it was registered in Canada on July 30, 1921, so it may be assumed that this burner is entirely a twentieth-century product.

As noted in chapter 9, the Ontario Lantern Company was established in Hamilton in 1892, and became the Ontario Lantern & Lamp Co. in 1905. Atwood-type burners were manufactured under both names; those marked "O.L. CO." may bear the trade name "SUNLIGHT," whereas those marked "O.L. & L. CO." usually are stamped "BANNER." Obviously the latter may be dated as twentieth century on the evidence of both maker's name and trade name.

Without changing the basic structure of the Atwood burner, several inventors devised modifications that are worthy of note. Spafford W. Lamberton of Newark, N.J., obtained a patent[3] for an extinguisher, which consisted of a sleeve fitting loosely around the wick tube, and weighted at the bottom by a lead disc about the size of a 50-cent piece. A simple wire lever projecting beyond the rim of the burner enabled the user to raise the sleeve so as to enclose and smother the flame; on release, the weight brought the sleeve back to its original position. The Lamberton patent also described a filler tube, projecting outward and upward from the rim of the burner, and opening into the font through a semicircular hole in the burner base. The outer end of this tube has a small brass cap.

133
Lamberton burner, 1887
Preston, Ont. LSR 81

An example of the Lamberton burner (LSR 81; figure 133) was purchased from Mr. Stan Ashbury of Preston, Ont. It fits the patent description very closely. The filler tube appears to be cast in white metal, and added to the finished burner. The disc on the extinguisher tube is marked "PHOENIX M'F'G / CO. / PAT. OCT. 18. / 1887." The thumb wheel is marked "PAT. JAN. 16. 83 FEB. 11. 73." These latter are dates of Atwood patents, and indicate that some, at least, of the Lamberton burners were made under an arrangement with the Plume & Atwood Company.

On another example (LSR 236), however, the thumb wheel is marked "PHOENIX M'F'G. CO. / PAT. OCT. 18. 87." This was obtained from Mr. and Mrs. Paul Shelley of East Aurora, N.Y. It lacks the extinguisher tube and the filler-tube cap. The burner is somewhat larger than the example from Preston, but otherwise similar. Just who were the Phoenix Manufacturing Company and where they were located is not yet clear, but a possible clue is that Lamberton assigned two-thirds of his patent rights to William P. Cleaver and Julia W. Cleaver of Newark, N.J.

134
Taplin burner
1896; Richmond Hill, Ont. LSR 97

The name of Taplin reappears on a burner dated 1896 (LSR 97; figure 134), which was obtained from Mr. W. M. Bell of Richmond Hill, Ont. This is an Atwood-type burner, but the chimney holder consists of 3 L-shaped prongs which are spring-loaded, so that without a chimney the prongs incline inwards. Pushing a chimney down over them depresses the horizontal branch of the "L" and causes the vertical branch to press against the inside of the chimney. The thumb wheel bears the incised legend "C. A. TAPLIN / MFG. CO. / PAT'D / 8.23.96." Unfortunately I have been unable to find any U.S. or Canadian patent for that date. The nearest date on which U.S. patents were issued was August 25, and none of this group corresponds to the burner described above.

Another well-marked Atwood-type burner (LSR 275) for which the patents have not been found was purchased from Mrs. Rill Brown of Richmond Hill, Ont. From the base, on either side of the wick opening, 2 strips of thin copper, reinforced on the edges by folded strips of tin, project down 2½ inches. Presumably they were to prevent fouling of the wick inside the font. One of the copper strips is stamped "PAT^D APR. 27–1897." To make it more confusing, the thumb wheel is marked "PAT. FEB. 16. 99."

Burners of Atwood type with glass deflectors are not uncommon. Presumably the idea was to get light from that portion of the flame below the blaze hole as well as from that above. The deflectors were cast in two halves, which are held together by a ring of strip brass. Each half of the deflector is marked "BING." The U.S. Registry of Trade Names lists this name as the property of the Bing Burner Co. of Minneapolis, Minn., and the date of registration as January 8, 1907, with usage dating from June 1, 1903. It may be assumed, therefore, that all such burners were made in the twentieth century. Most examples have nothing on the thumb wheel, but one was seen in which the wheel was marked "O.L. & L. CO.," so it would appear that some Bing burners were made in Hamilton, presumably using imported deflectors. The idea of transparent deflectors in glass or mica appeared in 1875 in a patent[4] by Henry Taylor of Richmond Hill, Ont., but I have no evidence that burners based on this patent were ever manufactured.

One of the last lamp patents bearing the name of L. J. Atwood was taken out in association with Frederick W. Tobey of Waterbury, Conn.[5] It was intended for large burners, especially those with two wick tubes. The patent claims a number of modifications to burner construction, most of them intended to reduce heating. The type appears in the Plume & Atwood catalogue of 1908 under the names "Eagle" (single wick) and "Climax" (double wick). It has a distinctive chimney holder, suggesting the coronet of earlier burners or of those imported from Europe. The most distinctive internal feature is in the base of the burner; the wick tube or tubes terminate in a brass disc or diaphragm just below the wick wheels, and the lower part of the base is an open conoid shell. This shell is threaded for both small and large collars. The burner described in the patent has an extinguisher device, a metal flap operated by an external lever, which closes over the wick tube, but this feature is not listed among the claims.

135
LEFT: *Metal table lamp with "Climax" burner*, 1890; *purchased in Hillsville, Va.* LSR 17

Two examples have been examined. One came with an all-metal lamp (LSR 17; figure 135) from Hillsville, Va. It lacks the extinguisher, but has the thumb wheel marked "CLIMAX / PAT. JAN. 21, 90 / MADE IN U.S.A." The second example is on a lamp (LSR 19) from Martinsburg, W. Va, and has the thumb-wheel inscription "EAGLE / MADE IN U.S.A." Both these burners have single wick tubes. Two lamps in the National Museum of Canada collection have burners of this type with double wick tubes and the lever-operated extinguisher.

The Plume & Atwood catalogue for 1908 illustrates three sizes of "Sun Hinge" burner. They belong to the same class as the Marcy and Taplin models, in which the deflector assembly hinges on the base plate. When this particular burner was introduced is not clear, but it was certainly available in the 1890s and later. Two examples (LSR 65 and LSR 169) were obtained from Mr. Stan Ashbury of Preston, Ont. They appear to be unused, as if from a dealer's stock. The deflector, the wide flange for the chimney to rest on, and the low, plain coronet, have been stamped from one piece of brass. The base plate is cup-shaped, with large rectangular openings on the inclined sides, and a closely perforated distributor plate on top. A Baldwin vapour vent is attached to the wick tube. The distinguishing feature appears to be in the hinge. It is a conventional hinge with two outer "eyes" attached to the base plate, and a long middle "eye" riveted to the chimney-supporting flange. The piece of brass that forms the middle "eye" is doubled back, and the free end rolled into an open cylinder which forms a hinge stop like Taplin's projecting tab. This prevents the deflector assembly from being swung back more than 90°. In the closed position the assembly is secured by a bent brass clip, as in the Marcy and Taplin burners.

CENTRE-DRAFT BURNERS   In the 1870s the Argand-type burner had been revived in the Kleeman student lamp and in the

136
Rochester-type table lamp, ca. 1890
purchased in East Aurora, N.Y.
LSR 390. ROM *photo*

ingenious folded-wick burners that did not require a draft tube up the centre of the lamp body. A final resurgence of the centre-draft burner appeared in the 1880s with the invention of the "Rochester" lamp. The story of the origin of this lamp has been told in some detail.[6] Charles Stanford Upton, of Spencerport, N.Y., presumably some time in 1883, got the idea for an improvement in the centre-draft burner, which he discussed with his friend Leonard Henkle of Rochester. Henkle was an experienced machinist, who already had patents for lanterns to his credit, and he suggested further elaboration. The two friends went out and purchased some tin spittoons, and in Mr. Henkle's workshop they fabricated them into the prototype of what came to be called the Rochester lamp.

The burner resembled the burners of those astral lamps in which the "Liverpool button" deflected the air of the central draft laterally onto the flame. But instead of a simple disc mounted on a rod, the deflector devised by Upton and Henkle was another tube, closed and perforated at the top, and mounted within the centre-draft tube so that some of the air passed up between the tubes to the base of the flame, and some came up the inner tube to spray out radially through the perforations onto the upper part of the flame.

Although the accounts agree that the original idea came from Upton, the patent for this new type of burner was issued to Henkle.[7] The inner tube as described in the patent had a dome-shaped top, and was appropriately called a thimble. Many variations of this shape subsequently appeared: cylindrical (figure 136), cylindrical with flange, inverted conical, mushroom-shaped (figure 137). The standard name for this part soon became "flame-spreader."

The manufacture and sale of the new lamp was undertaken by Upton, who formed a company with his two brothers. Instead of operating in Rochester, they set up headquarters in New York City, and had their lamps manufactured by various Connecticut lamp-

137
Bradley & Hubbard
Rochester-type burner, 1890s
purchased in United States. NMC H-15

makers, of whom Edward Miller of Meriden appears to have been the first. However, they retained the name "Rochester Lamp" for all those made under the Henkle patent, and this is a source of confusion, especially as there was a Rochester Burner Company in Rochester, which had no connection with the Upton group but which by the late 1880s was also making a centre-draft lamp with a flame spreader.

In his original patent Henkle did not describe a method of adjusting the wick. But at an early stage a new device for this purpose was added, sometimes called the draw-bar wick-lift. It consisted of a thin metal sleeve around the outside of the centre-draft tube, loose enough to slide up and down, and with projections of some sort to grip the tubular wick which fitted either over or inside it. If the wick were outside, the lower part of it had to be split to fit around the attachment of the draw-bar. In a primitive version of the Rochester lamp

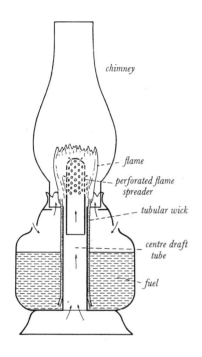

chimney

flame

perforated flame spreader

tubular wick

centre draft tube

fuel

in the collection of the Rochester Historical Society the "draw-bar" is actually a stout strip of metal projecting up at the margin of the burner. Usually, however, it was a true bar, emerging from the shoulder of the font, curving outward at the top, and terminating in a ball for easy gripping (figure 136). At the lower end, inside the font, the bar was L-shaped, the horizontal branch going to the tube that gripped the wick. This simple draw-bar was retained in a number of Rochester-type lamps, such as the early versions of the "Royal" lamp made by Plume & Atwood.

Often, however, the draw-bar was modified, usually so that the wick could be raised or lowered by a thumb wheel. The simplest way of doing this was to put teeth on one side of the draw-bar, so that it became a rack, into which a pinion, turned by the thumb wheel, meshed. This arrangement appears in the later versions of the "Royal" lamps of Plume & Atwood and in Rochester lamps made by Bradley & Hubbard of Waterbury, Conn. In these the rack and pinion device is mounted on the shoulder of the font, but in the "Rayo" lamps, apparently a late product of the Miller Company, the mechanism is within the base assembly of the burner.

A slightly more complicated way of operating the draw-bar appears in the "Miller" burner, made by that company in Meridan. The draw-bar is shaped like an inverted "U." The inner arm is the real draw-bar. The outer arm pasess down through a knurled wheel on the shoulder of the font, and is threaded below, so that turning the wheel raises or lowers the threaded arm and hence the whole wick mechanism. Another Miller burner, the "Juno," has what appears to be a simple draw-bar, but this is obliquely toothed below. A thumb wheel with an oblique shaft turns a pinion, which meshes with the draw-bar and permits it to be racked up and down.

The Bradley & Hubbard catalogue of 1885[8] does not show Rochester-type lamps, but in the 1890s this company produced a number of elaborate table and hanging lamps using the Rochester burner. A pair of bronze "reception" lamps in the National Museum of Canada (NMC H-15; figure 137) have mushroom-shaped flame spreaders. The draw-bar is shaped like an inverted "U," as in the "Miller" burner, but is tangentially, rather than radially, orientated to the burner. The mechanism is a rack and pinion, but is on the arm that is not attached to the wick holder.

The Bridgeport Brass Company of Bridgeport, Conn., manufactured what they called the "New Rochester" lamp. Its flame spreader had a convex overhang, so that some of the draft was directed down onto the flame. There was no draw-bar. Instead a thumb wheel was set obliquely on the shoulder of the font, from which a shaft extended down diagonally through the font and terminated in a gear wheel. The teeth of this wheel meshed with diagonally arranged perforations on a sleeve surrounding the centre-draft tube. This sleeve was the wick support, and motion imparted by the gear wheel caused support and wick to rise or descend spirally. The "New Rochester" lamp has not been found in Canada yet, but there is an excellent example in the collection of the Rochester Historical Society.

Lamps of the Rochester type, because of their late appearance, are well documented by manufacturers' catalogues, although not all of these publications are accurately dated. But the acquisition of working examples has been surprisingly difficult. One reason is that many surviving lamps have been mutilated; the flame spreader has been removed and replaced with an electric light socket. This is particularly true of those seen in Canada, with the result that, in order to compile the above account, it was necessary to purchase a number of examples in New York State. Now that the characteristics of the main types have been established, it is hoped that some will be recognized on the Canadian side of the border.

MINIATURE BURNERS Small lamps intended as night lights were common in the late nineteenth century and miniature burners were made especially for them. Most such burners have few clues as to their manufacturer but those made by Plume & Atwood are readily recognized. The first of these to be developed was called the "Nutmeg" burner and was based on a patent by L. J. Atwood in 1877.[9] The features claimed by this patent are well shown by an example (LSR 80; figure 138) purchased from Mr. John Player of Mallorytown, Ont. The base plate is only 1¼ inches wide.

It is in the form of a conoid chamber enclosing the single wick wheel; the wick tube extends through it and well above it. Immediately on top of this chamber and surrounding the wick tube is a horizontally placed brass disc with numerous perforations, called the "open-work guide" in the patent specifications. The deflector and coronet are in one piece, and from the latter a perforated cylinder extends down over ½ inch. When in place it encloses the space between basal chamber and perforated disc. The deflector/coronet assembly can be lifted off with the chimney, exposing the wick for trimming and the burner interior for cleaning. The thumb wheel is marked "PAT. FEB'Y. 27. 1877" This burner is part of a small hand lamp the body of which is described in the section on night lamps.

Even more common, but evidently of later development, is the P. & A. "Acorn" burner. An example (LSR 142) is shown in figure 139. It is on a miniature metal lamp body, the whole having been obtained from Mr. Phillip Shackleton of Manotick, Ont. The burner is 1³⁄₁₆ inches in diameter. The deflector is relatively high, perforated at the bottom, and flared out to form a flange on which the chimney rests. The coronet has 12 prongs, which are bent inward. The base plate is a flaring cup, with a row of perforations. The thumb wheel is marked "THE P. & A. M'F'G. CO / ACORN."

A third type of miniature burner made by Plume & Atwood was the "Hornet." This is rarer today than the other two; I have seen only two examples in Canada. One of them is shown in figure 140 (LSR 402). It was purchased from Mrs. Allie Hazelgrove of Kingston, Ont. It resembles the "Acorn" burner in form but is distinctly larger, the outer diameter of the coronet being 1⅝ inches. Also the prongs of the coronet are relatively higher and have a large, keyhole-shaped slit. The thumb wheel is marked " P & A / HORNET." The lamp body that came with this burner is of pressed copper, in 3 pieces. Such a body does not appear in the Plume & Atwood catalogues available to me, but it closely resembles the less ornate versions of the full-size table lamps produced by that company.

LAMP BODIES

During this period the composite lamp, at least in its original form, was unimportant, and those that were made were very different from their predecessors. They were replaced in part by the all-metal table lamp, which was best suited to take the popular centre-draft, Rochester-type, burner. Lamps with painted glass or china fonts were common; some of these were adapted to the centre-draft burner by having a true font or oil pot of metal, fitted inside the apparent font. But lamps varied so widely in form and use during this period that it is difficult to generalize. Perhaps that was the most characteristic feature of the time, the adaptation of the kerosene lamp to a wide variety of purposes, both useful and ornamental.

HAND LAMPS   Hand lamps were the least modified of all kerosene lamps during the nineteenth century. The basic form of a low glass font with a loop-shaped handle persisted. Cylindrical and octagonal varieties were both common, but perhaps the feature which most clearly distinguished this from earlier periods was that the font did not usually rest directly on the table or shelf. It had a distinct base,

140
"Hornet" burner,
1890s; Kingston district, Ont. LSR 402

even though there was little or no stem. This form can be appreciated by considering some typical hand lamps of the period.

The lamp shown in figure 141 (LSR 56) was purchased from Mrs. L. Baker, Orton, Ont. It is low and globose. The base consists of a projecting rim at the bottom of the font. The handle projects from the side of the font and one of the mould seams continues around its outer rim. Around the font is a pattern of 12 bull's-eyes separated by 3-pointed inverted fronds. This pattern appears on a series of lamps, from this low hand model to the tall table variety described below.

An intermediate size in this series is represented by a hand lamp (LSR 313; figure 142) purchased from Mrs. Mary Ryan of O'Regans, Codroy Valley, Nfld. Its font rests on a pyramid-like hollow base. The sides of the base are concave; each bears a bull's-eye, and where the sides meet is the inverted frond, but with 11 points instead of 3. The font, with its pattern, is like that of the previous example. The handle, however, is attached to the base at one of its corners and is shaped like a question mark.

On both lamps the fonts have 3 mould seams and were evidently mould-blown. In making the smaller of the two the handle part of the mould was filled with molten glass which was allowed to stiffen before the main part was blown. On the taller lamp the handle and base were evidently press-moulded, after which the font was blown on top. The base pattern is distinctly sharper than that of the font.

In Gerald Stevens' *Early Canadian Glass* (pp. 56–57; pl. 19), this pattern appears on a table lamp attributed to the Burlington Glass Company. Shards showing it have been found on the site once occupied by that company's factory in Hamilton. In the catalogue of a glass exhibition at the Royal Ontario Museum, prepared in 1964 under Mr. Stevens' direction,[10] the pattern is called "Bull's Eye," but it is obviously not the same as the Bull's Eye patterns described by Mrs. Lee.[11] The Museum guide book attributes footed hand lamps with this pattern to the Sydenham Glass Company of Wallaceburg and the Jefferson Glass Company of Toronto as well as the Burlington Glass Company.

A catalogue of the Jefferson Glass Company (established in Toronto in 1913) illustrates both types of hand lamp described above.[12] The low

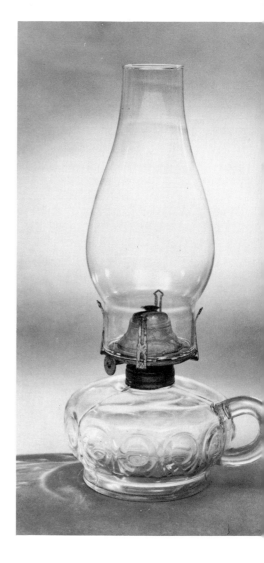

141
Glass hand lamp, "Bull's Eye"
probably 1890s; *purchased at Orton, Ont.*
LSR 56. ROM *photo*

142
Combination hand and table lamp
"Bull's Eye"; from a home at O'Regans
Codroy Valley, Nfld. LSR 313

lamp is called simply "Hand Lamp," the taller one, "Footed Hand Lamp." No name is given to the pattern but evidently it was a Canadian one, appearing on lamps about 1890 and continuing well into the 20th century. Lamps of very similar shape but without the pattern are shown in the T. Eaton Company Limited catalogue for the spring and summer of 1898.

Brass or brass-coated hand lamps were used in the 1890s and later. They had low fonts, shaped like a cut-off cone, a metal-strip handle, and a burner which used a rope wick adjusted by a wick wheel. Complete examples have a brass cap on a chain, like the burning-fluid lamps, but they are more often mistaken for whale-oil lamps. Actually they burned kerosene. Plume & Atwood made and sold this type as "Planter's Hand Lamp," the burner being called "Pet Ratchet." A similar lamp appears in the Bristol Brass catalogue of 1889 as the "Union Ratchet Hand Lamp." The E. Miller Company also had their version. One of these (LSR 119; fig. 143), purchased at Aberfoyle, Ont., was tried with kerosene and the original wick. When the top of the wick was kept at about the level of the wick-tube opening, a smokeless flame about half an inch high was obtained. Any greater exposure of wick resulted in a smoky flame. Plume & Atwood also made metal hand lamps with their "Royal" centre-draft burner.

143
LEFT: *Brass hand lamp, 1890s purchased at Aberfoyle, Ont.* LSR 119. ROM *photo*

144
RIGHT: *Glass table lamp, "Bull's Eye" probably 1890s; purchased at Orton, Ont.* LSR 57. ROM *photo*

TABLE LAMPS Probably the commonest and most versatile kerosene lamp of the 1890s and later was the all-glass table lamp. It was cheap, convenient to carry, tall enough to illuminate a useful area, and relatively easy to clean. It held a place of honour at the dinner table, was carried afterwards to the kitchen for the dishwashing, back to the dining room for homework and the newspaper, then to the bedroom for retiring. Most of these lamps were plain, with globose font, simple stem, and conoid, hollow base. But with elaborate pressed patterns on font, base, and sometimes chimney, they could compete even with ornate vase lamps as parlour ornaments.

These lamps were all so much alike in principle, yet so different in detail, that in figures 144 to 146 a series from Canadian sources has been illustrated as the best way of describing them. Scarcity of catalogues for the period makes it impossible to identify most of them as to date and maker, but it is certain that they were all used in some part of Canada in the 1890s or the early part of the twentieth century. Notice particularly the lamp in figure 144 (LSR 57). It is the table version of the two hand lamps previously described and shows the same "Bull's Eye" pattern, but there is a three-inch stem between font and base, with four curved and ribbed vertical flanges. These not only were ornamental but provided a firmer grip than would a simple cylindrical stem.

Another pattern that appeared frequently on lamps used in Canada is shown in figure 145 (LSR 139); it is usually called "Waterfall." It is made up of six panels of drape-like waves separated by narrow ribbed panels. This lamp is unusual in that it came with a moulded chimney showing the same pattern. A similar lamp, but without the moulded chimney, is in the National Museum of Canada (NMC D-39); the glass is deep blue. Coloured glass was widely used in lamp bodies during this period, and these are more sought after by collectors than those of clear glass. The table lamp shown in figure 146

145
LEFT: *Glass table lamp, "Waterfall"*
with moulded chimney, probably 1890s
purchased at Woodbridge, Ont.
LSR 139. ROM *photo*

146
RIGHT: *Green glass table lamp, probably*
1890s
purchased at Bruce Mines, Ont.
LSR 177. ROM *photo*

147
FAR RIGHT: *Composite table lamp*
with painted Ives shade, ca. 1890
purchased at Foxboro, Ont. NMC D-602

(LSR 177) has simple lines; the pattern is confined to the base, and the glass is emerald green.

Although the all-glass table lamp displaced the composite lamp as the common household light, it had competition as an ornamental object from a peculiar type of composite lamp that appeared in the 1880s and was popular in the 1890s.

148
LEFT: *Composite table lamp, early 1890s purchased at Markham, Ont.*
LSR 50A. ROM *photo*

149
RIGHT: *Figure-stem lamp, probably 1890s purchased at Bowmanville, Ont.*
NMC D-544

A fine example (NMC D-602; figure 147) was obtained from Mrs. Bert Wannamaker of Foxboro, Ont. The hemispherical font is of amber glass, with a fine diamond pattern, and has a channel on the top to catch oil drip. The stem is a painted glass cylinder, with brass connectors above and below. The square, bevelled base is of cast iron, painted black. This particular lamp came with the Ives combination of chimney and shade (see page 228) and the opal glass "Vienna" shade has been decorated. A very similar lamp is represented on page 199 of the T. Eaton Company Limited catalogue for spring and summer, 1897, and Freeman (p. 51) reproduced a page of the Bradley & Hubbard catalogue showing a number of such lamps. It is evident that various styles of font and stem could be interchanged.

A similar type of composite lamp appeared with a stem of moulded glass. An example (LSR 50A; figure 148), purchased from Mrs. Margaret Philip of Markham, Ont., has a vase-shaped stem of pale yellow glass, painted with green leaves and pink flowers. The base is a low cone of iron, with an acanthus-leaf pattern and its edges scalloped so that the weight rests on four points. The font is of clear glass, with a pattern of a zig-zag band and fine diamonds. A similar lamp, but evidently taller, was illustrated as the "Como Banquet Lamp" in the T. Eaton Company catalogue for 1892–93.

A third type of composite lamp is called figure stem by Freeman (pp. 53, 88, 89). The stem is a metal casting representing a human figure or head. An example in the National Museum of Canada (NMC D-544; figure 149) was obtained from Mrs. Verne Johnson of South Bowmanville, Ont. It has a depressed globose font of frosted glass, a square iron base, and a stem in the form of a female head and bust. Another example (NMC D-999), obtained from Mrs. W. D. Carrothers of North Gower, Ont., has a female figure as a stem. The figure-stem lamps illustrated by Freeman were made by R. P. Wallace & Company of Pittsburgh, Pa., but similar lamps no doubt were produced by other companies.

All-metal table lamps were widely manufactured and used in the period under review. Although the finish varied from plain to elaborately ornamented, the general form did not differ very much: a spheroid font joined by a concave-sided stem to an inverted-bowl base. The metal was usually nickel-plated brass. On some examples the base is cast iron. The all-metal lamp body was most commonly used with a centre-draft burner, and body and burner came as a unit. This was the case with the Rochester lamp and its numerous modifications. The all-metal construction made it relatively easy to provide a centre-draft tube and a special type of wick raiser. As the burner was an almost integral part of the lamp, it was necessary to provide an external filler opening on the shoulder of the font.

BANQUET LAMPS The class called banquet lamp varied greatly in style and construction, but had one thing in common: a relatively high stem. The extra height permitted illumination of a large area, and reduced the shadows cast by other objects on the table.

The glass banquet lamp shown in figure 150 (LSR 107) was purchased from Mr. and Mrs. Gordon McNair of Ilderton, Ont. The font is a depressed spheroid, with a distinct shoulder and peripheral keel. The outer surface is smooth, but the inside of the font has a series of low vertical undulations. The stem is cylindrical above, curving into the conoid base. The pattern on stem and base is dominated by ovoid depressed areas, each outlined by a raised rim with ribbing. Font and stem are joined by a short, nickel-plated tube, with annular grooves above and below to hold the cement. This would have permitted other combinations of font and stem/base, but an example in the National Museum of Canada (NMC D-601) is identical.

A truly composite banquet lamp (LSR 120; figure 151) was purchased from Mr. Don Van Buren of Port Hope, Ont., and was obtained by him at Peterborough. The font is opaque white glass in a depressed "turnip shape," with a flat top of cream-coloured glass put on after the original pressing. The shoulder of the font has a pressed pattern of hook-like forms, from which rows of little knobs descend spirally. Four panels have been painted buff, and between them are painted flowers and leaves. The stem is a tall brass tube, with collars where it joins font and base. The base is of cast brass, with open-work decoration; the four corners serve as legs.

150
Glass banquet lamp
1890s; purchased in Ilderton, Ont.
LSR 107. ROM *photo*

151
FAR RIGHT: *Composite banquet lamp*
early 1890s; Peterborough district, Ont.
LSR 120. ROM *photo*

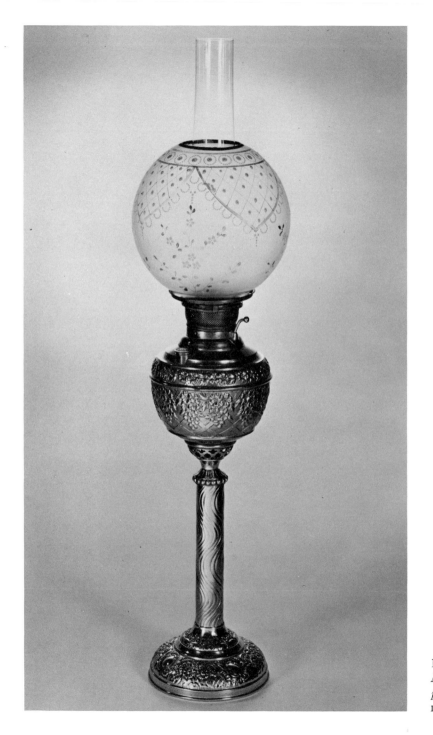

152
*Metal banquet lamp, late 1890s
purchased at Aylesford,* N.S.
LSR 303. ROM *photo*

Metal construction made it possible to have banquet lamps with centre-draft burners. The models usually pictured in old catalogues were of this type.

An example (LSR 303; figure 152) was purchased from Mr. William Meister of Aylesford, N.S. It has a Rochester-type burner with simple draw-bar, and a globose font. Air for the centre draft entered through openings in the cup on which the font rests. This cup in turn rests on a high tubular stem which is supported by an inverted-bowl base. Ornamentation consists of an intricate pattern of roses, leaves, and lattice on the font, wavy grooves on the stem, and daisies and leaves on the base. All parts but the burner are nickel-plated. Both burner and filler-cap bear the name "Rayo," but the shoulder of the font is marked "THE / JUNO LAMP / MADE IN / U.S.A." The name "Juno" was used by the E. Miller Company for one of its centre-draft burners (p. 243), but I have not found a record of the name "Rayo." A banquet lamp of this type was advertised in the T. Eaton Company catalogue for spring and summer, 1897.

VASE LAMPS With such a variety of lamp types in use during the last fifteen years of the nineteenth century, it is difficult to decide which was the most characteristic. Probably the honour should go to the vase lamp. Intended more as an ornament than as a source of light, the vase lamp, along with the library lamp to be described, reflected the ostentation so characteristic of late-Victorian home furnishing.

The distinctive feature of the vase lamp was the font, or more often the apparent font, which was like a globular or egg-shaped vase, supported on a low metal base, with little or no stem. What appeared to be the font was usually a shell of opaque glass, painted by hand in some floral or scenic design. The shade was either spherical or hemispherical, and was painted with the same design. Variants had frosted rather than painted glass, or fonts of china or metal. In some vase lamps the lower part or vase really was the font, but in the majority the true font was a separate receptacle called an oil pot, which was suspended inside the glass or china vase.

The idea for such a combination first appeared in 1883, in the patent of James H. White of New York City.[13] In his version a metal canister was set into the false font; the true font, which was a glass vessel with a metal cover holding the collar for the burner, fitted into the canister, and was suspended there by the overhanging rim of the cover. The metallic oil pot was patented less than a year later by Charles B. Boyle of New York City.[14] His design had a tube up the centre; air entered through holes in the brass bottom of the false font and passed up this tube to provide the centre draft for an Argand-type burner, usually the Rochester kind. Some oil pots, however, were simple cans without the centre-draft tube, and these used a flat-wick burner such as the Plume & Atwood "Climax."

Although the vase lamp reached its peak of popularity in the 1890s, an early version appeared in an English advertisement of 1879.[15] The high font and conical "Vienna" shade were painted in matching design. It was fitted with a double-wick burner in which the wick wheels had coaxial shafts.

Three styles of vase lamps from the 1890s are represented in figures 131, 153, and 154. The first (NMC A-1344) was purchased from Mr. Martin Beattie of Huntingdon, Que. The font is a depressed globe, with the burner collar attached by a large brass flange. This is the true font, and it had to be filled through the collar. The font is supported on a short brass stem attached to an open-work, four-footed base. The shade is spherical and, like the font, is of opaque white glass. Both are painted with a spirited scene obviously derived from Landseer's "Stag at Bay."

The second (NMC D-880; figure 153) was purchased from Mr. T. G. Wrightmeyer of Belleville, Ont., and is said to have been used in Hastings County. In general form it is similar to that previously described. However, the pink and green floral design on the yellowish "font" and shade

153
Vase lamp, moulded and painted glass, 1890s
purchased in Belleville, Ont. NMC D-880

154
Vase lamp, moulded and etched glass
1890s; purchased in Deseronto, Ont.
NMC D-1023

are raised on the glass, as well as painted. The true font or oil pot is a cylindical can that fits snugly into a receptacle inside the glass "font," and it has a separate filler opening. The bottom of the apparent font is open and a centre-draft oil pot could have been used, but the one present has no central tube, and the burner has a single flat wick. The wick wheel is marked "NEW YORK — B. B. CO," presumably standing for Bristol Brass and Clock Company.

The third example (NMC D-1023; figure 154) was obtained from Mr. Don McNeish of Deseronto, Ont. The separate oil pot is provided with a centre-draft tube which permits the use of a Rochester-type burner. The one on the lamp is a Plume & Atwood "Royal." The top of the oil pot is of heavy brass, pressed in an ornamental design. The apparent font is of an inverted pear shape and, like the spherical shade, is frosted glass with an elaborate raised pattern of flowers and leaves. There is no painting.[16]

Vase lamps were made by a number of manufacturers in the north-eastern United States. The Bristol Brass and Clock Company in its catalogue of 1889[17] devoted 21 pages of illustrations to such lamps. It is said[18] that the finest painted lamps were produced by the P. J. Handel Company of Meridan, Conn., which employed a staff of trained artists, mostly from Germany.

In recent years the painted vase lamp has become much sought after. Rather easy to convert into an electric lamp, it may even be provided in its new role with a light inside the font, a gilding of the lily that was not possible in its original form. Many surviving vase lamps have lost the matching shade, and there are dealers who will arrange to have the design of the font copied onto a new shade.

Part of this modern popularity resulted from a preposterous anachronism. In the motion picture "Gone with the Wind," based on the novel by Margaret Mitchell, lavish use was made of vase lamps to convey the impression of the opulent "before-the-war" southern mansion. The designers completely ignored the fact that such lamps did not appear until twenty or more years after the period represented by the story. So the awkward and ridiculous name, "Gone-with-the-wind lamp," became attached to the late nineteenth-century vase lamp, and appears likely to persist among dealers and collectors long after the origin of the name, and the error involved, are forgotten. Serious students of lighting, however, will continue to use the neat and descriptive name that was applied by the people who made, sold, and used these lamps.

STUDENT LAMPS The popularity of the Kleeman "study lamp" and its various modifications continued throughout this period and on into the twentieth century. Variants appeared in the form of double lamps with single reservoir, double hanging lamps, sconce lamps, and a grotesque version called a parlour lamp of cast bronze in the shape of a cornucopia. Unlike the original Kleeman lamp and its immediate imitations, the later student lamps had the shade support attached to the burner rather than to the upright.

A good example (NMC B-25; figure 155) was obtained from Mr. Dana L. Sweeny of Mahone Bay, N.S. It has a fine finish of nickel plate, and a corrugated milk-glass shade which rests on a brass ring supported by three wires from a collar around the burner. Probably the most radical departure from the Kleeman lamp is the presence of a perforated flame spreader, as in the Rochester burner. The wick is raised and lowered, not by turning the burner or the air-intake cup, but by means of the wick-wheel and thumb-wheel arrangement of a flatwick burner.

FLOOR LAMPS The unique contribution of this period to domestic lighting was the floor lamp. With one or two rare exceptions, nothing similar had been used since the eighteenth century, when adjustable wooden floor stands for candles were common. It was the Rochester-type centre-draft burner that helped to make the floor

155
Student lamp, style of the 1890s; purchased at Mahone Bay, N.S. said to be from a home in Lunenburg.
NMC B-25

lamp popular. Some floor lamps, however, did use double flat-wick burners.

In all the contemporary North American catalogues examined, the late nineteenth-century floor lamp is called a piano lamp. It is a confusing name, suggesting a lamp that stood on top of the piano, rather than alongside it on the floor. Basically the piano lamp consisted of a three-legged or four-legged stand, supporting a vertical rod which could be adjusted for height. At the top of the rod was a bowl-shaped false font, containing the oil pot with its burner, chimney, and shade.

The type of piano lamp most commonly illustrated in the catalogues of the 1890s had four spreading legs attached to a small, square onyx or marble table top. A spirally grooved tube, supported below, passed through this top. Inside it was a rod that engaged the spiral groove and supported the lamp proper. By turning the rod, the false font could be raised and lowered, and clamped into position by a screw collar. Such a lamp was depicted in the T. Eaton Company fall and winter catalogue of 1894–95. It was very popular in its decade but today examples are rare and expensive. Several Canadian dealers report having had them at one time, and I saw one in Kingston converted into a fern stand, but I have been unable to obtain an example. Even among American dealers they are not readily available. This may be because they were easily converted into attractive electric floor lamps. The tripod type of piano lamp, although perhaps not as popular in its day, is now more common.

An example (LSR 258; figure 156) was purchased from Mr. William Cole of Huntsville, Ont. It is said to have belonged to a family that lived near Baysville. The lamp is almost entirely constructed of brass. The 3 legs are simple spreading rods, braced below by an ornamented triangular plate, and terminating above in a perforated and scalloped disc. A smooth brass tube rests on the plate and extends through the disc. Inside it is a steel tube, which contains a spring and a gripping mechanism. A

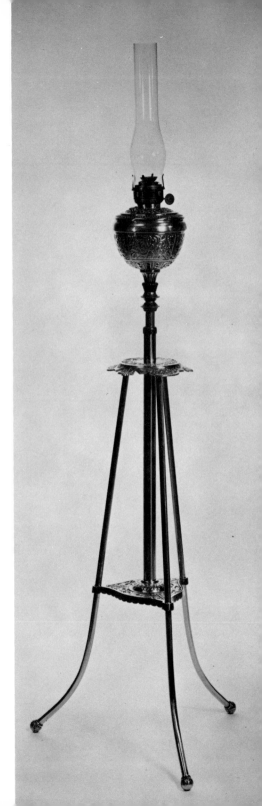

LEFT: *Piano lamp, tripod type*
1890s; from a home near Baysville, Ont.
LSR 258. ROM *photo*

flat steel rod, attached to the bottom of the brass tube, runs up the centre of the steel tube. When the steel tube is raised, the spring-loaded grip engages the central rod and holds the steel tube at the desired height. The grip is released by pressing down a brass ring at the top of the steel tube. The steel tube, of course, bears the false font, a bowl-shaped container of ornamentally pressed brass, with perforations at the bottom. The oil pot, a plain cylinder, has an ornamented cover which fits over the top of the false font. A centre-draft tube passes through the oil pot and extends above it for about 1½ inches. Over this the burner fits. There is a filler opening, with screw cap, on the cover of the oil pot.

The maker has not been identified. The thumb wheel of the burner is inscribed "THE / DAYLIGHT / C. & K." but the initials do not fit the name of any of the better-known lamp manufacturers. The top of the flame spreader is marked "ALWAYS RUB WICK EVEN / NEVER CUT." A picture of a piano lamp with a similar type of lift mechanism is reproduced by Freeman (p. 95) from a Bradley & Hubbard catalogue. Similar lamps but with slightly different lift mechanisms were sold by Edward Miller & Company of Meriden, Conn., and the Haida Lamp and China Company of New York City.[19]

The piano lamps seen today are usually provided with a globular glass shade. This may have been the style towards the close of the period, but about 1890 the characteristic shade was a conoid affair of paper, silk, or linen.

WALL LAMPS   Wall-mounted kerosene lamps were more characteristic of shops and workrooms than of homes, but they did occur in houses, especially in the kitchens. Simple forms were made of sheet-metal, possibly by the local tinsmith. They were similar to the old candle sconces, with a back plate to hang against the wall and a can-like font to replace the candle tray. The example shown in figure 157 (NMC N-266) is from Newfoundland. The font was made from a can that originally contained lobster.

Another seemingly improvised wall lamp (NMC D-1225; figure 158)

158
BELOW: *Wall lamp, sheet metal, ca.* 1900
purchased at Sheffield, Ont. NMC D-1225

159
LEFT: *Wall lamp with sconce, 1890s*
purchased at Danville, Que. NMC A-918

160
*Wall lamp with bracket and reflector
late 1890s; from a home in Hamilton, Ont.*
LSR 128

was obtained from Mr. R. L. Donaldson of Sheffield, Ont. The font is of sheet metal, shaped like a covered plate standing on its edge. A metal tube has been soldered to what would be the under surface. This tube extends obliquely upward and outward to about the level of the upper rim of the font, and bears a "White Flame" burner. Since these burners were probably not made before 1900, there is doubt that this lamp is of 19th-century date.

Most wall lamps combined a glass font with a metal support. A simple but common type, intended for the kitchen, is shown in figure 159. (NMC A-918). It was purchased from the Misses Elliott of Danville, Que. The font is a low glass cylinder, held by two metal prongs which fit in a wide, flat groove around the font periphery. The prongs extend from the wall bracket, which is surmounted by a metal reflector, stamped in a design suggesting a scallop shell. The font can be pulled free readily for filling or cleaning. Similar lamps were made with handles, so that they could double as hand lamps. Some used a metal belt instead of prongs, with a device for loosening or tightening.

Commonest of the wall lamps were those in which the font sat in a cast-iron ring attached to the bracket and reflector. Fonts of such lamps narrowed below the shoulder, which projected to rest on the ring. In other examples the font sat in an open-work iron cup.

An elaborate example of the latter type (LSR 128; figure 160) was purchased from Mr. Harold Luscombe of Hamilton, Ont., and is said to have been used in the home of a prominent local merchant. The lower part of the font is like a cup with concave sides; above the shoulder the font is dome-shaped. There are two mould seams on the upper part, one around the shoulder, and none below. The burner is a conventional Atwood, almost identical with the Plume & Atwood "Banner" but marked on the thumb wheel "ONT. L. CO. / HAMILTON." The Ontario Lantern Company of Hamilton became the Ontario Lantern & Lamp Company in 1905; since lamps are seldom younger than their burners, it may be assumed that this lamp is older than 1905, probably dating from the late 1890s. The support consists of a cast-iron cup with solid bottom and widely open sides. The font actually rests only on the rim. A hole in the bottom of the cup fits over a low pin on the end of the bracket. The bracket is an elaborate frame of cast iron, shaped like a recumbent "S" with flourishes. From a point opposite the font cup a simple iron rod curves outward, then straight upward, to support the reflector. At the very back of the bracket is a small finial, the lower end of which fits into a hole in a small escutcheon which can be screwed to a wall. Thus the bracket was supported at right angles to the wall and could be swung in a horizontal plane. The reflector is a concave, hollow glass disc, free-blown and coated internally with mercury. It is attached at the back to a small sheet-metal cylinder from which a tube extends down to fit over the vertical rod on the bracket. By this means the reflector, as well as the bracket, can be swivelled. The peculiar chimney came with the lamp and is discussed in the section on chimneys.

ANGLE LAMPS   These unusual devices were made both as wall lamps and as hanging lamps. The design first appeared in a U.S. patent by George C. Berry of New York City and Thomas M. Fell of Tenefly, N.J.[20] Three years later an improved version was more elaborately described and illustrated in a Canadian patent by John U. Bauchelle of Elizabeth, N.J., and Thomas M. Fell.[21] The lamps were sold by the Angle Lamp Company of New York City.

The basic idea was to tilt the burner sharply so that instead of being vertical it was less than 30° from the horizontal. Used with a modified form of the Ives combination chimney and shade, this arrangement directed most of the light downward, free of the shadow of font and support produced by the conventional lamp.

The example shown in figure 161 (NMC D-991) was purchased from Mr. and Mrs. Gordon McNair, then of Ailsa Craig, Ont. It has a cylindrical tin font, which is suspended by a harp-shaped handle. The font contains a reservoir, with valve opening at the bottom, and the whole

161
Double hanging angle lamp
1893; *purchased at Ailsa Craig, Ont.*
NMC D-991

arrangement is the familiar "bird bath" used in the student lamp and the original Argands. From near the base, and on opposite sides of the font, two tubes project at an angle to the horizontal. Each tube ends in a burner having a coronet and set-screw arrangement for holding the chimney. The latter is hemispherical and of clear glass, and supports on its upper rim a conoid shade of white opaque glass. This is the Ives combination of 1878 (see page 228) except that the lower, clear part is attached to the burner at its side, rather than at its bottom.

Single-burner angle lamps were made as wall lamps; the font hung from a nail in the wall, like a simple sconce lamp. An example of such a lamp is in the Huron County Museum at Goderich, Ont. One in the National Museum of Canada (NMC H-15) was purchased in Hallidaysburg, Pa. It has a spherical font, with a pressed-pattern ornamentation, and an inverted finial at the bottom. Such elaborate fonts were also used in hanging models.

A catalogue of the Angle Lamp Company, preserved in the Metropolitan Museum of Art, shows the variations and uses of these lamps. Models are illustrated with plain cylindrical, ornamented cylindrical, or ornamented spherical fonts. Hanging lamps with three and four burners are shown. Four illustrations depict various models in their settings, three of which are homes, the fourth a store. This disposes of the idea held by some that the angle lamp was intended only for use in stores and workshops. The slogan of the catalogue is "The Light that never fails   No Danger   No Smoke   No Odor   No Shadow."

HANGING LAMPS   Two distinct types of hanging lamps were popular in the period under discussion, the hall lamp and the library lamp. Both were in use earlier, but not so commonly or in such ornate form. As noted previously (p. 223), the hall lamp or hall light is distinguished by the fact that font, burner, and chimney are all enclosed within the shade, which is suspended by some form of chain or rod arrangement. The earlier forms, with the shade shaped like a six-sided prism, persisted into this period, as shown by the T. Eaton Company fall und winter catalogue of 1892–93. In the same company's catalogue for 1896–97 that style of shade is replaced by one shaped like an inverted vase. Evidently mould-blown, it has a pattern of faint vertical ribs. A shade of this type (LSR 287) was purchased from Mrs. Anne Beaulieu of North Hatley, Que. It is of deep red ("cranberry") glass, and has twenty vertical ribs which are slightly askew at the top as if the blower had given it a twirl before it was quite hard. The overall height of the shade is 8⅝ inches. The upper opening, which is rimless, is 2¾ inches in diameter, and the lower opening, which has a vertical collar, is 3¾ inches.

The manner in which a hall lamp was adjusted can be seen from the example shown in figure 162 (LSR 6), which was donated by the Trinket and Treasure Antique Shop of Kingston, Ont. The shade is relatively

162
Hall lamp, "cranberry" glass, 1890s
Kingston district, Ont. LSR 6

163
RIGHT: *Library lamp, 1890s*
purchased in Peterborough, Ont.
NMC D-990

small and pear-shaped and is of purplish red ("ruby") glass, with a swirl pattern. The lower opening, with its collar, rests on a brass cup, which holds a simple cylindrical font with burner and chimney. From this cup two chains extend upward to a pair of pulleys in a concave brass disc, then down to attach to a flaring brass collar which is secured by bent projections to the upper, rimless opening of the shade. This arrangement does not permit any adjustment of the height of the lamp, as is possible with counterweight hanging lamps (p. 223), but when the bottom ring is pulled down, the lower cup descends and at the same time the shade rises, so that the lamp inside can be reached for lighting, adjusting, or cleaning.

The library lamp is an entirely different type of hanging lamp, and it competed with the vase lamp as the most ornate illuminating device of the late nineteenth century. Actually it was only an elaboration of the hanging lamp described for the previous period (p. 221), but the elaboration gives it a quite distinctive character. The basic features are a hemispherical shade of translucent glass, with or without pendants, a metal framework to support font and shade, and a system of chains and pulleys to suspend and to adjust the height of the lamp.

Such lamps appear in the T. Eaton Company fall and winter catalogue of 1893–94. They could have been made by one of several manufacturers in the United States, but Edward Miller & Company of Meriden, Conn., had thirty pages illustrating library lamps in their catalogue of about 1895.[22]

A handsome example of a library lamp is shown in figure 163 (NMC D-990). It was purchased from Mrs. Mabel J. Sissons of Peterborough, Ont. The hemispherical shade is made of translucent white glass, with painted decoration of red roses and green leaves. The shade is supported on an ornamental brass ring from which hang 30 glass pendants. The same ring is attached by 2 pairs of chains, each pair coming together above at the opposite ends of a balanced arm. This arm in turn is suspended by 2 chains which are partly wound on pulleys inside the cup-shaped ceiling attachment. The pulleys are spring-loaded, permitting the lamp to be raised and lowered like a window blind.

Below the shade ring is an ornate, strap-metal framework, at the centre of which is a metal bowl into which the font fits, secured by 2 set-screws. The font is of translucent white glass, like the shade, and is painted in the same design.

Variations on this type of library lamp were almost infinite, because of the many styles of shade and font available. In some the lamp was suspended from inside the shade, and there was no ring to support pendants. Usually there was a small inverted cup suspended above the chimney, called a smoke bell. Presumably this caught the ascending soot, which could be cleaned off at intervals. The counter-balanced suspension seen in the hanging lamps of the late 1870s was unusual in the more ornate lamps of the 1890s.

Hanging lamps with metal fonts were made by Plume & Atwood and probably by other manufacturers. They had false fonts with oil pots, like piano lamps, and could be used with the centre-draft Rochester-type burner. The false font was suspended at its base or periphery from a metal frame or harp.

An outsize variant of this style was produced by a number of manufacturers under the name of "Mammoth lamp." Apart from largeness, their main feature seems to have been the wick-raising draw-bar, which was adjusted from below the font and secured by a set-screw. The mammoth lamps all had true fonts, there being no possibility of having an oil pot with this wick mechanism. Commonly, but not invariably, they had a broad, conical, sheet-metal shade, which rested on shoulders on the harp. Mammoth lamps were made by Plume & Atwood and by the Bristol Brass and Clock Company. The example shown in figure 164 (NMC D-995) was made by Bradley & Hubbard, and is labelled "RADIANT." It was purchased from Mr. and Mrs. Gordon McNair, then of Ailsa Craig, now of Ilderton, Ont. The

164
"Mammoth" lamp, 1890s
purchased at Ailsa Craig, Ont.
NMC D-995

165
RIGHT: "Guardian Angel" night lamp,
1890s
purchased at Danville, Que. NMC A-915

plain form and large size of mammoth lamps suggests that they were used in stores, halls, or other public places. However, the more ornate models may have been intended for home use.

NIGHT LAMPS Miniature glass lamps for bedroom use go back to burning-fluid days but were particularly common in the late nineteenth century. Many were handsome and they are much sought by collectors. Unfortunately, few have makers' names or patent dates, so that they are an unsatisfactory group to study. Perhaps the best documented is the small hand lamp known as the Guardian Angel.

The example shown in figure 165 (NMC A-915) was purchased from the Misses Elliott of Danville, Que. The chimney is of yellow glass and globular shape, and rests on a brass ring clamped to the wick tube. The burner is of the type called "Pet Ratchet" in the Plume & Atwood catalogue. The low cylindrical glass font is 3½ inches in diameter and has a single applied handle. On the impressed periphery is inscribed in raised letters "L'ANGE GARDIEN / EXTRA / BINKS & CO. MONTREAL."

Very similar lamps are known without this inscription (e.g., NMC A-916), and the globular chimneys also occur in deep red and in blue glass. It was long assumed that these little lamps were made in Montreal for the Quebec trade, and that they had some religious significance. Gerald Stevens (pp. 53–55; fig. 18) discovered shards of such lamps, however, in the dump of the Burlington Glass Company and argued that some, at least, were made in Hamilton for G. H. Binks of Montreal. The problem has been discussed by the Spences (p. 41; pl. 15), who show two such lamps with fonts as well as chimneys of coloured glass. Their use in religious ceremonies has not been described. Certainly they would have made an attractive and effective night lamp, as the name seems to suggest.

Plume & Atwood made a number of miniature burners for use in night lamps, as has been mentioned previously (p. 245). They also made lamp bodies suitable for one or more of these burners. The lamp shown in figure 166 (NMC N-217) was obtained from Mr. William Fifford of Sandy Cove, Nfld. It has a low, cylindrical, blue glass font bearing the word "NUTMEG" on the left side. The handle is formed from a narrow strip of brass, bent to form a ring just under the shoulder of the font, and with the ends clamped together to make a hook-shaped loop for gripping. The burner is a typical "Nutmeg," as described previously. Such a lamp is illustrated on page 40 of the Plume & Atwood catalogue, the only one shown with a glass font. The caption states that it is available "in assorted colors, Flint, Opal, and Blue."

The glass and metal miniature lamp shown in figure 167 (LSR 80) may also be of Plume & Atwood manufacture but of earlier date. It bears the patented Atwood burner which came to be called "Nutmeg," but this example bears only the patent date. The font is of deep blue glass, tapering a little from bottom to top. There is an expansion around the shoulder, and another just above the bottom. Below the lower expansion the font is narrower, and has an annular groove. On the side of the font

166
BELOW LEFT: *Miniature hand lamp with "Nutmeg" burner, ca. 1890*
from a home in Sandy Cove, Nfld.
NMC N-217

167
BELOW: *"Little Duchess" miniature hand lamp*
ca. 1885, with "Nutmeg" burner
Kingston district, Ont. LSR 80

is the inscription "LITTLE DUCHESS," the two words being separated on each side by three stars. The font fits into a brass base with metal-strip handle, like the tray of a candle holder, but instead of the central tube there is a coiled spring bent in the form of a circle. Into this circle the narrow base of the font fits snugly, the groove serving to make a secure attachment but the spring permitting easy removal. Because the burner lacks the trade name, I suspect that this lamp dates from before 1886, but in the absence of more definite proof it is included here with other night lamps.

A very handsome little lamp bearing a Plume & Atwood "Acorn" burner (NMC A-917; figure 168) was purchased from the Misses Elliott of Danville, Que. Both font and shade are globular and have a pressed pattern suggesting an artichoke. The font is 4 inches in diameter and is made of opalescent light-green glass. The shade is brown above, white below.

A pair of small metal lamps with "Acorn" burners (LSR 142 and 143; figure 169 were obtained from Mr. Phillip Shackleton of Manotick, Ont. The yellow-painted bodies are like miniatures of the metal table lamps, with depressed-spheroid fonts and curved-conoid bases. No such lamp is illustrated in the Plume & Atwood catalogues studied.

168
ABOVE: *"Artichoke" miniature lamp probably 1890s; purchased at Danville, Que.*
NMC A-917

169
Miniature metal lamp with "Acorn" burner, 1890s purchased at Manotick, Ont. LSR 142

VAPO-CRESOLENE LAMP. A night lamp that would supply some illumination but was principally intended for medicinal purposes was the Vapo-Cresolene lamp. Examples are common in antique shops in Canada and the United States, but few are complete, as is the one in figure 170 (LSR 92).

It was purchased from the Trillium House Antiques of Toronto. The lamp proper has a simple glass font with an overhanging shoulder. Above the shoulder is the legend "VAPO CRESOLENE," and below, "USE KEROSENE." The burner has a threaded collar which fits over the threaded glass neck of the font. There is a small cylindrical wick tube for the cord-like wick and an open-work coronet for the little milk-glass chimney. The font sits in a brass-ring base, from which an elaborately ornamented upright rises to a height of 6 inches. An arm of the upright ends in a circular ring, which supports the vaporizer. The latter is in 3 parts. What might be called the bell is a shallow conoid hood directly above the lamp chimney. It extends as a threaded, closed tube through the ring. There are 4 holes on the side of the tube. Screwing over the threaded part of the tube is the lower opening of a cup-shaped vessel, the upper rim of which is vertical, with 4 holes. In this "cup" sits a "saucer," a simple concave dish about the size and shape of a chemist's watch-glass.

Another example of this lamp (LSR 24), purchased in the United States, is incomplete, but has the original package with claims and directions. The vapour created by this lamp, its makers stated, was remedial for "Whooping Cough, Spasmodic Croup, Asthma, Catarrh, Colds, Bronchitis, Coughs, Hay Fever, Sore Throat, Broncho Pneumonia, The Bronchial Complications of Scarlet Fever and Measles and as an aid in the treatment of Diphtheria." The instructions for use read in part:
Fill the lamp with the best Kerosene (Petroleum) Oil obtainable. Alcohol will explode the lamp if used in it. Light the lamp allowing as large a flame as possible; but care must be taken for the first fifteen

170
"Vapo-Cresolene" medicinal lamp
1880s and later
purchased in Toronto, Ont. LSR 92

minutes to see that it does not smoke. Place the lamp under the Vaporizer. Place the Vaporizer in a tin or crockery dish to guard against overturning, and set the same on a table near the bed. Lastly fill the removable cup with CRESOLENE. *Tarry sediment remaining in the cup may be removed with alcohol.*

The directions go on to recommend that the device be used in a closed room, preferably at night. The odour of the vapour could be removed by thorough airing in the morning.

A number of dates of registration in different countries are given on the package, that for France, May 1, 1884, being the earliest. The Canadian date is April 12, 1893. The Canadian agent is given as Leeming Miles Co. Ltd. of Montreal.

A third example (LSR 329) of the Vapo-Cresolene outfit was purchased from Mr. William Cole of Huntsville, Ont. This one also includes the box with the printed directions, and an unopened bottle of "Vapo-Cresolene," a dark brown liquid with an odour like that of phenol. The more modern style of printing, and the use of half-tone illustrations in the accompanying folder, suggest that this particular example was made in the twentieth century.

All three vaporizers have the same inscription on the side of the "cup," between two of the holes: "PATENTED / AUG.4.85 – AUG.8.88." The second date does not seem to be that of a patent, as the nearest date of issue was August 7, 1888. It may refer to a reissue. The first date is that of a patent by James H. Valentine of Stanley, N.J., for a vaporizer.[23] From the description and illustrations it is clear that this is the "Vapo-Cresolene" lamp, although the ornamentation shown on the upright is different from that on the actual lamp. Valentine described his design as an improvement on that patented by George Shepard Page and himself in 1881. On examination it turns out that the earlier patent was by Elias H. Carpenter of Providence, R.I.,[24] who assigned it to Valentine, who in turn assigned a half-interest to Page, also of Stanley, N.J.

The Carpenter patent describes a shallow dish supported over a miniature lamp by a tripod or a single upright. A disc-shaped baffle, or "deflector," placed below the dish and above the lamp, prevented too intense heating of the liquid. This principle of indirect heating was elaborated in the Valentine patent of 1885. The heat would enter the "cup" via the "bell" at the bottom, pass across the under surface of the "saucer" and emerge through the four holes on the side. There was also provision in the Valentine patent for attaching the vaporizer to a gas jet.

The questions remain: what was "Vapo-Cresolene," and what remedial properties, if any, did it have as an inhalant? For the answers I went to Professor G. R. Paterson of the School of Pharmacy, University of Toronto, who is an enthusiastic student of the history of pharmacy. Dr. Paterson searched the records and consulted with his colleagues, and found the answer just as I was about to submit the newly acquired bottle of "Vapo-Cresolene" to him for analysis. The answers appeared in the *American Medical Association Journal* for 1908.[25] A correspondent in Tennessee had written to ask, "What can you tell me about Vapo-Cresolene?" The editor in reply quotes some of the claims of the manufacturer and refers to an analysis carried out in the A.M.A. laboratory. "From the examination we concluded that Vapo-Cresolene is essentially cresol and corresponds in every respect to cresol U.S.P. (Physician's Manual, page 36)." In both the Carpenter and the Valentine patents it is stated explicitly that Vapo-Cresolene or Cresolene is cresylic acid, the old name for cresol.

The verdict of the editor on the therapeutics of the substance was disillusioning. "This report indicates that Vapo-Cresolene is a member of that class of proprieties in which an ordinary product is endowed, by its manufacturer, with extraordinary virtues. The type is so common and has been referred to so frequently that but for the dangers intendant on the inhalation of any of the phenols, this particular product need not have been mentioned." Oh well, the little lamp is pretty.

MECHANICAL LAMPS It may be assumed that the Hitchcock lamps continued to be made and used well into the 1880s and probably later. However, from 1886 on they had competition, at least in Canada, from a very similar device known as the Wanzer lamp. This was actually invented by Abel (or Able) Grove Heath, of New York City,[26] but the Canadian patent was assigned to Richard Mott Wanzer of Hamilton, Ont.

Wanzer was a successful manufacturer of sewing machines, whose third factory still stands in Hamilton, on Barton Street between Mary and Elgin, with his name spelled out vertically on the brick chimney. The Wanzer sewing machines were based on the Singer patents, and

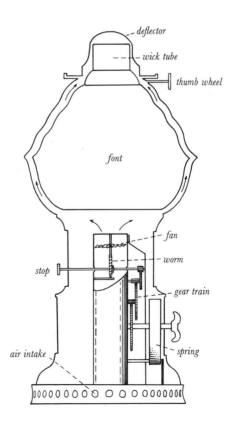

were the first of their type to be introduced into Canada and many other parts of the world. Wanzer came to Hamilton from Buffalo in 1859, and set up a small factory which prospered until the owner became one of the wealthiest men in his city. His venture into the lamp business also must have prospered for a time, as the Wanzer is still represented by numerous examples in Canada. I have never seen one in American antique shops or collections, however. As will be seen, the differences between the lamp patented by Heath and that invented by Hitchock are slight, and it is difficult to see how the Heath patent could have been granted in the first place. Certainly in any legal action the priority of the Hitchcock lamp would have been upheld. It is possible, therefore, that Wanzer restricted the sale of his lamps to Canada and Great Britain, even though some were made in the United States. Hitchcock, as noted, took out a Canadian patent in 1874, but perhaps his Canadian sales were too small to make litigation worthwhile.

In his later years Wanzer tried to expand into the electric light business, but overextended his credit and had to liquidate his business in 1890. Senator W. E. Sanford bought the rights to the Wanzer lamp and gave them back to his friend, and Wanzer made a modest financial recovery by resuming its manufacture. While seeking additional capital in New York in 1900, he suddenly was stricken with pneumonia and died in his eighty-second year.[27]

It is appropriate that three fine examples of the Wanzer lamp are preserved in the Dundas Historical Society Museum, a few miles from the Wanzer factory. One was made in Philadelphia, one in Niagara Falls, N.Y. (presumably at the Oneida Lamp Company), and one in Hamilton. The Hamilton example (figure 171) is of further interest in carrying the heater attachment patented by Wanzer[28] but actually invented by John Bessemer of New York City. This was a kind of stove lid supported over the lamp flame.

171
Wanzer lamp, 1886
with Bessemer heater attachment
Dundas Historical Society Museum
Dundas, Ont.

The Wanzer lamps resemble the Hitchcock lamps superficially, especially those Hitchcock models in which the motor is wound from the side. The Wanzer lamp is a little more squat in its proportions. Like the Hitchcock, it is made of pressed brass, nickel-plated. The base is high and cone-like, with a number of steps. At the narrow top it receives the bottom of the font, which is inverted-conoid below, passing into the main part which is depressed-globular. Removal of the burner discloses that the apparent font is really an outer shell, and the real oil font is an inner vessel. The space between them opens below into the interior of the base.

The burner is a flatwick type, with the usual thumb wheel for adjustment. There is no chimney holder, only a horizontal shelf with a slight rim. The shelf could support a shade.

The motor and fan mechanism is housed in the lower part of the base. An incomplete lamp (LSR 279), presented by Mr. John Player of Mallorytown, Ont., was dissected and the blower mechanism (shown in figure 172) studied in detail. It is mounted on a heavy vertical tube, which is secured to a perforated brass plate near the bottom of the lamp base. On one side of the tube is a powerful coiled spring, with ratchet wheel and pawl. The axle of this spring passes transversely through the tube, and on the other side bears a large gear wheel, part of a train of 3 accelerating gears, each large one engaging a small pinion on the axle of the next gear. The last and smallest pinion, near the top of the tube, is on an axle that passes transversely into the tube but to one side of its centre. On the end of this axle is a gear wheel that engages a vertical worm, which is in the long axis of the tube. The shaft of this worm has needle bearings above and below, and near the upper end a horizontal fan with 10 triangular blades. The spring power, transmitted through the gear train, makes the fan rotate very fast but with so little power that a slight misalignment of the axle will stop the whole mechanism.

There are a few differences in this actual motor and the drawings in Heath's patent. The patent motor has the spring and the gears on the same side of the tube, and there is a small handle extending out through the side of the stem, opposite the winding key, which acts as a stop, permitting the movement to be turned off when the lamp is not in use. This stop has not been observed on any of the Wanzer lamps studied by the writer.

172
Motor and fan mechanism from a
Wanzer lamp
from Mallorytown, Ont. LSR 279

The three Wanzer lamps in the Dundas Museum, although almost identical in appearance, bear different inscriptions on the shelf that supports the shade. The lamp catalogued as No. 1954–15 has the legend "THE WANZER LAMP C^O LIM^{TD} PHILADELPHIA PA. U.S.A. PAT.MCH. 22 1887." The second lamp, no. 64–62, is labelled "WANZER LAMP CO. NIAGARA FALLS U.S.A. PAT. Mch. 22 1887." The third lamp, with the heater attachment (figure 171; no catalogue number), is marked R. M. WANZER & C^O HAMILTON ONT. CANADA. THE WANZER LAMP PAT. 1888 – ." The year should read 1886 for the Canadian patent.

A Wanzer lamp in the National Museum of Canada (NMC A-1338) was purchased from Mr. L. Leclerc of Quebec City. It has the Philadelphia inscription on the shade holder. The main part of the base is cylindrical, corresponding to the shape shown in both the Canadian and American patents. This suggests that the National Museum lamp is older than those in the Dundas Museum. It came with the Ives 2-part chimney/shade, as shown in figure 173.

Wanzer lamps must have been operated in much the same way as some Hitchcock lamps. The first step, of course, would be to fill the font with kerosene. With motor wound and fan running, the wick is lit. A small but adequate current of air is drawn by the fan up through the motor tube and driven on up through the space between true font and outside shell. From here it passes into the space within the burner deflector, providing the additional draft needed to make a chimney unnecessary.

CHIMNEYS AND SHADES

CHIMNEYS The simple glass chimney, with straight lower section for the burner prongs, expanded middle, and tapering top, continued to be used widely to the end of the nineteenth century and beyond. But the trend towards elegance affected even chimneys, and many,

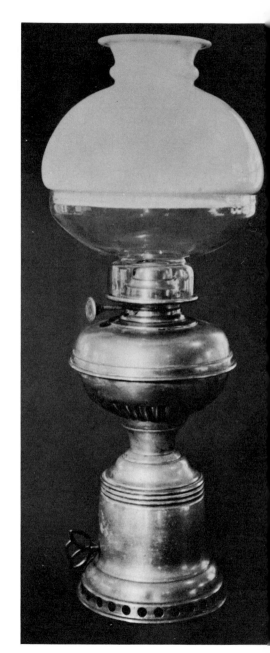

173
LEFT: *Wanzer lamp
with Ives chimney and shade
purchased in Quebec City, Que.*
NMC A-1338

174
*Chimney, "Empire Flint"
with "Sun Hinge"-type base and
"crimped" top, 1890s
purchased at Morristown,* N.Y. LSR 154

perhaps most, of those in the last fifteen years of the century had a restricted neck and a flaring upper rim, decorated by intricate scallops or beads. In addition to making the chimney prettier, these elaborations made it easier to handle, especially during cleaning. According to information supplied by the Corning Glass Museum, these types of chimneys appeared about 1885. An advertisement of a heater attachment for a kerosene lamp in the *Ontario Gazetteer and Directory for 1887* shows a chimney with a scalloped upper rim.

Trade catalogues of the time name the different chimney patterns. A scalloped upper rim was called a "crimped top." A ring of bead-like serrations produced a "pearl top." A simple flaring rim appears in one advertisement on a chimney called a "Quaker flint," presumably because it was plain. Just how universal these names were is not clear; they may have been used only by certain manufacturers.

Not uncommon was a combination of the expanded, ornamented upper rim with a flaring lower rim like those of chimneys used in the 1860s on Marcy and similar burners. Burners using a coronet and set-screw to secure the chimney (for example, the Plume & Atwood Sun Hinge) were made and used on into the twentieth century, and these anachronistic-looking chimneys were probably made for them. One such chimney (LSR 154; figure 174) obtained from Holly's Antiques, Morristown, N.Y., still has the maker's sticker attached. It reads simply "EMPIRE FLINT." An advertisement in the Corning Glass Museum library has "Empire" as one of the trade names for chimneys made by the MacBeath-Evans Glass Company of Pittsburgh.

Some chimneys of this period had even more peculiar shapes. That on the glass banquet lamp (LSR 107) shown in figure 150 has the expansion of the middle and the constriction of the neck exaggerated. The chimney seems short for such a tall lamp, but perhaps a regular chimney would have made the whole lamp much too high. The chimney on the wall lamp (LSR 128) of figure 160 is like three glass tubes

Lamp and Gas Fixtures.

PRICES SUBJECT TO CHANGE WITHOUT NOTICE.

Hall and Hanging Lamps.

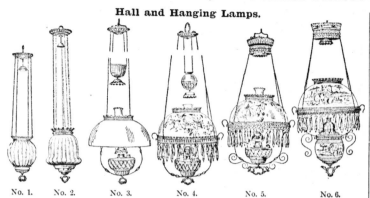

No. 1.　　No. 2.　　No. 3.　　　No. 4.　　　No. 5.　　　No. 6.

Above cut represents six of our very best lamps. They are made for service as well as ornament.

No. 1. Hall lamp, gilt lacquered chain and mountings, rose or ruby globe, $1.65.

No. 2. Hall lamp, larger size, gilt lacquered chain and mountings, rose or ruby, $2.50.

No. 3. Hanging lamp, glass fount, large-sized burner, 14-inch plain opal, dome-shaped shade, weight balance, brass mountings, $2.15; with decorated shade, $2.50.

No. 4. Hanging lamp, glass fount, brass mountings, weight balance, decorated shade, 30 prisms, $4.00.

No. 5. Hanging lamp, glass fount, with fine gilt lacquered frame, decorated and tinted shade, spring balance, $5.00.

No. 6. Hanging lamp, polished bronze metal, rich gold finish, improved spring extension, length closed 36 inches, extends to 72 inches, removable oil pot, handsome bisque-finished 14-inch dome, shade and fount to match, hand-decorated, centre draught burner, 75 candle-power, can be lighted without removing chimney, 30 crystal prisms, $6.50.

Hall Lamps.

With gilt lacquered chain and mountings, chimney and burner, complete, and very handsome globes, $2.00 each.

Fancy brass frames, large fancy globes, large burner and chimney, $3.50, 4.00, 4.50, 5.00 each.

Vase Lamps.

No. 1.　　No. 2.　　No. 3.

No. 1. Brass foot, large-sized burner, 7-inch dome shade, decorated to match fount, tinted pink, blue or yellow, complete with chimney and wick, $1.25 each.

No. 2. Brass foot, with 10-inch dome and bowl to match, large-sized burner, pretty decorations, complete with chimney and wick, $1.75 each.

No. 3. Brass foot, dome and bowl to match, removable fount, Climax burner, height 21 inches, beautiful decorations, a very handsome ornament as well as most serviceable article, special $2.25 each.

Also a fine assortment of vase lamps, in newest designs and decorations, from $5.00 to 12.00 ea.

All glass parlor lamp, opal, decorated globe and pedestal to match, brass fount removable, and brass foot, climax burner, $3.00 each.

Banquet Lamps.

No. 1　　　No. 2.

No. 1. Embossed brass, with open-work foot, guaranteed, centre draft burner, complete, with new device for lighting, $1.75, 2.00 each.

Banquet lamp, No. 2, cupid pedestal, fount not detachable, silver or gilt figure, ornamental foot, centre draft burner, complete with chimney, $2.50 each.

Embossed brass, with onyx or handsome brass pedestal and open-work foot, with movable fount, centre draft burner, most beautiful designs, $3.75, 4.50, 5.00 each.

Gold lacquered, full size, open-work, cast heads, fine imperial or onyx pedestals, with 75 candle-power burner, $6.00, 7.00, 8.00, 10.00, 15.00 each.

All banquet lamps are complete with 4-inch ring for shade or globe.

Lamp Globes.

This style of shade has driven silk shades entirely out of the market, and we have some very pretty decorations at prices ranging from $1.25 to 12.00 each.

Piano Lamps.

All gilt, onyx top, patent extension rod, with automatic fastener, removable fount, round plain legs, complete with chimney, $10.00 each.

Brass table, onyx top, removable fount, cast bowl and legs, $14.00, 15.00, 20.00 each.

Wrought iron piano lamps, extension rod, removable founts, circular burner, automatic stop, complete with chimney, special, $8.50, 10.00, 12.00 each.

No. 1.　　　　No. 2.

Glass bracket lamps, with large sized burner and chimney, 25c each; with self-filling cap, 30c each; with self-filling cap and handle, 35c each.

Lamp brackets for above, 10c, 15c, 25c.

Bracket lamps, complete, as cut No. 1, 65c each.

Glass bowl, decorated, colored glass pedestal, heavy iron foot, complete, with large burner, 85c each.

Glass Lamps.

No. 1.　No. 2.　No. 3.　No. 4.　No. 5.　No. 6.　No. 7.　No. 8.

No. 1. Complete, with A burner, chimney and wick, 18c each.

No. 2. Complete, with A burner, chimney and wick, 20c each.

No. 3. Complete, with A burner, chimney and wick, 25c each.

No. 4. Complete, with A burner, chimney and wick, 25c each.

No. 5. Complete, with B burner, chimney and wick, 30c each.

No. 6. Complete, with B burner, chimney and wick, 35c each.

No. 7. Complete, with B burner, chimney and wick, 40c each.

No. 8. Complete, with B burner, chimney and wick, 45c each.

of different diameter joined together. The lower part, for the prongs, is moderately wide. The middle part, near the flame, is wider but with straight sides. The upper part, also straight, is the narrowest.

Most chimneys of this period were free blown, the traditional method of fabrication, but the ornamented upper rim must have been shaped by reheating and pressing against an open mould. True mould-blown chimneys are also known. The handsome "waterfall" lamp (LSR 139) shown in figure 145 has a matching chimney, moulded in the same pattern. The upper rim has a beaded ring about $\frac{3}{16}$ of an inch below the top, an arrangement that would provide a shelf on which to rest the wire frame for a shade. Another mould-blown chimney with a pattern of vertical rows of beads is in the National Museum of Canada collection (NMC A-1527). It came with a lamp having a very different pattern, the whole being obtained from Mr. Roger Berger, St. Scholastique, Que.

The Ives combination chimney and shade (see p. 228), with its clear lower bowl and opaque conical shade, continued to be popular, not only for student lamps, but also on such diverse innovations as the angle lamp and the Wanzer lamp.

Coloured glass chimneys were used mainly on night lamps, where subdued light was desired. Most of these served as both chimney and shade. Examples are shown in the illustrations of night lamps.

SHADES   The principal innovation in shades during this period was the hand-painting of those used on vase and library lamps. Shades for vase lamps were either globular or hemispherical, but on library lamps the hemispherical was the rule. A few vase-lamp shades, such as those shown in figures 153 and 154, have pressed patterns, with or without painting. Elaborate pressed patterns appear on shades of library lamps, the commonest being a type called "hob-nail."

Some banquet lamps used globular shades with etched rather than

OPPOSITE: *T. Eaton Co. Limited catalogue Fall and Winter 1899–1900*

painted decoration, probably because such lamps were expected to provide good light. But the T. Eaton Company fall and winter catalogue for 1892–93 shows the "Como Banquet Lamp" with a conical shade of pleated linen. Such seemingly dangerous fabric shades were very popular, and the Eaton catalogues of 1893–94 offers them in stiff paper, conical or dome-shaped, and in pleated linen or Parisian silk. Frames for the do-it-yourself shade maker are also listed. The 1893–94 catalogue of the Haida Lamp and China Company of New York City shows four different shapes of such frames, the smallest being twelve inches in diameter. They were most common on piano lamps of the early 1890s, and the flouncy shades shown in pictures of floor lamps of that time would make an insurance underwriter squirm. Towards the end of the decade they seem to have been replaced by the painted-globe type of shade.

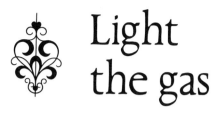

CHAPTER XI

Light the gas

ALL THROUGH THE kerosene era, and for almost half a century before it, gas had been used for lighting. Its development as a practical illuminant began about the same time as the introduction of the scientifically designed oil lamp. Natural gas of course had long been known in various parts of the world where it seeped up from underground, and it had played a part in religious ceremonies. In 1799, however, artificially manufactured gas was offered to the world for the first time as an illuminating fuel. From then on, with some vicissitudes, the organization of facilities for providing gas for lighting increased rapidly. By the middle of the nineteenth century most cities in Europe and North America lit their streets by gas, and many of their more prosperous homes as well.

The success of kerosene as a lamp fuel temporarily set gas back in domestic lighting, but the invention of the incandescent mantle in 1885 gave it new impetus. This popularity was short-lived. Electric lighting was coming in, and eventually proved more convenient and economical. However, there was a concurrent shift in the use of gas from lighting to heating, and with the widespread introduction of natural gas in place of the manufactured product, the industry today is a flourishing one.

INVENTION AND DEVELOPMENT

Assigning credit to the original inventor of gas lighting is a matter of deciding what is a gas light, a decision, unfortunately, that tends to be influenced a little by national pride. Nevertheless, d'Allemagne (pp. 551–60) has made a good case for awarding the distinction to Philippe Lebon, who was born in France on May 29, 1767. When Lebon was twenty-four years old he began work on a project to burn wood in a closed furnace and to collect the gas given off in a vessel over water. Thus he devised primitive forms of what were later called producers and gasometers. He obtained a patent[1] in 1799, which, like the Argand patent of 1784, marks an officially dated beginning for the development of a new form of lighting.

The Lebon patent emphasized the importance of his gas not only for lighting but also for heating, and referred to valuable by-products. He demonstrated its use in a single lamp ("thermolampe") and in the lighting of public buildings. He recognized the possibility of obtaining the gas from coal, but in his demonstrations he prepared it from wood. Then, in 1804, he was murdered on a Paris street. The project was carried on for a time by his widow, but it remained for others to devise more practical production and distribution of the gas, and to promote its public use.

The manufacture of illuminating gas from coal, and its distribution from a central reservoir to a number of outlets, was first achieved by William Murdoch, an engineer employed by James Watt, inventor of the steam engine. Murdoch's early experiments were carried out in 1782, while he was directing mining operations in Cornwall. Instead of a furnace he used a retort, the coal being brought to gas-producing temperature by a separate source of heat. In 1798 he installed gas lighting in a factory in London, and four years later gave his first public demonstration.

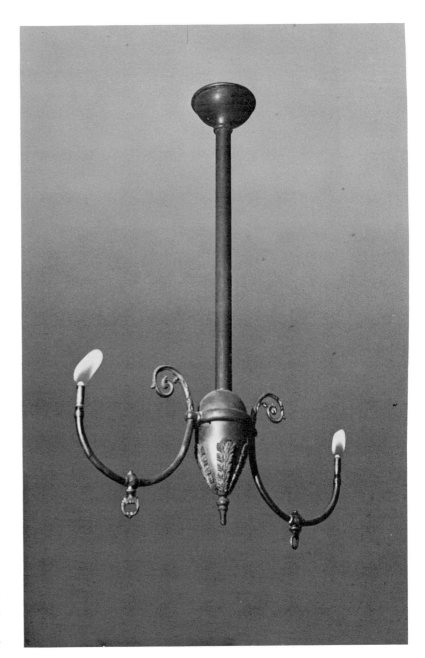

175
Double gas fixture in dining room of
William Lyon Mackenzie House
Toronto, Ont.
burners have steatite tips

289 LIGHT THE GAS

The great *entrepreneur* of gas illumination was Frederic Albert Winzer, a native of Moravia, who tried to introduce the Lebon process in various parts of Germany. In 1803 he came to London and learned of the work of Murdoch. It seemed so promising that he decided to stay in England, become a naturalized citizen, and anglicize his name to Winsor. He gave public demonstrations of the new method of lighting, took out a patent on the manufacture of gas, and persistently tried to organize a company that would produce and distribute gas for public use. After several set-backs he was finally succesful in 1810. Part of the credit must go to his chief engineer, Samuel Clegg, who had been associated in Murdoch's early installations. Clegg produced a number of devices to overcome the technical difficulties of gas distribution, and some that served merely to meet the exaggerated safety requirements of the authorities. These and other achievements were recorded by his son, Samuel Clegg, Jr. (pp. 1–11), in what is probably the first treatise on the illuminating gas industry.

With the success of gas in London, particularly for street lighting, its use spread quickly to other cities. Winsor tried to introduce it in Paris, but it was not until 1824 that the industry was established there by a French group with royal support. Credit for the first gas lighting in America is given to David Melville of Newport, R.I., who obtained a patent on the process in 1810.[2] The city of Baltimore was the site of the first American public gas works six years later. Gas companies were established in various Canadian cities in the 1840s, beginning with Montreal in 1840, followed by Toronto in 1841. Both companies were organized by Albert Furniss. The Consumers' Gas Company of Toronto was established in 1847.[3] The following June it advertised:[4]

NOTICE

PATTERN Books of Gas Fittings &c, lie for inspection at this Office. Individuals wishing a superior style of gas Lustre,

Pendent, Pillar or Bracket Light, for a private house, church, public hall, or place of business, by arranging with the Company's Secretary, may have an order for such transmitted along with the general order of the Company, which will be despatched in a few days.

Individuals may employ any competent tradesman to fit up their Gas pipes, &c, which must be examined and proved Gas-tight by the Company's Inspector, before the Gas can be turned on.

By Order of the Board

JOHN WATSON

Secretary

Consumers' Gas Co's Office
Toronto, June 15, 1848.

Saint John, N.B., had a public gas system in operation in 1845. Hamilton, Ont., got its gas company in 1850. By 1858 even far away St. John's Nfld., was using gas illumination. Before the kerosene lamp became widespread, illuminating gas was available in every city and most towns of Canada.

PRODUCTION OF ILLUMINATING GAS

For many years illuminating gas was manufactured by a process that was only a refinement of the Murdoch system. Retorts of brick or iron were charged with coal, and were then heated by an external fire to a temperature of between 1000° and 1800° Fahrenheit. Under these conditions the coal decomposed into a series of gaseous and liquid derivatives, leaving a solid residue of coke.[5] Principal constituents of the gas from the retort were hydrocarbons such as methane, ethylene, and acetylene, but there were also less desirable products – volatile liquids and tar, and the gases ammonia, hydrogen sulphide, and carbon dioxide. The raw gas was fed through a condenser to remove the liquid substance, then through an apparatus called a scrubber where water spray or steam absorbed the ammonia. The hydrogen sulphide was removed by passing the gas through ferrous oxide, and the carbon dioxide by contact with moist lime (calcium hydroxide). The purified gas was stored in a gasholder or "gasometer," which consisted of a huge cylindrical vessel held inverted in water by a giant framework. The gas bubbled up through the water and was trapped in the inverted container, which rose as the gas content increased. As long as the rim of the container remained below water the gas would be safely stored. These structures were familiar features of the urban landscape, and marked the less desirable residential area as the "gas-house" district.

Almost all the substances extracted from the gas during purification had value. The seemingly endless series of chemical products from coal tar became the basis of great nineteenth-century chemical industries. The ammonia and the sulphur were employed in other ways. Even the coke was in demand for blast furnaces. But the installation and operation of a coal-gas plant were major undertakings. There was a demand as well for gas in moderate amounts, either for small communities or for factories, and also as a supplement to coal gas in periods of peak demand. This requirement was met about the middle of the century by a revival of the Lebon process. A furnace of iron or brick called the producer was charged with coal or other carbonaceous matter, which was ignited and allowed to burn in a reduced supply of oxygen. The "producer gas" that resulted consisted mainly of carbon monoxide and gaseous hydrocarbons, with the residual nitrogen of the air.

Gas was also manufactured from oil for small-scale use and for enrichment of coal gas. The technique had been tried early in the century with oils of animal or vegetable origin, but was not eco-

Eight-burner "gasselier" in living room
William Lyon Mackenzie House, Toronto

nomical. In the 1870s petroleum, or its derivatives, was used, the oil being heated in a suitable retort. The process had some applications, but the gas was too rich for ordinary uses. More important was the development of water gas by T. S. C. Lowe of Norristown, Pa., starting with patents in 1872.[6] In his process, superheated steam was introduced into the producer during combustion of coal, coke, or petroleum. In addition to the components of producer gas, water gas contained a large proportion of hydrogen, which added greatly to its efficiency as a fuel. Water gas came into widespread use in the United States, but in Canada it was mostly a supplement to coal gas. One objection to its use, shared with producer gas, was the insidiously poisonous nature of the carbon monoxide it contained.

GAS FITTINGS AND BURNERS

A BASIC TYPE of gas light for home use was established early and continued with little change until after 1885. It consisted simply of a nozzle with an adjustable stopcock, which connected through a pipe with the gas distributing system. Probably the finest existing examples of mid-nineteenth-century gas fixtures in Canada are in the William Lyon Mackenzie House in Toronto, the one-time dwelling of the fiery political reformer which has been refurnished in the style of his time. The fittings, all functioning, were restored and installed by the Consumers' Gas Company for the Toronto Historical Board. The simplest are in the downstairs kitchen and dining room (figure 175); they are shaped each like an inverted letter "T," the vertical arm being attached to the ceiling, and the horizontal arms terminating in stopcock and jet. Somewhat more elaborate fixtures in the upstairs bedrooms have glass shades. The front parlour on the main floor has an elaborate "gasselier," with eight burners on ornate metal pipes, and decorated glass shades (figure 176). The burners of these ornate fixtures have to be turned on and off with a special device called a gas lighter. This consists of two long, parallel metal tubes on a wooden handle. One tube ends in a kind of wrench that serves to turn the stopcock, the other carries a length of wax taper, by means of which flame can be transmitted to the gas. The main-floor hall has a hanging light (figure 177) that closely resembles the kerosene-burning hall lamp, and may have been copied from it, or vice versa.

By the 1880s the common gas fixture was a wall bracket, which in its simplest form was just a brass pipe projecting from the wall, with a stopcock at the wall end and a jet at the other. There was usually a simple ornamentation of pattern and finials. More elaborate versions had a joint at the wall, so that the pipe could be swivelled horizontally, or even two joints, as in the example shown in figure 178 (LSR 21). It was purchased in West Virginia, but except for the burner is similar to fixtures shown in the catalogue of the James Morrison Brass Manufacturing Company Ltd. of Toronto in 1896.

In gas fixtures of the type described above, there is a threaded end, on to which is screwed the burner proper, a tubular device with an opening for the gas jet at the top.[7] The first burners had a simple round hole, but about 1810 the "batwing" burner was introduced. It had a dome-shaped top with a slit-like opening. The burning gas issuing from the slit assumed a wide, thin, fan shape, with a fancied resemblance to a bat's wing, and so increased the area of luminosity. About 1820 a different way of obtaining a flat flame was devised. This involved a burner that was flat or slightly concave on top, with two fine tubular openings pointed obtusely towards each other. Gas jets from the two orifices impinged and mutually spread the flame into a shape higher and narrower than the earlier "batwing." These burners were called "fish-tail" or "union jet."

177
Gas hall light at
William Lyon Mackenzie House, Toronto

From this stage on, the changes in gas burners were matters of refinement. Since the metal tip dissipated heat and so decreased luminosity, tips of steatite, a kind of soapstone, were introduced. To keep the gas flow uniform, and at optimum pressure, various devices were installed within the burner. One of these consisted of a washer with a narrow opening, through which the gas emerged into a much larger chamber above. Another had a filter of muslin, through which the gas had to pass to the main chamber of the burner. The best known of these regulated burners were the Bray Burners, a few of which are shown in the Morrison catalogue already mentioned. This firm was established in Toronto in 1894 and continued into the twentieth century.

Gas burners using the centre-draft principle, and actually called Argand burners, were introduced very early and were revived from time to time, but until the appearance of the incandescent mantle they were not as luminous as the flat-flame burners.

178
Double-jointed gas bracket with shade
ca. 1895; purchased in Martinsburg,
W. Va. LSR 21

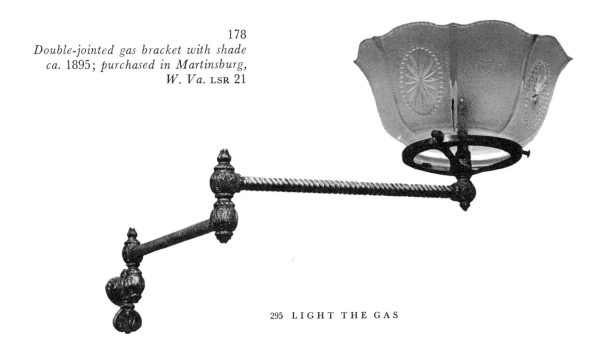

Portability was one of the principal advantages the kerosene lamp had over the gas light. Efforts to meet this competition produced gas lamps connected to the outlet by flexible rubber hose. The example shown in figure 179 (NMC D-1240) is reminiscent of the figure-stem lamps of the 1880s. Even more curious is the gas light shown in figure 180 (NMC H-45). It is from West Winfield, N.Y., but no doubt similar lamps were used in Canada. The base of iron and brass, the long stem, and the globular shade all suggest a kerosene lamp, as does the burner with its flame spreader. Most extraordinary is the globular "font" of ruby glass, which serves only as decoration and as a reminder of the familiar kerosene lamp. It recalls the famous anachronism of the buggy-whip socket on the dash-board of the early automobiles.

THE WELSBACH MANTLE

Prior to 1885 the luminosity of the gas flame was due mainly to the presence of incandescent, unburned particles of carbon, most of which came from the ethylene and acetylene. The use of such a flame for heating would result in some deposition of soot on the object to be heated.

In 1855 R. W. von Bunsen, Professor of Chemistry at Heidelberg, devised a gas burner in which a jet of gas was mixed with a controlled current of air before being burned. With proper adjustment the resultant flame is pale blue, almost invisible, and sootless. Commemorated in the Bunsen burner of the chemistry laboratory, his invention also made possible the gas stove and fireplace.

The adaptation of the almost colourless Bunsen flame to lighting was the work of one of his students, Karl Auer von Welsbach, an Austrian mentioned in chapter 2 as the inventor of the sparking "Auer Metal." Welsbach was a student of the "rare-earth" metals,

179
Figure-stem portable gas lamp, 1880s
Ontario. NMC D-1240

180
RIGHT: *Portable gas table lamp with burner for incandescent mantle* ca. 1895; *purchased at West Winfield,* N.Y.
NMC H-45

and made many important scientific discoveries concerning them. He also produced three valuable inventions in the field of lighting based on his chemical findings. The first was the incandescent or Welsbach gas mantle. This consisted of a cotton fabric hood impregnated with the oxides of thorium and cerium. When it was appropriately mounted over a Bunsen-type gas burner, and the fabric burned away, it could be heated by the gas flame to incandescence, producing an intense white light.

This sensational innovation seems to have spread rather slowly in Canada. It was still being treated as a novelty in some cities as late as 1895, as shown by the following advertisement.[8]

STOREKEEPERS

Why Not Use the Cheapest and Most Powerful Light?

THE AUER LIGHT — 50 Candle Power

Incandescent Burner consumes only 3 feet of gas per hour.

25,000 now in use in Montreal

Call and see Messrs. R. S. Williams & Son's New Store Bank

Street considered the best and cheapest lighted shop in the

city.

Apply to Ottawa Gas Company for all particulars.

A mantle of the type that may have been used on such a light is shown in figure 181 (LSR 175). This example was purchased from Mr. Stan Ashbury of Preston, Ont. It came in its original box, a cardboard tube bearing a label that reads " 'The Best' / LIGHT / ONE / NUMBER 1 / MANTLE / STRONG DURABLE AND / WILL NOT SHRINK. / The Best Light Co. / OFFICES WORKS & FOUNDARY / 776–800 EAST 5TH STREET / CANTON OHIO U.S.A.!" The mantle stands about 3¾ inches high, and is 1¼ inches in greatest diameter at the bottom. Its golden yellow colour may be the product of age; modern mantles are white.

The flame to activate the Welsbach mantle must be cylindrical rather than spreading, and so the burners for it were flat on top, with a number of circular perforations. Farther down the burner tube are the air-intake openings and characteristic Bunsen jet.

The pre-Welsbach gas burners with their spreading flame had to have a wide, usually globular shade. In the burner with a Welsbach mantle there was little flame, and the source of light was high and narrow. This permitted the use of a narrow glass chimney, which accentuated the draft and hence the combustion. An example of one of these chimneys (LSR 174; figure 182) also came from Mr. Ashbury. The height is eight inches and the diameter is just under two inches. The lower 1½ inches of outer surface is etched. Near the upper rim is an etched legend in small letters: "THE 'BEST' LIGHT / BEST LEAD GLASS."

181
"The Best" incandescent gas mantle ca. 1895; purchased in Preston, Ont. LSR 175. ROM *photo*

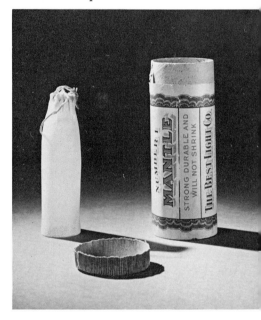

NATURAL GAS

Gas occurs in nature under geological conditions similar to those of petroleum, and the two are often associated. The principal component of most natural gas is methane, the basic hydrocarbon, but with this may be various proportions of other gaseous and light liquid hydrocarbons, hydrogen, carbon dioxide, nitrogen, and even helium. The last three minor constituents are non-combustible

Though natural gas had been known from antiquity; commercial production did not begin until 1875, in western Pennsylvania. In 1888 Eugene Coste of Toronto obtained gas from a well drilled in Essex County, southwestern Ontario. This led to the development of a commercial gas field, from which gas was exported to Detroit in the 1890s. In 1889 a second Canadian field was located in Welland County, at the southeastern corner of the Niagara peninsula, which for a time supplied gas to Buffalo, N.Y. Early in the twentieth century these fields began to decline, but their place was taken by other areas of production, and natural gas remained an important fuel for home and industry in southern Ontario.[9]

The great gas fields of western Canada were not discovered until after the Second World War, but production there began in 1901 at Medicine Hat, Alta. This led to the development of ceramic and glass industries, as well as the provision of gas for municipal and domestic use.

The equipment for burning natural gas for lighting or heating is the same as that used for artificial gas, the only alteration necessary being in the parts that control the proportions of air to gas. The biggest change is the elimination of the large and expensive retorts and gasometers. Another important difference is that artificial gas usually has oily constituents, which help to seal imperfect connections, whereas natural gas is dry or is made so by condensation of liquid constituents. As a result, the natural product requires completely gas-tight lines and connections.

ACETYLENE LIGHTING

Acetylene is a hydrocarbon gas analogous to methane but with the formula C_2H_2. It was discovered in 1836 by Edmond Davy of Dublin, who noted its combustible and explosive nature. The present name for it was given by P. E. M. Berthelot of Paris in 1860. In 1862 Friedrich Wöhler of Göttingen made calcium carbide and found that it reacted with water to produce acetylene.[10] It remained for a Canadian to make this process a practical source of the gas as an illuminant.

Thomas Leopold Willson was a self-taught electrical engineer, whose inventions laid the foundations of the great North American

182
Chimney for incandescent-mantle gas burner
ca. 1895; *purchased in Preston, Ont.*
LSR 174. ROM *photo*

electrochemical industry. He was born at Princeton, a village between Woodstock and Paris, Ont., in 1860. While still a student at the Hamilton Collegiate, he became interested in the electric arc as a means of promoting chemical processes. Failing to find an opportunity to pursue his investigations in Canada, he went to New York City and engaged in various experimental and business activities. In 1894 he was in Spray, N.C., conducting metallurgical experiments with the electric arc. In an effort to prepare metallic calcium by fusing lime with coal tar, he discovered a cheap new process of manufacturing calcium carbide. Wöhler's method of making acetylene was now available on a commercial scale.

Willson's discovery led to a major production of "carbide" in the United States and Canada. Acetylene generated either in the lamp or in a central apparatus became a popular illuminant for automobile and bicycle lamps, miner's lamps, and navigation buoys. It was not successful as a domestic lamp fuel, because of the messy and corrosive nature of calcium carbide and the unpleasant odour of acetylene. But it did have a passing popularity in the late 1890s for lighting public buildings, such as hotels and theatres, where numerous lamps could be supplied from a common generator. The flame was brilliant white, but required careful adjustment of the air supply.

In addition to its use as an illuminant, acetylene was soon found to have important industrial applications, as in welding. Also, calcium carbide was found to be the basic reagent for the manufacture of artificial nitrogen fertilizers. Willson became wealthy and for a time the head of a large hydroelectric syndicate. He spent his later years in Ottawa, where he continued his experiments and his industrial promotions until his death on December 20, 1915, in New York City.[11]

Acetylene bicycle lamps and miner's lamps are still readily available, although long since replaced by electrical substitutes. They have a double reservoir, the lower chamber for the calcium carbide, the upper for water. A controlled drip from the upper chamber starts the generation of acetylene, which passes to a jet where it can be ignited, usually by rotating a toothed steel wheel against a piece of sparking metal. Acetylene household lamps were also made and should be sought.

VAPOUR LAMPS

The more volatile lamp fuels, such as burning fluid and gasoline, could be vaporised in suitable lamps and burned like a gas. Such an arrangement did away with the normal wick and reduced the danger of transmitting flame to the font. These lamps were in effect miniature gas generators, using a volatile liquid instead of a solid as the source of gas, and operating at a moderate heat.

Apparently the first vapour lamp was that patented by Isaiah Jennings, the inventor of burning fluid.[12] His lamp had a tall wick tube, which was closed at the top except for one small opening. Other small perforations were drilled in the wick tube near its base. Burning fluid brought up the wick by capillarity would generate fumes, which would come through the perforations and could be lit. The wick tube would then become a generator, and a flame of useful size would issue from the top.

A similar idea appeared in the vapour lamp patented by S. W. Lowe of Philadelphia, Pa., in 1860.[13] Whether or not this ever went into production, it is typical of the vapour lamps using burning fluid. The patent model in the U.S. National Museum (USNM 331114; figure 183) is made of Britannia metal. From the egg-shaped font a large wick tube rises, closed at the top by a dome-shaped cap with a row of small perforations across it. In operation this tube was stuffed with a loosely twisted wick, which splayed out into a wire bag con-

183
Low vapour lamp, for burning fluid patent model, 1860
USNM 331114

184
Vapour lamp for burning fluid
purchased in Hudson Heights, Que.
LSR 411. ROM *photo*

taining raw cotton. Burning fluid was introduced through a stoppered opening in the base, saturating the cotton and the wick, and omitting vapour through the perforations. There it could be ignited to produce a fan-shaped flame.

A vapour lamp of this sort but with a different shape of burner was purchased from Mr. Jacques Rivard of Hudson Heights, Que. (LSR 411; figure 184). It was obtained by him in Ottawa.

The body is that of a typical "Sandwich" all-glass burning fluid lamp. The base is a hollow square, merging into the conoid, 8-sided stem. The font is cylindroid, with a ring of 8 ovoid facets around the upper and lower part. The top is low and conoid and evidently free-formed. The burner is of brass and is relatively heavy. The base plate, which screws into the collar of the font, is similar to that of burning-fluid burners, but there is only one wick tube, $1\frac{13}{16}$ inches high and $\frac{3}{8}$ inch in diameter. Screwed over the upper end is a cap consisting of a lower projecting ring, a short tubular middle portion, and a wide, flat top. The tubular middle part is perforated by 6 small holes. The wick, which is original, consists of a number of cotton strings loosely twisted together and threaded through the loop end of a wire that projects down from the wick tube. The strings are folded up on each side and the loose ends inserted in the wick tube, presumably to the top. Height of the lamp with burner is $12\frac{1}{4}$ inches. The operation would have been similar to that of the Jennings and Lowe lamps but the flame would have been crown-shaped, made up of 6 small jets directed radially.

After 1860 the refining of petroleum made available a new fuel for vapour lamps, the pre-kerosene fraction of the distillate. Known at first as light hydrocarbon or volatile hydrocarbon, it was being made and used by 1872 as gasoline.[14] Most vapour lamps of this period used a burner very similar to that of the lamp from Hudson; an example (NMC D-634; figure 185) was obtained from Mr. T. G. Wright-meyer, then of Belleville, Ont. The body is that of a composite lamp of the early 1860s, although the milk-glass font is unusual. The wick tube is relatively higher and narrower than in the Hudson lamp, and the cap has two simple flanges. There are six perforations between the flanges. That this lamp worked on gasoline rather than burning fluid is suggested by the post-1860 lamp body and by the fact that similar burners were described for use with the hydrocarbon fuel.

A modification of such a burner was patented by T. S. Doane of New York, N.Y.[15] It had the double-flange cap, but the true wick tube was enclosed in a similar but slightly larger tube, like a sleeve. The ends of the tubes were designed so that rotation of the sleeve tube on the wick tube opened and closed the perforations in the cap.

Various vapour lamps were developed in which the tube from font to burner passed near the flame so as to vaporize the fuel, or in which the fuel, under pressure, was sprayed into a hot generator, but these date from the twentieth century.

185
*Vapour lamp for gasoline or naphtha,
ca. 1870; purchased in Belleville, Ont.*
NMC D-634

CHAPTER XII

Thank you, Mr. Edison

LIGHTING BY ELECTRICITY began when Sir Humphrey Davy discovered in 1808 that an electric current could be made to cross a gap between two carbon points, and in so doing create an intense white light. The luminous path of the current was curved, hence the name "electric arc." From Davy's initial experiment the arc light developed. The composition of the carbon electrodes was improved, and electromechanical devices were designed to maintain the proper gap as the carbon was consumed. But for many years the only – though inefficient – source of the electric current was the chemical cell or battery. In 1831 Faraday showed that an electric current could be produced by motion of a conductor in a magnetic field, a discovery that led eventually to the development of the electric generator or dynamo. By 1857 such devices were powerful enough to supply the current for practical arc lights, which were installed first in lighthouses, and later in public buildings.[1]

The electric arc was impractical for home use because of the intensity of its light. Hence inventors became very interested in the problem of "subdividing" the electric light. The solution was found in the use of an incandescent conductor.

Credit for the first incandescent electric light is commonly given to

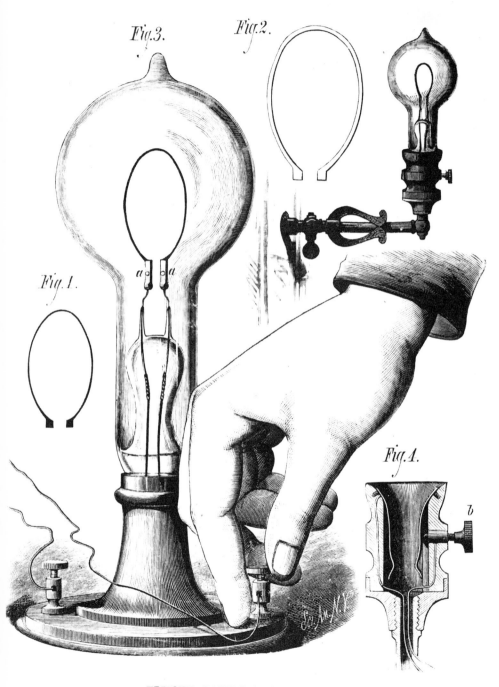

Fig.3.

Fig.2.

Fig.1.

Fig.4.

EDISON'S LATEST ELECTRIC LAMP.

Edison's first carbon-filament electric light
From The Scientific American, *January 10, 1880*
(Toronto Public Library)

Thomas Alva Edison, the famous American inventor, but this honour must be awarded with reservation. The circumstances of the invention, from the American viewpoint, were summarized by Pope. Early experiments in the United States, England, and Canada[2] involved wires of platinum or iridium, sealed in a glass vessel from which the air was exhausted; even Edison was trying to perfect this approach as late as 1879.[3] Meanwhile, however, Joseph Swan in England, and William Edward Sawyer and Albon Mann in the United States had produced working electric lights by using a conductor or filament of carbonized paper. Carbon, having a much higher resistance to electric current than metals, can be brought to incandescence with less electric power. In 1879 Edison finally abandoned the metallic filament in favour of carbonized paper,[4] and on January 1, 1880, was able to offer a public demonstration of electric lighting at his laboratory in Menlo Park, N.J. Practical electric lighting may be considered to date from that occasion. The event caught the imagination of the public, who had been going through a period of anticipation and disappointment. So sensational were the reports that a drastic, if temporary, decline in the value of gas company shares occurred in both the United States and England.

It is of interest that Edison obtained a Canadian patent[5] for his carbon-filament light two months before his American patent[6] was granted. Accordingly, five years later when the Canadian patent expired, under the then existing U.S. patent regulations his American right automatically lapsed, whereas they might otherwise have gone on for another two years.

The credit for making the first successful incandescent carbon filament must go to Swan in England and Sawyer and Mann in America. Edison's version may have been a little simpler and easier to make, but it was his appreciation of practical aspects and the value of publicity, aided by the powerful financial interest behind him, that made his version the basis of the electric-light industry. The speed at which he worked is also noteworthy. It was only in September 1879 that he finally abandoned hope of perfecting the metallic filament, and by November of that year he had a carbon-filament light working satisfactorily. For these reasons we can acknowledge Edison as the inventor, if not the discoverer, of the practical electric light.

THE DISTRIBUTION OF ELECTRICITY

In spite of, or perhaps because of, Edison's appreciation of the practical application of his inventions, he had a blind spot to the value of some contributions by other people. Many years later he made disparaging remarks about the future of radio broadcasting, then just starting as a medium of entertainment. Probably he feared competition for the phonograph. In the 1880s, as the demand for electricity mushroomed, Edison strongly advocated the transmission of the power in the form of direct, rather than alternating, current.

At the risk of discussing what is generally well known, it might be in order to consider the nature of direct and alternating current, and the effects that result from transmission over distance. The early experiments on current electricity almost all depended on the output of the chemical cell. As this was a steady, one-way flaw, most electrical developments were designed to use this so-called direct current. Faraday's discovery of the electromechanical generator, however, made alternating current available. If we consider a simple generator, consisting of a coil of wire rotating in a steady magnetic field, we find that electricity will flow through the coil and its output circuit in a peculiar manner. As the coil goes through one complete rotation the electric pressure and the flow of current build up from zero to a maximum, fall off to zero, rise to a second, opposite maximum, and again fall off to zero. The rapidity or "frequency" of the alteration will depend on the speed at which the coil is rotated.

Alternating current is the normal output of the rotating generator. To make a generator produce direct current it is necessary to add a kind of rotary switch called a commutator, which reverses the direction of current flow in the second half of the cycle. Even then we have pulsating direct current, unlike the steady current of the chemical cell.

Direct current is entirely satisfactory for local applications, where the generator and the device that it supplies with current are close together. But voltage loss due to resistance in the transmission wires is proportional to wire length, and if it were desired to have a central generator supply a number of widely spaced devices, the drop in voltage could be serious. Electric lights, for example, would be dimmer the farther away they were from the power source. No amount of ingenuity could overcome this fundamental limitation.

Alternating current, because of its constantly changing nature, can be passed from one circuit to another by electromagnetic induction. In the device known as the transformer, the input current flows through a coil of wire called the primary, wound on an iron core. A secondary coil on the same core will receive an induced current, and the relationship of the pressure or voltage of the primary and secondary currents will be the same as the ratio of the number of turns of wire on the two coils. So losses in voltage due to line resistance can be corrected by means of an appropriate transformer at the far end. Furthermore, if the current is sent through the wire at voltages higher than that needed at the end, the loss through resistance is smaller proportionally to this voltage, a proportion that is retained when the voltage is changed to the lower, usable value in the transformer.

Although these advantages were strongly urged by George Westinghouse in the 1880s, the Edison interests put up a bitter fight against the use of alternating current. A pamphlet[7] put out by them in 1887 or 1888 gives, among other dire warnings, a grim picture of the disasters that would result from the use of high-voltage alternating current. It is true that many people have lost their lives over the years by coming in contact with high-voltage transmission lines, but the voltage used in urban distribution, 220 volts, is not excessively dangerous, and is in fact the normal household voltage in many parts of Europe.

The most effective attempt to overcome the disadvantages of direct-current distribution was the development by Edison of the ingenious "three-wire system." This involved two direct-current generators, each at 110 volts. The positive output of one generator was joined to the negative output of the other, and from this common lead the middle or "neutral" wire of the circuit was taken off. The two outside terminals, with a combined potential difference between them of 220 volts, were connected to the other two wires of the distribution system. If about the same number of lamps were on each side of the circuit, the amount of current in the common "neutral" wire would be small, and the system would enjoy the advantages of the higher voltage in overcoming line resistance.

The doom of direct-current distribution resulted from the development of water power as a means of generating electricity on a large scale. Sites where such power might be developed – Niagara Falls, for example – were seldom close to cities where there was a large demand for such power. The long-distance transmission that was required was only practical if alternating current were used. In 1896 power was sent from Niagara Falls, N.Y., to Buffalo in sufficient amount to meet the domestic, municipal, and industrial needs of that city. This demonstration of the possibility of long-distance transmission of electric power tipped the balance of opinion in favour of alternating current. It also had much to do with starting the movement that led to the establishment of the Ontario Hydro Electric Power Commission in 1905.[8]

ELECTRIC LIGHTING COMES TO CANADA

The first electric lights in Canada are said to have been individual arcs installed in Montreal in 1878 and 1879. Most other early installations were for street lighting by electric arc. But in 1880 Edison installed incandescent electric lighting in a factory in Montreal, and the demand for the new form began to grow during the next decade. It was obvious from the start that the flameless electric bulb would be ideal in industries which involved flammable material. In homes too, as well as factories, the incandescent bulb met the demand for brighter, more convenient lighting. Small to medium electric generators were built, operated by steam engines or water wheels. An advertisement of 1888 lists thirteen Ontario communities that had installed generators built by the Ball Electric Co. Ltd. of Toronto, and it may be assumed that there were many others provided by rival manufacturers.[9] By the end of the decade the incandescent light was available for home use in most of the settled parts of Canada.

Expansion and consolidation continued in the 1890s. New requirements for electric power developed. It was soon as important for operating machinery as for lighting. A network of suburban electric railways sprang up and became the principal means of short-distance transportation, and in some cities the electric railway company also provided the electricity for domestic lighting. Most of the large generating plants set up at this time used steam engines fuelled by coal. In central Canada the coal had to be transported long distances. Costs were accordingly high, and supply uncertain. Meanwhile, hydroelectric power was being developed in the United States. In Canada a demand arose for a government-operated utility, or at least for close government control. How these demands were met is part of the twentieth-century record.

ELECTRIC LIGHTS FOR DOMESTIC USE

Apparently all examples of the original Edison electric lights of early 1880 have been lost. Even the U.S. National Museum in Washington and the Edison Museum at Menlo Park, N.J., have only replicas. But shortly before the famous public demonstration Edison gave a preview to a reporter from the *Scientific American*, and ten days after the demonstration that journal published a full description with illustrations of the new light.[10] These illustrations are reproduced page 306.

It will be seen that the filament was contained in a glass vessel shaped like an inverted Florence flask ("Fig. 3"). In the neck of the vessel was a glass pedestal, through which two platinum wires extended. Edison used platinum because it expands and contracts at about the same rate as glass with changes of temperature. The ends of the carbon filament were attached to the two wires by means of tiny platinum clamps. The glass bulb was exhausted of air by means of a mercury pump, the last vestiges being removed while electric current flowed in the filament. The tip on the bulb marked the point where the exhaust tube was sealed off. The two platinum wires were connected to copper wires which projected from the open end and were folded back and held by tape. The socket for the light contained two copper strips ("Fig. 4"). When the lamp base was inserted in the socket, these two strips touched the two copper wires. The lamp was secured and the light turned on by tightening the thumb screw "b," and so completing the circuit.

186
*Carbon-filament electric light
with Edison base,* 1890
Ontario Hydro Museum no. 447

187
*Carbon-filament electric light
with Thompson-Houston base,* 1885-90
Ontario Hydro Museum no. 449

188
TOP: *Carbon-filament electric light with Westinghouse base,* 1900
Ontario Hydro Museum no. 376

189
Carbon-filament electric light with Ediswan base, 1900
Ontario Hydro Museum no. 352

The filament was prepared from a horseshoe-shaped piece of Bristol board ("Fig. 2"), a kind of cardboard, and carbonized by roasting in an oven. The resultant loop of carbon ("Fig. 1") was surprisingly tough. In the drawing the lamp is shown inserted in a table socket ("Fig. 3"), and also in a converted gas wall bracket. In the famous outdoor demonstration of January 1, 1880, the lights were mounted on poles.[11]

Before the end of 1880, when people were finding this crude method of inserting the lamp in the socket awkward for replacing bulbs, Edison produced a new design. The base of the glass was cemented into a spool-shaped piece of wood, around which was placed a copper shell with a spiral thread. The shell could be screwed into a correspondingly threaded socket, thus making one of the electric connections while securing the lamp. The other was made by a metal stud projecting from the bottom of the "spool" and touching a plate at the bottom of the socket. By 1881 this improvement had been modified into the familiar Edison screw base (figure 186), which has been changed very little since.

In 1883, competition began from other manufacturers of incandescent electric lights. Each had its own type of lamp base.[12] The Thompson-Houston base (figure 187) was the reverse of the Edison; the outer shell had no thread, but the central terminal, instead of being a projecting stud, was a recessed brass tube, threaded on the inside, which screwed onto a bolt-like pin projecting from the bottom of the socket. The Westinghouse base (figure 188) was not screwed into the socket, but simply pushed in. It was held in place by the springy sides of the socket. The second contact was a pin on the base which fitted a hole in the bottom of the socket. A bayonet type of base, like those still used on automobile lights, characterized the Ediswan lamps made in England, some of which were sold in North America (figure 189). Around the turn of the century there was a general swing towards the Edison base but meanwhile adapters had been produced to make bases and sockets interchangeable (figure 190).

Paper filaments burned out far too quickly. Edison directed an intensive search for a material that would make a stronger, longer-lasting filament. His final choice was carbonized bamboo fibre. This was more flexible than paper and filaments with two or more loops were introduced; because they were longer they gave more light. Meanwhile other inventors, dissatisfied with any form of carbon, were returning to metallic filaments. One of the first to succeed was Auer von Welbach, who made a filament of osmium in 1897. Fine wires of tantalum were also tried. But all other forms, including carbon, were displaced when the tungsten filament became available after 1908.

The flask-shaped bulb gave way in the late 1880s to a conoid shape with the base at the narrow end and the wide end rounded. As long as the filament was arranged in an elongated pattern this remained the standard shape of bulb. Tightly coiled filaments, introduced in the 1920s, led to a return to the flask-shaped or more globular bulb.

The manufacture of incandescent elctric lamps began in Canada early in the twentieth century in Hamilton and St. Catharines, Ont. Up until then all electric lamps were imported, most of them being the Edison type.

The early incandescent lights sat on a table or hung from the ceiling. But electric lighting was introduced at a time when kerosene lamps were becoming very ornate. By the 1890s the simple hanging light could be replaced with an elaborate "electrolier." Ornate bracket lights took the place of the kerosene wall lamps. The portability of the kerosene lamp was approached by using well-insulated flexible wires, making it possible to have electric table lights and floor lights, much the same in form as the lamps they were supplanting. Just as solar lamps were converted to use kerosene, so kerosene lamps were made into electric lights, and by the end of the century parts were available to make this conversion simple. Today the interest in "antiques" has led to a widespread conversion of old kerosene lamps to electricity, but in the 1890 it was utility, rather than ornamentation, that inspired such change.

In twenty years Canada, like the rest of the civilized world, moved from the age of fuel lamps to the age of electricity. For the first time man had a source of artificial light that did not require combustion. The Argand lamp had displaced the grease lamp, kerosene had made the burning-fluid and whale-oil lamps obsolete, and now the electric light promised to sweep away all forms of flame light, and to make it possible for artificial lighting to be built into the home, along with the windows and the plumbing.

190
Carbon-filament electric light
with Edison base, and adaptor
for Thompson-Houston socket, ca. 1900
Ontario Hydro Museum

Epilogue

THE SUPREMACY of electric lighting that could be foreseen in the 1890s became real in the twentieth century. Yet the conquest was not immediate. Kerosene fought a rear-guard action with the Aladdin lamp, in which the Welsbach mantle was combined with an Argand-type burner. The Coleman lamps burned vaporized kerosene or gasoline, and using a Welsbach mantle, gave a brilliant light. In the more remote parts of Canada the ordinary "coal-oil" lamp held out. The prairie farmer was in the kerosene age until the 1920s. First to breach his isolation was the Delco Light plant, which used a 32-volt generator driven by a gasoline engine. But it was not until cheap hydro or steam power made possible the distribution of electricity to the farms as well as the cities that the kerosene lamp finally went up into the attic.

Finally? Not quite. Canadians today have become conscious of their interesting past, and like to have in their homes some link with it. Often this is a kerosene lamp, inherited from grandmother or bought at an antique show. The old burner may be gone to make way for an electric-light socket, or the lamp may still be intact. Even modern versions of the kerosene lamp can be bought, with coloured glass fonts and chimneys and even coloured kerosene. If you have a kerosene lamp, fetch it out and make it ready. Then some stormy night when the power fails, light it and look into the golden flame. If your mind's eye is keen you will see some interesting pictures. There is poor, cheated Ami Argand, fitting a glass tube over his circular flame and making the first lamp chimney. The man with the German accent, pleading his case before a committee of the House of Lords, is Frederic Albert Winsor, trying to get support for his scheme for lighting the streets of London by gas. The man in the frock-coat, watching an iron retort on a stove, is Dr. Abraham Gesner of Nova Scotia, distilling coal to make the first kerosene. Peering down a hole on a muddy Ontario plain is a dignified gentleman with magnificent mutton-chop whiskers; he is James Miller Williams of Hamilton, Ont., supervising the digging of the world's first oil well. A trim-bearded man with a stand-up collar and a workman's apron is tinkering with a brass object; he is Lewis John Atwood in his Water-bury, Conn., workshop, making his famous burner. Another bearded man from Hamilton, Richard Mott Wanzer, is winding the motor of a larger, clumsy lamp, which will then burn brightly without a chimney.

Suddenly the lights come on again, but at the instant you may see a group of reporters and visitors in a cold New Jersey courtyard, marvelling at a Christmas-like display of glowing electric lights, while the proprietor of the show, Thomas Alva Edison, glows almost as warmly at the exclamations of wonder and delight.

The nineteenth century was the age of lighting. Man did more in those hundred years to push back the darkness than in all his time before. Canada and Canadians shared in this festival of light, and more than once contributed to it.

GLOSSARY

ONE OF THE MINOR difficulties in making use of the many excellent books and articles on lighting has been the lack of uniformity in naming the devices and their parts. This has resulted in a confusion of terminology by curators and dealers. The first attempt to overcome this was the illustrated glossary in *Flickering Flames*,[1] which provided names and definitions for most of the known lighting devices. A more recent, expanded version has been compiled by Darbee, and the nomenclature used has been followed for the most part in the present work. A standard system for naming the parts of lamps is still lacking. So that there will be no doubt about what is meant in the preceding chapters, the following annotated classification of lighting devices, and glossary of lamp parts, are appended.

CLASSIFICATION OF LIGHTING DEVICES

A scheme that attempts to classify all devices for providing artificial lighting is more uniform if based on the source of the light rather the physical design of the device. The latter can be the basis of the more detailed subdivisions. Such a system of classification is not perfect, because some lamps work with more than one kind of fuel, and an arbitrary choice has to be made. In general, however, there is a close relationship between the source of the light and the physical form of the device that uses it.

The following scheme includes only those lighting devices that were used or may have been used in North American homes, but it could be expanded easily to a much wider application.

I SOLID-FUEL DEVICES The fuel is sufficiently rigid to support itself, requiring only a device to hold it in position.

A *Torch holders.* A burning piece of wood or bundle of rushes makes a torch. A tubular or frame holder enables it to be carried or placed in a fixed position. Torches, usually called links, have a long history of use in Europe, but were seldom more than an impromptu means of lighting in North America.

B *Splint holders.* Splints are miniature torches, slivers of resinous wood such as pine. They could be held in rushlight holders, but there were special splint holders of slotted or folded metal.

C *Rushlight holders.* The rushlight was formed from the stem of the common rush (*Juncus effusus*) by peeling the outer fibrous layer except for a narrow strip, and then dipping the pithy rod that remained in melted tallow or lard. Convenient lengths of this impregnated stem were held at an angle in the rushlight holder, which is an iron device like a pair of pincers, held closed by a counterweight. The base may be of iron, wood, or cork. Some have an auxiliary socket thought to be a candle holder.

D *Taper holders.* The taper resembles the candle, into which it apparently evolved, but differs in that the wick is impregnated with, rather than imbedded in, the solid fuel. Tapers holders are gripping devices, like rushlight holders, but some have a reel on which the taper is wound and unreeled as needed.

E *Candle holders.* Candles are distinguished by having a sufficiently thick mass of solid fuel around the wick that they can stand vertically, given some basal support. Candle holders provide this. They are of two types, those that have a socket or tube into which the candle fits, and those which have a spike to impale the base of the candle (pricket).

II SEMI-LIQUID FUEL DEVICES   The fuel melts at a relatively low temperature and so must be contained in a vessel. Lard, tallow, or other animal fats were the usual fuels.

A *Crusies.* Open pans, with one or more angular projections of the rim, in which the wick lies.

B *Betty lamps.* These have a separate trough to support the wick. The font is usually, but not always, covered.

C *Lard lamps.* This term is applied to a variety of lamps, which have a closed font with projecting vertical wick tube or tubes. In some there is an arrangement to conduct heat from flame to fuel; others have a mechanical means of forcing the fuel to the wick.

D *Solar lamps.* Tubular-wick lamps without separate reservoirs; the distinctive deflector is a low dome with circular opening. They could burn whale oil but were commonly used with lard oil or lard.

III LIQUID-FUEL DEVICES   These resemble lard lamps in having closed fonts and wick tubes, but they require no heat feed-back to melt the fuel. They can be further subdivided on the basis of the kind of liquid fuel normally used.

A *Whale-oil lamps.* Using this term in the broad sense to include all lamps that normally burned whale oil, the group may be subdivided on the physical form of burners and reservoirs.

1 Simple whale-oil lamps: Glass or metal bodies with one or two short wick tubes, which may or may not be attached firmly to the font. Such lamps were also used with seal oil and olive oil.

2 Argand lamps: Argand burners have a tubular wick, which is supported between two metal tubes so that air is fed to the inside as well as the outside of the circular flame. This principle is used in many different lamps. The original Argand lamps were made of sheet metal, and the wick was adjusted by hand. The reservoir is separate, and feeds fuel to font and burner on the bird-bath principle.

3 Mantel lamps: Ornate versions of the Argand lamp, of cast brass, with urn-shaped reservoir feeding one or two fonts and burners. The wick was adjusted by twisting the burner.

4 Astral lamps: the name was originally used for hanging lamps with a ring-shaped reservoir but was later applied to table lamps of the same design. *Sinumbra lamps* are astrals in which the ring-shaped reservoir has a stream-lined shape in cross-section. These reservoir shapes were intended to reduce shadow.

5 Rumford lamps: An early flatwick lamp with offset reservoir. The wick is supported on a frame which is raised and lowered by a rack-and-pinion mechanism.

B *Colza-oil lamps.* Designed to burn the heavy oil pressed from rape seed, these lamps could also use the heavier grades of whale oil. The common version was the *moderator lamp*, a tall device in which a spring-loaded piston forced the fuel through an elaborate control mechanism to an Argand-type burner.

C *Camphene lamps.* Designed to burn rectified turpentine. They have an Argand burner without separate reservoir, and a button-shaped deflector to spread the flame. The name is often used erroneously for burning-fluid lamps.

D *Rosin-oil lamps.* Similar to camphene lamps but designed to burn the oil distilled from rosin. The air supply is capable of critical adjustment.

E *Burning-fluid lamps.* Designed to burn a mixture of 95% alcohol and redistilled turpentine (camphene). Burners typically have two high, diverging and tapering wick tubes, with caps. Fonts are high and narrow, usually of pressed glass, but also of tin and pewter.

F *Kerosene lamps.* Designed to burn the light hydrocarbon oil distilled from coal or petroleum. Used flat or tubular wicks, with a device for adjusting the height. There is usually a deflector to direct the air to the flame and a chimney to concentrate the draft.

1 Hand lamps: The font usually forms the bottom of the lamp, and there are one or more handles for carrying.

2 Table lamps: These have distinct font, stem, and base. Those with very tall stems are called *banquet lamps*.

3 Student lamps: A revival of the Argand lamp, with separate burner/font and reservoir, the two being balanced on opposite sides of an upright, their height being adjustable.

4 Wall lamps: The font is attached to, or supported by, some form of bracket, by means of which it can be hung on a wall. There is usually a reflector on the bracket, behind the lamp.

5 Hanging lamps: Designed to hang from the ceiling and to cast most of the light downward. *Library lamps* have the shade mounted over the font and burner; *hall lamps* have the font and burner inside the shade.

6 Floor lamps: The lamp proper is mounted on the top of a vertical rod supported by a table or a tripod, and is capable of height adjustment. In North America they were known as *piano lamps*.

7 Night lamps: Miniature lamps intended to supply a subdued light and to burn safely all night.

8 Mechanical lamps: A spring-driven fan in the base provides an acceledated current of air to the flame, making a chimney unnecessary.

IV GAS-FUEL DEVICES The fuel being already vaporized, these devices have no need for a burning wick.

A *Gas burners.* In simplest form these are open ends or tips of the gas line, with some device to control or shut off the flow. There may be an arrangement to adjust the amount of air to the flame. Later examples used the Welsbach incandescent mantle. Principal fuels were coal gas, water gas, and natural gas.

B *Acetylene lamps.* The hydrocarbon gas acetylene is made by bringing water into contact with calcium carbide. Lamps have a container for the "carbide," a reservoir of water with a controlled drip, and a nozzle, at the end of which the gas is burned. More common as lanterns and carriage lamps than as domestic lights.

C   *Vapour lamps.* These use a liquid fuel, which at some stage of its passage to the point of combustion is converted into a vapour. Welsbach mantles were used in later types.

V   ELECTRICAL DEVICES   Passage of an electrical current through an imperfect conductor produces heat, and if the resistance is high enough, also light.

A   *Arc lights.* The electric current is made to traverse an air gap between two electrodes, usually of carbon. The air in the gap as well as the tips of the electrodes become heated to a brilliant white incandescence. Such lights had little application to the home, but the modern fluorescent tube is an analogous device.

B   *Incandescent-filament lights.* A fine carbon or metal conductor is heated to incandescence by passage of an electric current, and is protected from combustion by being sealed in a glass vessel from which the air, or at least the oxygen, has been removed.

A NOMENCLATURE FOR LAMP PARTS

The simplest lamp consists of a vessel or font for the fuel and a wick or similar device to bring the fuel to a point where it can be vaporized and burned. More advanced lamps have a distinct burner, which not only holds the wick safely, but also increases the supply of air to the flame by means of ducts, deflectors, or chimneys. In some kerosene lamps the burner is a complex structure. The font, which originally made up almost the entire lamp, becomes only a part of the lamp body, together with the stem, base, and handle. Nearly all the names in the following glossary were previously employed in patents or technical descriptions of the time concerned. Where the contemporary term is unknown, one used in the better works on lighting is accepted. A few original names had to be found, which, it is hoped, are simple and appropriate.

Base. That part of the lamp that is normally in contact with the table or floor; it may be the bottom of the font, or a separate expansion connected to the font by the stem.

Base plate. A part of the burner, disc- or cup-shaped, which is attached

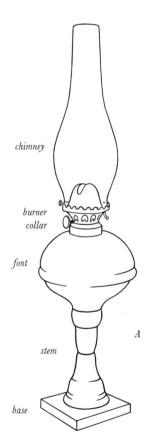

chimney

burner
collar

font

stem

A

base

to the screen below, is perforated for the wick tube, and supports the deflector, if any; in lamps with chimneys it is pierced for the passage of air, or is made of metallic gauze.

Blaze hole. An opening in the deflector through which the flame emerges.

Body. All of the lamp below the burner, consisting of the font, and possibly a stem, base, and handle.

Burner. That part of the lamp which supports and permits adjustment of the wick, and is the seat of the combustion that provides the light.

Chimney. A tubular device of glass, metal, or mica which extends upward from the rim of the burner and concentrates the hot air rising from the flame, thus producing a draft.

Chimney holder. That portion of the burner that receives and secures the chimney; commonest type consists of four spring-metal prongs which grasp the lower part of the chimney.

Collar. A ring-shaped attachment, usually of brass, which surrounds the opening of the font, and is threaded inside to receive the screw of the burner.

Coronet. A type of chimney holder consisting of a ring of short, spring-metal serrations, sometimes ornamentally shaped and pierced, into which the lower rim of the chimney fits. Additional securing may be provided by a set-screw or a spring-loaded clip.

Deflector. A disc, cone, or dome, usually of metal, which directs a current of air onto the flame.

Filler hole. A separate opening on the font or burner for the introduction of fuel into the font; usually provided with a cap.

Flame-spreader. A type of deflector used with the late tubular-wick lamps; it consists of a tube, capped and perforated at the top, through which part of the centre draft rises and is directed onto the flame.

Flange. That portion of the burner base plate not covered by the deflector.

Font. The fuel container that supports the burner and receives the lower part of the wick; usually an integral part of the body.

Handle. Commonly a loop of glass or metal attached to font or base.

Oil pot. A type of font, usually of metal, which fits into and is largely concealed by another receptable of metal, glass, or china that appears

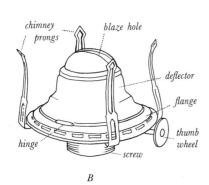

B

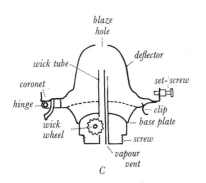

C

to be the font, which actually serves only for support and decoration.

Reservoir. A fuel container distinct from the font, and not bearing a burner; from it the fuel is automatically or manually supplied to the font as required.

Sconce. A frame or plate which can be attached to the wall, and which has a support for the body of the lamp; usually with a reflector behind the burner.

Screw. A short threaded tube at the bottom of the burner, which can be screwed into the collar of the font.

Shade. An attachment of glass, metal, or fabric which surrounds the chimney and burner and reduces or deflects the light; characteristically conical, hemispherical, or globular.

Shade holder. A support for the shade, consisting of a ring-shaped channel, a wire frame, or both.

Stem. A constricted portion of the lamp body joining font to base; characteristic of table lamps.

Thumb wheel. A disc-shaped wheel at the outer end of a shaft, by means of which the shaft and its wick wheel or wheels can be turned manually; in some burners a simple loop of the shaft replaces the wheel.

Vapour vent. A tubular opening through the base plate, usually attached to the wick tube, to permit escape of vapour from the font.

Wick. A cord, ribbon, or tube of fabric which extends from the fuel in the font through the wick tube to protrude at the top; fuel rises in the wick by capillary action and is vaporized and burned at the upper end; usually made of twisted or woven cotton, but may be of asbestos.

Wick tube. A circular or flattened-ovoid tube extending through the base plate, and housing the wick; combustion of fuel and wick takes place at the top of the tube; usually associated with a wick-raising mechanism.

Wick wheel. One or more toothed discs on a shaft attached to the base plate, the teeth projecting into the wick tube through a slot; rotary motion of thumbwheel and shaft causes the teeth of the wick wheel to raise or lower the wick, thus controlling the amount that is exposed for combustion.

NOTES

CHAPTER ONE

1 Thwing, p. 7; but see also *Rushlight*, II, no. 1 (1936), pp. 4, 5.
2 *Rushlight*, I, no. 1 (Nov. 1934), p. 2; XVIII, no. 4 (1952), pp. 10, 11.
3 *Rushlight*, II, no. 2 (1936), pp. 3, 4.
4 For permission to describe and figure this holder I am indebted to Dr. H. J. Newman, Director of the Halton County Museum.
5 O'Dea, p. 33; Thwing, p. 91.
6 Thwing, p. 106.
7 Child, p. 114.
8 Darbee, p. 1.
9 Groves and Thorp, II, p. 70.
10 *Novascotian or Colonial Herald*, Halifax, II, no. 55 (Nov. 30, 1826), p. 415.
11 *Public Ledger and Newfoundland General Advertiser*, St. Johns, XXXVIII, no. 288 (April 9, 1858), p. 3.
12 H. H. Langton, p. 91.
13 *Ibid.*, p. 137.
14 *Ibid.*, p. 156.
15 Guillet, *Pioneer Farmer*, II, p. 245.
16 Traill, *Emigrant's Guide*, pp. 168–70; *Canadian Settler's Guide*, pp. 168–70.
17 Traill, *Backwoods of Canada*, pp. 323–24.
18 For additional directions for making candles by the old-time methods under modern conditions, see the excellent article by Sarah C. Robb, *Rushlight*, XXI, no. 3 (Aug. 1955), pp. 13–15, 2 figs.
19 Thwing, p. 104.
20 For 19th-century accounts of commercial candle-making, see *Scientific American*, n.s., I, no. 11 (1859), pp. 162–63; VII, no. 23 (1862), p. 354.
21 Lee; Revi.
22 Pierce; Stevens, *Early Canadian Glass*, pp. 76–78.
23 *Rushlight* XIV, no. 2 (1948), pp. 1–9.

CHAPTER TWO

1 *Scientific American*, n.s., XV (1866), p. 199.
2 *Ibid.*
3 *Rushlight*, XVIII, no. 4 (1952), p. 9.
4 Guillet, *Pioneer Farmer*, p. 68.
5 U.S. Patent, no number (Oct. 25, 1816).
6 *Rushlight*, I, no. 2 (Dec. 1934), p. 2.
7 *Ibid.*
8 Christy, p. 12.
9 *Ibid.*, p. 13.
10 O'Dea, pl. opp. p. 17.
11 *Scientific American*, n.s. II (1860), p. 101.
12 Christy, p. 14.
13 *Scientific American*, n.s., II (1860), p. 101.

14 Christy, pp. 15, 168.
15 U.S. Patent no. 40,258 (Oct. 13, 1863).
16 Eggleston, p. 96.
17 Canadian Patent no. 17,206 (July 19, 1887).

CHAPTER THREE

1 Thwing, p. 21.
2 *Ibid.*, p. 37.

CHAPTER FOUR

1 These data and much other information on the old-time whaling industry were obtained from Chambers, pp. 111–27. For a more recent account, see Ashley.
2 *Novascotian or Colonial Herald, Halifax*, I, no. 10 (March 6, 1829), p. 79.
3 Brandt, p. 212.
4 Chambers, p. 127.
5 *Daily Witness*, Montreal (Nov. 4, 1865).
6 *Public Ledger and Newfoundland General Advertiser*, XXXVIII, no. 2894 (May 25, 1858), p. 3.
7 *Montreal Gazette* (June 22, 1858).
8 *Rushlight*, XV, no. 1 (1949), pp. 8–9.
9 *Montreal Gazette* (Jan. 11, 1855).
10 *Groves and Thorp*, II, p. 250, figs. 173–75.
11 *Globe*, Toronto (Sept. 25, 1844).
12 Thwing, pl. 60.

13 Lee, *Sandwich Glass*.
14 Hayward, 1962.
15 Lee, *Sandwich Glass*, pl. 189.
16 Watkins, pl. 3.
17 Hayward, 1962, pl. 82.
18 *Ibid.*, p. 37.
19 Thwing, p. 47.
20 *Rushlight*, XIX, no. 2 (1953), pp. 12–15.
21 Hayward, 1962, pl. 31.
22 *Novascotian or Colonial Herald*, III, no. 22 (May 31, 1827).
23 Hayward, 1962, pls. 35, 37.
24 Thwing, pl. 8.
25 *Ibid.*, pp. 11–15.
26 Clipping in the Barnett Collection, Univ. Western Ontario, dated 1851.
27 British Patent no. 1591 (March 9, 1787).
28 *Rushlight*, XIX, no. 3 (1953), pp. 11–12.
29 Thwing, pls. 54, 55.
30 British Patent no. 1425 (July 3, 1784).
31 For a detailed account of Argand, see d'Allemagne, pp. 372–80.
32 Thwing, pl. 52.
33 British Patent no. 4388 (Dec. 24, 1819).
34 Thwing, p. 75.
35 French Patent no. 999 (April 13, 1809).
36 d'Allemagne, p. 508, illus.
37 British Patent no. 4475 (Aug. 15, 1820).
38 Groves and Thorp, II, p. 250, fig. 179.
39 French Patent no. 1170 (Sept. 2, 1820).

40 Groves and Thorp, II, p. 255, fig. 181.
41 British Patent no. 7908 (Dec. 17, 1838).
42 Groves and Thorp, II, p. 258, figs. 184–86.
43 British Patent no. 9446 (Feb. 15, 1843).
44 Russell, p. 10.
45 H. H. Langton, p. 169.
46 As quoted in the *Jour. Franklin Inst. of Philadelphia*, LI (1852), pp. 341–42, fig. 4.

CHAPTER FIVE

1 *Scientific American*, n.s., II, no. 14 (March 31, 1860), p. 215.
2 Freedley, p. 146.
3 *Ibid.*, p. 147.
4 Hare, p. 172; *Rushlight*, IV, no. 2 (1958).
5 U.S. Patent, no number (Oct. 16, 1830).
6 Lower Canada, Patent no. 25 Oct. 3, 1831).
7 *Jour. Franklin Inst. of Philadelphia*, XI, n.s. 7 (1831), p. 76.
8 U.S. Patent, no number (March 17, 1834).
9 U.S. Patent, no number (April 3, 1835).
10 Lower Canada, Patent no. 110 (April 15, 1847).
11 U.S. Patent no. 1,453 (Dec. 31, 1839).
12 Lee, *Pressed Glass*, p. 141.
13 Hayward, 1962, pl. 87; Lee, *Sandwich Glass*, pl. 192.
14 Hayward, 1962, pl. 80

15 *Scientific American*, VII, no. 36 (May 22, 1852), p. 282.

16 *Quebec Mercury* (March 6, 1845), as quoted in *Globe*, Toronto (March 25, 1845).

17 *Globe*, Toronto (Oct. 20, 1856), p. 2.

18 *Quebec Gazette* (June 15, 1846).

19 *United Service Magazine*, as quoted by *Charlottetown Islander* (Sept. 18, 1846).

20 U.S. Patent, no number (Aug. 1, 1831).

21 U.S. Patent no. 29 (Sept. 22, 1836).

22 U.S. Patent no. 8,630 (Jan. 6, 1852).

23 U.S. Patent no. 10,099 (Oct. 4, 1853).

24 Hayward, 1962, p. 131.

25 Hamilton, p. 419.

26 U.S. Patent no. 12,814 (May 8, 1855).

27 British Patent no. 1,095 (May 14, 1855).

28 U.S. Patent no. 13,860 (Nov. 27, 1855).

29 *Globe*, Toronto (Nov. 22, 1856), p. 3.

30 U.S. Patent no. 1,082 (Feb. 19, 1839).

31 U.S. Patent no. 1,083 (Feb. 19, 1839).

32 U.S. Patent no. 7,667 (Sept. 24, 1850).

33 Ripley and Dana, p. 441.

34 U.S. Patent no. 13,259 (July 17, 1855).

35 U.S. Patent no. 14,369 (March 4, 1856).

36 U.S. Patent no. 14,478 (March 18, 1856).

CHAPTER SIX

1 Traill, *Emigrant's Guide*, p. 95.

2 Groves and Thorp, II, p. 42.

3 *Ibid.*, p. 43.

4 *Rushlight*, XX, no. 1, (1954), pp. 15–20; XXII, no. 1 (1956) pp. 6–10; also Watkins, pp. 401–3.

5 U.S. Patent no. 2,604 (May 4, 1842).

6 U.S. Patetn no. 11,497 (Aug. 8, 1854).

7 U.S. Patent no. 2,763 (Aug. 25, 1842).

8 *Rushlight*, XX, no. 1 (1954), p. 17; XXII, no. 1 (1956), p. 7.

9 U.S. Patent no. 11,633 (Aug. 29, 1854).

10 U.S. Patent no. 13,170 (July 3, 1855).

11 U.S. Patent, no. 2,703 (July 2, 1842).

12 U.S. Patent no. 7,921 (Feb. 4, 1851).

13 U.S. Patent no. 14,806 (May 6, 1856).

14 *Rushlight*, I, no. 2 (1934), pp. 2–3.

15 U.S. Patent no. 27,248 (Feb. 21, 1860).

16 U.S. Patent no 27,500 (March 13, 1860).

17 Groves and Thorp, II, p. 258.

18 *Ibid.*

19 *Ibid.*

20 *Globe*, Toronto (Oct. 6, 1847).

21 U.S. Patent no. 3,028 (April 6, 1843).

22 Freedley, p. 356.

23 Seen in the Metropolitan Mus. of Art, New York City.

CHAPTER SEVEN

1 Biographical data on Abraham Gesner were obtained from the following sources listed in the bibliography: G. W. Gesner, Matthew, MacKenzie, Sclanders, Beaton and Squires.

2 *Scientific American*, n.s., V (1861), p. 378; Partington, p. 108.

3 A. Gesner, 1861, pp. 61, 65; Groves and Thorp, II, pp. 311–12.

4 *Can. Jour. of Industry, Science & Art*, III (1854), pp. 66–67.

5 British Patent no. 13,292 (Oct. 7, 1850).

6 U.S. Patent no. 8,833 (March 23, 1852).

7 *Dictionary of Natl. Biography*.

8 U.S. Patent no. 11,203 (June 27, 1854).

9 Advertisement of John M'Grath in *Saint John and Fredericton Business Directory, 1862*.

10 Advertisement of John Rhynas in *Montreal Transcript* (April 20, 1866).

11 *Globe*, Toronto (Nov. 10, 1857), p. 3.

12 Advertisement of Brown & Co., *Public Ledger*, St. John's (Sept. 7, 1860), p. 3.

13 Advertisement of the New Brunswick Oil Works Company in *Monitor*, Charlottetown, P.E.I. (Sept. 17, 1857), p. 3.

14 *Scientific American*, n.s. V (1861), p. 266.

15 A. Gesner, 1861.

16 Nova Scotia Patent no. 108 (March 30, 1863).

17 A. Gesner, 1865.

18 Silliman.

19 The original petition is in the possession of Mr. Charles O. Fairbank, of Petrolia, Ont.

20 Cronin.

21 *Daily Spectator and Jour. of Commerce*, Hamilton (July 4, 1860).

22 Hunt, p. 248.

23 Hildreth, pp. 43–68.

24 The petition of the International Petroleum and Mining Company of Hamilton, C.W.–which I have seen–was applied for on Oct. 26 and granted on Dec. 18, 1854. The certificate of the Pennsylvania Rock Oil Company was filed in Albany, N.Y., on Dec. 30, 1854, and issued on Jan. 16, 1855 (Williamson & Daum, p. 68).

25 For a more detailed summary of these events, see Dickey; also Williamson & Daum, pp. 63–81.

26 Mitchell & Co.'s *County of Wentworth and Hamilton City Directory for 1865–66*, p. x.

27 Brown's *Toronto General Directory 1861*, p. 380.

28 Advertisement of G. S. Hobart, *Daily News*, Kingston (May 4, 1861).

29 Philip, p. 88.

30 A. Gesner, 1865, p. 11.

31 *Rushlight*, IV, no. 2 (1938), p. 5.

32 U.S. Patent no. 20,159 (May 4, 1858); reissue no. 648 (Jan. 11, 1859).

33 U.S. Patent no. 26,952 (Jan. 24, 1860).

34 U.S. Patent no. 21,576 (Sept. 21, 1858).

35 *Rushlight*, IV, no. 2 (1938), p. 5.

36 U.S. Patent no. 22,516 (Jan. 4, 1859).

37 U.S. Patent no. 23,160 (March 8, 1859).

38 U.S. Patent no. 23,832 (May 3, 1859).

39 Dietz, p. 95.

40 U.S. Patent no. 24,015 (May 17, 1859); no. 25,493 (Sept. 20, 1859).

41 *Scientific American*, n.s., I, no. 17 (Oct. 22, 1859), p. 280.

42 *Ibid.*, no. 19 (Nov. 5, 1859), p. 306.

43 U.S. Patent no. 24,397 (June 14, 1859).

44 Lee, *Sandwich Glass*, pls. 196, 197.

45 Hayward, 1923, pl. 78.

CHAPTER EIGHT

1 U.S. Patent no. 33,047 (Aug. 13, 1861).

2 *Scientific American*, VI, no. 10 (March 8, 1862), p. 152.

3 U.S. Patent no. 37,281 (Jan. 6, 1863).

4 U.S. Patent no. 39,320 (July 21, 1863).

5 U.S. Patent no. 71,949 (Dec. 10, 1867).

6 U.S. Patent no. 30,381 (Oct. 16, 1860).

7 U.S. Patent no. 36,680 (Oct. 14, 1862).

8 U.S. Patent no. 41,794 (March 1, 1864).

9 U.S. Patent no. 74,863 (Feb. 25, 1868).

10 U.S. Patent no. 35,552 (June 10, 1862).

11 U.S. Patent no. 42,262 (April 5, 1864).

12 Canadian Patent no. 1924 Nov. 23, 1865); no. 2040 May 14, 1866).

13 U.S. Patent no. 49,984 (Sept. 19, 1865).

14 U.S. Patent no. 74,049 (Feb. 4, 1868).

15 U.S. Patent no. 73,488 (Jan. 21, 1868).

16 U.S. Patent no. 40,226 (Oct. 13, 1863).

17 U.S. Patent no. 74,271 (Feb. 11, 1868).

18 U.S. Patent no. 80,843 (Aug. 11, 1868).

19 Anderson, chap. 22.

20 *Globe*, Toronto (March 25, 1856).

21 The first patented under U.S. Patent no. 36,493 (Sept. 16, 1862).

22 *Hamilton Spectator* (Aug. 7, 1920), p. 8.

23 *City of Hamilton Directory, 1856*, p. 98.

24 *Hutchinson's Hamilton Directory for 1862–63*, p. 7.

25 *Mitchell & Co.'s County of Wentworth and Hamilton City Directory, 1865–6*, p. 232.

26 *Brown's Toronto General Directory, 1861*, p. 380.

27 Revi, p. 25.

28 U.S. Patent no. 32,739 (July 2, 1861).

29 James Seaman Atterbury and Thomas Bakewell Atterbury were brothers.

30 U.S. Patents: no. 34,345 (Feb. 11, 1862; no. 35,429 (June 3, 1862); no. 35,430 (June 3, 1862).

31 U.S. Patent no. 37,267 (Jan. 6, 1863).

32 U.S. Patent no. 79,298 (June 30, 1868).

33 U.S. Patent no. 82,579 (Sept. 29, 1868).

34 U.S. Patent no. 73,122 (Jan. 7, 1868); reissued July 14 and Aug. 11, 1868.

35 Lee, *Pressed Glass*, p. 183, pl. 2.

36 *Scientific American*, n.s., XVII, no. 6 (1867), p. 88.

37 *Ibid.*, n.s. XXII, no. 6 (1869), p. 88.

38 U.S. Patent no. 33,428 (Oct. 8, 1861).

39 U.S. Patent no. 95,667 (Oct. 12, 1869).

40 U.S. Patent no. 86,291 (Jan. 26, 1869).

CHAPTER NINE

1 Williamson and Daum, pp. 371–551.

2 Anderson, II, pp. 361–63.

3 U.S. Patent no. 98,836 (Jan. 18, 1870).

4 U.S. Patent no. 106,303 (Aug. 16, 1870).

5 U.S. Patent no. 133,307 (Nov. 26, 1872).

6 U.S. Patent no. 135,749 (Feb. 11, 1873).

7 Canadian Patent no. 4768 June 4, 1875).

8 U.S. Patent no. 138,601 (May 6, 1873).

9 U.S. Patent no. 162,004 (April 13, 1875).

10 U.S. Patent no. 270,722 (Jan. 10, 1883).

11 U.S. Patent no. 324,067 (Aug. 11, 1885).

12 U.S. Patent no. 324,068 (Aug. 11, 1885).

13 U.S. Patent no. 324,069 (Aug. 11, 1885).

14 U.S. Patent no. 129,821 (July 23, 1872).

15 U.S. Patent no. 208,309 (Sept. 24, 1878).

16 U.S. Patent no. 210,236 (Nov. 26, 1878).

17 Anderson, II. chap. 18.

18 U.S. Patent no. 90,863 (June 1, 1869).

19 U.S. Patent no. 195,241 (Sept. 18, 1877).

20 *The Industries of Rochester* (Rochester, N.Y.: Elstner Publ. Co., 1888), p. 121.

21 U.S. Patent no. 91,208 (June 15, 1869).

22 U.S. Patent no. 103,213 (May 17, 1870).

23 *Scientific American*, n.s., XVI, no. 18 (May 4, 1867), p. 285.

24 *Ibid.*, n.s. XXV, no. 22 (Nov. 25, 1871), p. 350.

25 U.S. Patent no. 107,514 (Sept. 20, 1870).

26 Revi, p. 304.

27 Seen in the Metropolitan Museum of Art, New York City.

28 U.S. Patent no. 129,781 (July 23, 1872).

29 Revi, pp. 41–43.

30 U.S. Patent no. 181,618 (Aug. 29, 1876).

31 U.S. Patent no. 103,460 (May 24, 1870).

32 U.S. Patent no. 104,205 (June 14, 1870); no. 107,544 (Sept. 20, 1870).

33 U.S. Patent no. 249,676 (Nov. 15, 1881).

34 U.S. Patent no. 146,467 (Jan. 13, 1874).

35 Canadian Patent no. 6207 (June 16, 1876).

36 U.S. Patent no. 115,528 (May 30, 1871).

37 U.S. Patent no. 37,867 (March 10, 1863); reissued March 29, 1870.

38 U.S. Patent no. 75,479 (March 10, 1868).
39 U.S. Patent no. 102,163 (April 19, 1870).
40 Freeman, pp. 64–65.
41 U.S. Patent no. 30,466 (Oct. 23, 1860).
42 U.S. Patent no. 40,566 (Nov. 10, 1863).
43 U.S. Patent no. 125,954 (April 23, 1872).
44 U.S. Patent no. 134,547 (Jan. 7, 1873).
45 U.S. Patent no. 142,103 (Aug. 26, 1873).
46 U.S. Patent no. 145,176 (Dec. 2, 1873).
47 Canadian Patent no. 3138 (Feb. 24, 1874).
48 Since this was written, a detailed account of the Hitchcock lamp, by Mrs. Mabel S. Cooke, has appeared in *Rushlight*, xxxII, no. 4 (1966), pp. 3–11.
49 U.S. Patent no. 161,912 (April 13, 1875).
50 U.S. Patent no. 163,764 (June 22, 1875).
51 U.S. Patent no. 175,022 (March 21, 1876).
52 U.S. Patent no. 98,936 and no. 98,937 (Jan. 18, 1870).
53 U.S. Patent no. 100,637 (March 8, 1870).
54 *Scientific American*, n.s., xxxVI, no. 4 (Jan. 21, 1871), p. 47.
55 *Daily Globe*, Toronto (Nov. 6, 1875), p. 6.
56 U.S. Patent no. 208,396 (Sept. 24, 1878).
57 Cronin.
58 *Hamilton City Directory, 1875/6.*
59 *Daily Globe*, Toronto (Oct. 16 and Nov. 6, 1875).

CHAPTER TEN

1 Williamson and Daum, pp. 677-701.
2 Consulted in the Metropolitan Museum of Art, New York City.
3 U.S. Patent no. 371,894 (Oct. 18, 1887).
4 Canadian Patent no. 4576 (April 4, 1875).
5 U.S. Patent no. 419,747 (Jan. 21, 1890).
6 Seldon, pp. 196–97.
7 U.S. Patent no. 292,114 (Jan. 15, 1884).
8 In the Metropolitan Museum of Art, New York City.
9 U.S. Patent no. 187,800 (Feb. 27, 1877).
10 Stevens, *Canadian Glass, 1825–1925.*
11 Lee, *Pressed Glass*, pp. 153–61.
12 Lent by Mr. D. H. Kennedy, Weston, Ont.
13 U.S. Patent no. 283,177 (Aug. 14, 1883).
14 U.S. Patent no. 295,479 (March 18, 1884).
15 *London Reflector, Supplement* (Sept. 22, 1879).
16 Since this handsome lamp was photographed, it was lent to a motion picture company for use as a prop and the shade was broken.
17 In the Metropolitan Museum of Art, New York City.
18 *Meriden Record*, Conn. (Dec. 29, 1848), p. 9.
19 In the Metropolitan Museum of Art, New York City.
20 U.S. Patent no. 441,052 (Nov. 18, 1890).
21 Canadian Patent no. 44,933 (Dec. 20, 1893).
22 In the Metropolitan Museum of Art, New York City.
23 U.S. Patent no. 323,547 (Aug. 4, 1885).
24 U.S. Patent no. 247,480 (Sept. 23, 1881).
25 *Amer. Medical Assoc. Jour.*, L, no. 14 (April 4, 1908), p. 1135.
26 Canadian Patent no. 24,994 (Sept. 27, 1886) ; U.S. Patent no. 350,968 (March 22, 1887).
27 Most of these biographical details were obtained from *Hamilton Semi - Weekly Times* (March 27, 1900), and *Hamilton Spectator* (Oct. 4, 1941, and March 5, 1966), consulted in the Hamilton Public Library. There are slight discrepancies among these three accounts.
28 Canadian Patent no. 26,948 (June 14, 1887).

CHAPTER ELEVEN

1 French Patent no. 356 (Sept. 28, 1799).
2 U.S. Patent, no number (March 24, 1810).
3 *Globe*, Toronto (Sept. 25 and Nov. 3, 1847).
4 *Globe*, Toronto (June 17, 1848).
5 Groves and Thorp, III, p. 18 *et seq.*
6 U.S. Patent no. 130,382 (Aug. 13, 1872).
7 Most of the information on gas burners was obtained from Coe, p. 129 *et seq.*
8 *Daily Citizen*, Ottawa (Feb. 19, 1895).
9 Malcolm.
10 Partington, pp. 74, 324, 468–69.
11 Most of the biographical data on Willson were obtained from an article by Paul Montgomery in *Saturday Night*, Toronto (July 26, 1930).
12 U.S. Patent, no number (Aug. 1, 1831).
13 U.S. Patent no. 28,536 (May 29, 1860).
14 *Scientific American*, n.s. XXVI, supplement (May 18, 1872), pp. 335–42, 20 figs.
15 U.S. Patent no. 121,497 (Dec. 5, 1871).

CHAPTER TWELVE

1 Dunsheath.
2 Canadian Patent no. 3738 (Aug. 3, 1874).

3 *Scientific American*, n.s., XL, no. 12 (March 22, 1879), pp. 185–86; figs. 1–3.
4 *Scientific American*, n.s., XLII, no. 2 (Jan. 10, 1880), p. 19, figs. 1–4.
5 Canadian Patent no. 10,654 (Nov. 17, 1879).
6 U.S. Patent no. 223,898 (Jan. 27, 1880).
7 "A Warning from the Edison Electric Light Co.," 83 pp., 4 figs. In the library of Mr. Stan Ashbury, Preston, Ont.
8 Denison.
9 *Ontario Gazetteer and Directory, 1888–89.*
10 *Scientific American*, n.s., XLII, no. 2 (Jan. 10, 1880), p. 19, figs. 1–4.
11 Schroeder, p. 49.
12 *Ibid.*, pp. 56–61; Bright, p. 116.

GLOSSARY

1 Thwing, pp. 127–38.

BIBLIOGRAPHY

D'ALLEMAGNE, HENRY-RENÉ. *Histoire du luminaire depuis l'époque Romaine jusqu'au XIXe siècle*. Paris: Alphonse Picard, 1891. 702 pp., 80 text-figs., 80 pls.

ANDERSON, JOSEPH, ed. *The town and city of Waterbury, Connecticut, from the aboriginal period to the year eighteen hundred and ninety five*. New Haven, Conn.: The Price & Lee Co., 1896. Vol. I, 718 pp., vol. II, 560 pp., vol. III, 820 pp., illus.

ASHLEY, C. W. *The Yankee Whaler*. Boston: Houghton Mifflin Co., 1926. 379 pp., illus.

BEATON, KENDALL. "Dr. Gesner's Kerosene: The Start of American Oil Refining," *Business Hist. Rev.*, XXIX (March 1955), pp. 28–53.

BRANDT, KARL. *Whale Oil: An Economic Analysis*. Palo Alto, Calif.: Food Research Inst., Stanford Univ., 1940. 251 pp.

BRIGHT, ARTHUR A., JR. *The Electric Lamp Industry: Technological Change and Economic Development from 1800 to 1947*. New York: Macmillan Co., 1949. 526 pp., 43 figs.

CHAMBERS, WILLIAM, and ROBERT CHAMBERS. *Chamber's Information for the People: A Popular Encyclopaedia*. 15th Amer. ed. Philadelphia: Jas. B. Smith & Co., 1856. Vol. I, 840 pp., illus.

CHILD, MRS. *The American Frugal Housewife: Dedicated to those who are not Ashamed of Economy*. 22nd ed. enlarged and corrected by the author. New York: Samuel S. & William Wood, 1839.

CHRISTY, MILLER. *The Bryant and May Museum of Fire-making Appliances: Catalogue of the Exhibits*. London: Bryant & May Ltd., 1926. 255 pp., 32 pls. Supplement 1928, 76 pp., 7 pls.

CLEGG, SAMUEL, JR. *A Practical Treatise on the Manufacture and Distribution of Coal-gas, its Introduction and progressive Improvement*.

London: John Weale, 1853. 299 pp., 47 text-figs., 19 pls. (The first edition was published in 1841.)

COE, ARTHUR. *The Science and Practice of Gas Supply Including the Economics of Gas Supply.* Halifax, England: The Gas College, 1934. 919 pp., 730 figs.

CRONIN, FERGUS. "North America's Father of Oil," *Imperial Oil Rev.* (June 1958), pp. 22–25, 4 figs.

DARBEE, H. C. "A Glossary of Old Lamps," *Hist. News,* Amer. Assoc. for State & Local Hist., XX (Aug. 1965), Tech. Leaflet 30, 16 pp., 26 figs.

DENISON, MERRILL. *The People's Power.* Toronto: McClelland & Stewart Ltd., 1960. 295 pp., 2 pls., 2 maps.

DICKEY, P. C. "The First Oil Well." *Jour. Petrol. Technol.* (Jan. 1959), pp. 14–26, 7 figs.

DIETZ, FRED, ed. *1913, A Leaf from the Past: Dietz Then-and-Now: Origin of the late Robert Edwin Dietz—his Business Career, and some Interesting Facts about New York.* New York: R. E. Dietz Co., 1914. 194 pp., 89 text-figs., 4 pls.

DUNSHEATH, PERCY. *A History of Electrical Engineering.* London: Faber and Faber, 1962. 368 pp., 71 figs.

EGGLESTON, WILFRID. *The Queen's Choice: A Story of Canada's Capital.* Ottawa: Queen's Printer, 1961. 325 pp., illus.

ENGLAND, G. A. *Vikings of the Ice: Being the Log of a Tenderfoot on the Great Newfoundland Seal Hunt.* Garden City, N.Y.: Doubleday, Page & Co., 1924. 323 pp., 90 illus.

FERGUSON, JOHN. *Bibliotheca Chemica: A Catalogue of the Alchemical, Chemical and Pharmaceutical Books in the Collection of the late James Young of Kelly and Durris, Esq., LL.D., F.R.S., F.R.S.E.* Glasgow: James MacLehose, 1906. Vol. I, 487 pp., 1 pl., vol. II, 598 pp., 1 pl.

FREEDLEY, EDWIN T. *Philadelphia and its Manufactures: A hand-book exhibiting the Development, Variety, and Statistics of the Manufacturing Industry of Philadelphia in 1857.* Philadelphia: Edward Young, 1860. 504 pp., 1 text-fig., 5 pls.

FREEMAN, LARRY. *Light on Old Lamps.* Watkins Glen, N.Y.: Century House, 1944. 128 pp., illus.

GESNER, ABRAHAM. *A Practical Treatise on Coal, Petroleum, and other distilled Oils.* New York: Baillière Brothers, 1861. 134 pp., 18 figs.

——— *A Practical Treatise on Coal, Petroleum, and other distilled Oils.* 2nd. ed. revised and enlarged by GEORGE WELTDEN GESNER. New York: Baillière Brothers, 1865. 181 pp., illus.

GESNER, G. W. "Dr. Abraham Gesner—a Biographical Sketch," *Bull Nat.*

Hist. Soc. New Brunswick, no. 14, art. 1 (1896), pp. 3–11, 1 portrait.

GROVES, C. E., and WILLIAM THORP. *Chemical Technology or Chemistry in its Application to Arts and Manufactures*. Vol. II. *Lighting*. By W. E. DENT, J. MCARTHUR, L. FIELD, F. A. FIELD, B. REDWOOD, and D. A. LOUIS. Philadelphia: P. Blakiston, Son & Co., 1895. 398 pp., 358 figs.

———— *Chemical Technology or Chemistry in its Applications to Arts and Manufactures*. Vol. III. *Gas Lighting*. By CHARLES HUNT. Philadelphia: P. Blakiston's Sons & Co., 1900. 312 pp., 291 figs., 2 pls.

GUILLET, E. C. *Early Life in Upper Canada*. Toronto: Univ. Toronto Press, 1963. 728 pp., 302 illus.

———— *The Pioneer Farmer and Backwoodsman*. 2 vols. Toronto: Univ. Toronto Press, 1963. 372, 404 pp., illus.

HAMILTON, WILLIAM. "Report on Mr. Seth E. Winslow's Safety Can and Lamp for Spirit-gas," *Jour. Franklin Inst. of Philadelphia*, LXII (1857), p. 419.

HARE, ROBERT. "Means of Producing Light, &c.," *Amer. Jour. Sci. & Arts*, II (April 1820), p. 172.

HAYWARD, A. H. *Colonial Lighting*. Boston: B. J. Brimm Co., 1923. 159 pp., illus..

———— *Colonial Lighting*. 3rd enlarged ed. with a new Introduction and Supplement "Colonial Chandeliers" by JAMES R. MARSH. New York: Dover Publications, Inc., 1962. 198 pp., 47 pls.

HEBARD, HELEN B. *Early Lighting in New England 1620–1861*. Rutland, Vt.: Charles E. Tuttle Company, 1964. 88 pp., 45 illus.

HILDRETH, S. P. "Observations on the Bituminous Coal Deposits of the Valley of the Ohio, and the Accompanying Rock Strata; with Notices of the Fossil Organic Remains and the Relics of Vegetable and Animal Bodies, Illustrated by a Geological Map; by Numerous Drawings of Plants and Shells, and by Views of Interesting Scenery," *Amer. Jour. Sci.*, XXIX, art. 1 (Jan. 1836), pp. 1–54, figs. 1–19, 1 pl., 1 map.

HOUGH, WALTER. "Collection of Heating and Lighting Utensils in the United States National Museum," *U.S. Natl. Mus., Bull.*, no. 141 (1928), 113 pp., 99 pls.

HUNT, T. STERRY. "Notes on the History of Petroleum or Rock Oil," *Can. Naturalist and Geologist*, VI, 4 (Aug. 1861), pp. 241–55.

JEFFREYS, C. W. *The Picture Gallery of Canadian History*. Vol. II. *1763 to 1830*. Toronto: The Ryerson Press, 1945. 271 pp., 192 illus.

LANGTON, H. H. *A Gentlewoman in Upper Canada: The Journals of Anne Langton*. Toronto: Clarke, Irwin & Co. Ltd., 1950 (paperback 1964). 207 pp.

LANGTON, W. A. *Early Days in Upper Canada: Letters of John Langton from the Backwoods of Upper Canada and the Audit Office of the Province of Canada.* Toronto: The Macmillan Co. of Canada Ltd., 1926. 310 pp., 5 figs., 17 pls.

LEE, RUTH WEBB. *Sandwich Glass: The History of the Boston & Sandwich Glass Company.* 9th ed., revised and enlarged. Wellesley Hills, Mass.: Lee Publications, 1947. 590 pp., 228 illus.

———— *Early American Pressed Glass, Enlarged and Revised: A Classification of Patterns Collectible in Sets together with Individual Pieces for Table Decoration.* 35th ed. Wellesley Hills, Mass.: Lee Publications, 1960. 666 pp., 190 pls.

MACKENZIE, K. A. "Abraham Gesner, M.D., Surgeon Geologist, 1797–1864," *Can. Medical Assoc. Jour.*, LIX, 4 (Oct. 1948), pp. 384–87.

MALCOLM, WYATT. *The Oil and Gas Fields of Ontario and Quebec.* Ottawa: Geol. Surv., Canada, Memoir 81, 1915. 248 pp.

MATTHEW, G. F. "Abraham Gesner: A Review of his Scientific Work," *Bull. Nat. Hist. Soc. New Brunswick*, no. 15, art. 1 (1897), pp. 3–48, 2 figs., 2 maps.

MOODIE, SUSANNA [STRICKLAND]. *Roughing it in the Bush. Or Forest Life in Canada.* 2 vols. London: R. Bentley, 1852. 587 pp.

———— *Life in the Clearings versus the Bush.* London: R. Bentley, 1853. 384 pp.

O'DEA, W. T. *The Social History of Lighting.* London: Routledge and Kegan Paul, 1958. 254 pp., 59 figs., 32 pls.

PARTINGTON, J. R. *A History of Chemistry.* Vol. IV. London: Macmillan & Co. Ltd., 1964. 1007 pp., 91 figs.

PHILIP, CATHARINE. "The Crosses of Alberta," *Chatelaine*, XXXVIII, 6 (1965), pp. 32–33, 86–94, 96–97, 6 illus.

PIERCE, EDITH CHOWN. *Canadian Glass: A Footnote to History.* Toronto: privately printed, 1954. 11 pp., 1 pl.

POPE, F. L. *Evolution of the Electric Incandescent Lamp.* Elizabeth, N.J.: Henry Cook, 1889. 91 pp., 20 figs.

REVI, A. C. *American Pressed Glass and Figure Bottles.* New York: Thomas Nelson & Sons, 1964. 446 pp., numerous illus.

RIPLEY, GEORGE, and C. A. DANA, eds. *The American Cyclopaedia: A Popular Dictionary of General Knowledge.* New York: Appleton & Co., 1883, vol. XIV.

RUSSELL, L. S. *Lighting the Pioneer Ontario Home.* Toronto: Royal Ontario Museum, 1966. 16 pp., illus.

SCHROEDER, HENRY. "History of Electric Light," *Smithsonian Misc. Coll.*, LXXVI, 2 (1923), 94 pp., numerous illus.

SCLANDERS, IAN. "He Gave the World a Brighter Light," *Imperial Oil Rev.*, XXXIX (Feb. 1955), pp. 22–25, 6 figs.

SELDON, H. R. and G. B. "Some Rochester Inventions," *Rochester Hist. Soc. Publication Fund Series*, XIV (1963), pp. 192–211, 6 pls.

SILLIMAN, BENJAMIN. "Notice of a Fountain of Petroleum, called the Oil Spring," *Amer. Jour. Sci.*, XXIII, art. 15 (1833), pp. 97–102.

SPENCE, HILDA, and KELVIN SPENCE. *A Guide to Early Canadian Glass.* Toronto: Longmans Canada Ltd., 1966. 112 pp., 80 pls.

SQUIRES, W. AUSTIN. "Abraham Gesner: A Short Biography of New Brunswick's First Provincial Geologist," *Atlantic Advocate*, LIII (Jan. 1963), pp. 92–95, 1 fig.

STEVENS, GERALD. *Early Canadian Glass.* Toronto: The Ryerson Press, 1961. 184 pp., 46 pls.

———— *One Hundred Years of Canadian Glass, 1825–1925.* Toronto: Royal Ontario Museum, 1964. 13 pp., 1 pl.

STRICKLAND, [SAMUEL], MAJOR. *Twenty-seven Years in Canada West; or, the Experience of an Early Settler.* 2 vol. London: Richard Bentley, 1853. 655 pp.

THWING, LEROY L. *Flickering Flames: A History of Domestic Lighting through the Ages.* Rutland, Vt.: Charles E. Tuttle Company, 1958. 138 pp., 54 figs., 97 pls.

TRAILL, CATHARINE PARR [STRICKLAND]. *The Backwoods of Canada, Being Letters from the Wife of an Emigrant Officer.* London: Charles Knight, 1836. 351 pp., 20 illus.

———— *The Emigrant's Guide, and Hints on Canadian Housekeeping.* Toronto: MacLear and Co., 1854. 271 pp., 8 illus.

———— *The Canadian Settler's Guide.* 5th ed. Toronto: The Old Countryman Office, 1855. 262 pp., 6 illus.

———— *The Canadian Emigrant Housekeeper's Guide.* Toronto: Lovell & Gibson, 1862. 150 pp.

WATKINS, C. M. "Artificial Lighting in America: 1830–1860," *Ann. Rept. Smithsonian Inst. 1951*, 1952, pp. 385–407, 8 pls.

WILLIAMSON, H. F., and A. R. DAUM. *The American Petroleum Industry: The Age of Illumination 1859–1899.* Evanston, Ill.: Northwestern Univ. Press, 1959. 864 pp., illus.

INDEX

Figures in italic refer to illustration numbers